M. N. Roy

Pathfinders

Series Editor: **Dilip M. Menon**
Department of History, University of Delhi

This series explores the intellectual history of South Asia through the lives and ideas of significant individuals within a historical context. These 'pathfinders' are seen to represent a break with existing traditions, canons and inherited histories. In fact, even the idea of South Asia with its constituent regions and linguistic and religious divisions maybe thrown into crisis as we explore the idea of territory as generated by thought. It is not cartographic limits that determine thinking but the imagining of elective affinities across space, time and borders. These thinkers are necessarily cosmopolitan and engage with a miscegenation of ideas that recasts existing notions of schools of thinking, of the archive for a history of ideas, and indeed of the very notion of national and regional limits to intellectual activity. The books in this series try to think beyond the limited frameworks of colonialism and nationalism for the modern period and more generally of histories of societies that are told through the prism of the state, its institutions and ideologies.

These slim volumes written by leading scholars are intended for the intelligent layperson and expert alike, and written in an accessible, lively and authoritative prose. Through telling the lives of celebrated names and lesser known ones in context, this series will expand the repertoire of ideas and individuals that have shaped the history and culture of South Asia.

Also in the Series

Javed Majeed
Muhammad Iqbal: Islam, Aesthetics and Postcolonialism
ISBN: 978-0-415-44578-8

Lakshmi Subramanian
Veena Dhanammal: The Making of a Legend
ISBN: 978-0-415-44611-2

M. N. Roy
Marxism and Colonial Cosmopolitanism

Kris Manjapra

Routledge
Taylor & Francis Group
LONDON NEW YORK NEW DELHI

First published 2010
by Routledge
912 Tolstoy House, 15–17 Tolstoy Marg, New Delhi 110 001

Simultaneously published in the UK
by Routledge
2 Park Square, Milton Park, Abingdon, Oxon, OX14 4RN

Routledge is an imprint of the Taylor & Francis Group, an informa business

Transferred to Digital Printing 2010

© 2010 Kris Manjapra

Typeset by
Star Compugraphics Private Limited
D–156, Second Floor
Sector 7, Noida 201 301

British Library Cataloguing-in-Publication Data
A catalogue record of this book is available from the British Library

ISBN: 978-0-415-44603-7

For

Theodor Bergmann

and

Sibnarayan Ray

Contents

List of Illustrations

List of Acronyms

ACLU	American Civil Liberties Union
AICC	All India Congress Committee
AITUC	All India Trade Union Congress
CCF	The Congress for Cultural Freedom
CIA	Central Intelligence Agency (USA)
CID	Criminal Investigation Department of the Bengal Presidency
CPGB	Communist Party of Great Britain
CPI	Communist Party of India
Comintern	The Office of the Communist International
CSP	Congress Socialist Party
KPD	*Kommunistische Partei Deutschlands* (Communist Party of Germany)
KPD-O	*Kommunistische Partei-Opposition* (German Communist Party Opposition [Right Group])
IFL	Indian Federation of Labour
INA	Indian National Army (Azad Hind Fauj)
INC	Indian National Congress
INKOPP	*Internationale Nachrichten der Kommunistischen Opposition*
Inprecor	*International Press Correspondence*
Inprekorr	*Internationale Presse Korrespondenz*
RH	*Radical Humanist* magazine
WES	Western Bureau of the Communist International
WPP	Workers and Peasants Party

Acknowledgments

I wish to thank all those who helped me deepen my understanding of M. N. Roy and sharpen my view of the historical context. In this regard, I think especially of the scholars in Cambridge, Massachusetts: Sugata Bose, Ayesha Jalal, David Blackbourn, Peter Gordon, Daniel Mulholland, Neilesh Bose and Robert Fannion. Thanks to Sujit Raman for a seminal discussion many years ago. I wish to thank my colleagues in the History Department at Tufts University for their collegiality. Jeanne Penvenne helped me find a foothold quickly in my new institution. Elsewhere in the United States, I thank the members of the UCLA Mellon Postdoctoral Program in the Humanities, especially Françoise Lionnet, Shu-mei Shih, Sonali Pahwa and Sarah Valentine, as well as Mridu Rai at Yale University. Both UCLA and Yale providing me venues to present my work and obtain most beneficial feedback. I am grateful to Sanjay Subrahmanyam, Sudipta Kaviraj, Akhil Gupta and Aamir Mufti for our exchanges during my postdoctoral year. And thanks especially to Suzanne Marchand for her inspiring scholarship and friendly support.

In Europe, I offer my sincerest thanks to Theodor Bergmann in Stuttgart, who shared his memories of M. N. Roy with me, and helped me imagine the Weimar context. Thanks to Ravi Ahuja, Harald Fischer-Tiné, Benjamin Zachariah, Jürgen Lütt, Joachim Oesterheld, Hans Piazza, Mario Kessler, Gita Dharampal-Frick and the South Asia Institute at Heidelberg University. Javed Majeed's comments on a chapter of this work were very helpful to me. Astrid Eckert, who straddles the academic world between United States and Germany, offered me invaluable encouragement.

Heidemarie Dengl at the Zentrum Moderner Orient in Berlin and Mieke Ijzermans at the Institute for Social History in Amsterdam, have a special place in my memory for their tremendous kindness. And my visit to Moscow would not have been so illuminating without the help of Alexander Watlin.

This project only obtained its wings after a meeting with the most eminent and gracious scholar, Sibnarayan Ray, whom I first met in Kolkata. I am grateful for his willingness to share his vast knowledge, his interpretive finesse, and his largesse with me. Sibnarayan Ray's meticulous work on the oeuvre of M. N. Roy provided me a most firm foundation to begin my own explorations. Our long conversations in Kolkata and Shantiniketan were a reminder that scholarship is a wonderful inter-generational endeavour.

In India, I send my most respectful thanks to Amlan Datta, Samaren Roy and R. M. Pal for giving of their time and sharing their reminiscences. Amlan Datta's philosophical acumen and keen sense for history were particularly stimulating. Subhas Chakraborty of Presidency College, Kolkata, offered kindness, direction, and a wealth of historical knowledge. And Uma Dasgupta and Martin Kämpchen were and continue to be role models in many ways. I wish to thank the staff at the Indian National Library in Kolkata and the Nehru Memorial Museum and Library in Delhi for their unflagging assistance. And thanks also to Aditya Nigam for helping me navigate research in Delhi.

This book would not have come to fruition without the guidance, encouragement and vision of Dilip Menon. It is an honour to have written a book under his editorship. At Routledge India, special thanks to Nilanjan Sarkar and Rimina Mohapatra for their expertise and advocacy. Thanks to Kanai Paul at Renaissance Publishers for permission to use images.

And finally, a heartfelt thanks to my friends and family for sustaining me, especially Saugato Datta, Lucia Volk, Jeanile Manjapra, Thomas Brennan, Monika Golembiewski, James Savage, Julianna LeMieux and Abby Collins.

Introduction

Manabendranath Roy was an intermediary between many worlds. Writing his intellectual biography involves situating him beyond the regnant binaries of the 'local' versus 'global', or 'subaltern knowledge' versus 'Western episteme', in order to shed light on the historical significance of an interstitial thinker.[1] The case is strange indeed. As one of the premier international communists of the colonial world in the 1920s, he was an anti-colonial icon for a brief period in his life. In 1915, he scoured South East Asia for ammunition and funds as a lieutenant in one of the most powerful anti-colonial insurgency networks of Bengal.[2] By 1920, he had reached Moscow as a delegate to the Second Congress of the Communist International. His 1920 'supplementary theses on the colonial question' are included in official communist publications as an addendum to Lenin's own official writings on the subject, and the theses stimulated African, American, Indonesian and Egyptian rejoinders, among others.

Roy helped found the Mexican Communist Party and was a leading Comintern envoy to the revolutionary attempts in Germany in 1923 and China in 1926–27. He was briefly a member of the Institute for Social Research in Frankfurt (the Frankfurt School), collaborated with Max Horkheimer in 1930, and sought to establish a Frankfurt School of India in the 1940s. When M. N. Roy was imprisoned in India in 1931, an international campaign for his release drew the support of Jawaharlal Nehru, Albert Einstein and American Civil Liberties Union (ACLU) founder, Roger Baldwin. Upon his release from prison, he was, for a time, seriously considered for the post of president of the Indian National Congress, and went on to form the Indian Federation of Labour (IFL), one of the most important Indian trade union organisations of the war years. Roy's ideas contributed to the formation of the Congress Socialist Party, resonated with the contemporaneous All-Indian Progressive Writers' Association movement and influenced Jawaharlal Nehru. They also bore fruit in the perspectives of intellectuals outside India, such as the French–Caribbean poet, Aimé Césaire, or the German–Jewish political philosopher, August Thalheimer.[3] Roy was named vice–president of the International Humanist League in Amsterdam in 1952.

But if M. N. Roy was such a star in the mid-century internationalist firmament: writing a treatise alongside Lenin; plotting communist revolutions across continents; and collaborating closely with some of the most iconic intellectuals of Europe and India, then why do so few people know his name today? After all, in Indonesia, Tan Malaka, the leading Marxist cosmopolitan, inspired a whole genre of literature dedicated to fictive accounts of his life, known as the Tan Malaka novel;[4] in South America, anti-colonial communist intellectuals such as Martí and Mariátegui are invoked with canonical reverence. In the French-speaking world, world-travelling intellectuals associated with the left, such as Aimé Césaire, Frantz Fanon or Albert Memmi, are recognised as forefathers of postcolonialism. Elsewhere, in Asia, the young Marxist internationalists of the 1920s, such as Zhou Enlai, Deng Xiaoping and Ho Chi Minh became the leaders of postcolonial nation-states. Roy, as an anti-colonial cosmopolitan thinker of tremendous clout in mid-century, has been so lost to the historical record that this recently spurred a French documentary filmmaker to retrace Roy's travels across the globe.[5] This book argues that the forgetting of M. N. Roy, his place as an Indian cosmopolitan icon *manqué*, in fact constitutes an important element of his historical meaning.

Indian anti-colonial nationalists of the mid-century saw M. N. Roy as a Europhile who had spent long years outside of India, and who, upon return, refused to ascribe to accepted regimens of nationalist or internationalist identity. Roy's unpopularity stemmed from his strident attack on enshrined heroes and the pieties of international communism and mainstream Indian anti-colonialism, at the regional, national and international levels. He had come to be seen as a pariah figure already after his break with the increasingly orthodox Comintern in 1928. After 1939, following his open support for the British war effort against Fascism and Nazism, Roy set himself outside the bounds of mainstream Congress politics. In the midst of the Quit India Movement of 1942 , Roy argued that the victory of Hitler would be a far worse scenario than the temporary continuation of British rule in India. He viciously attacked the most prominent Congress leaders such as Nehru and Gandhi for their 'Quit India' politics in the context of the Second World War. Rhetoric was razor sharp and the stakes were high in the war years. Roy was labelled a 'British spy' and a 'traitor' by mainstream politicians, and was even thought to have gone mad by others.[6] And so, even while he was still alive, the forgetting of M. N. Roy in the realm of Indian high politics had already begun.

That forgetting of M. N. Roy is now almost complete. Sudipta Kaviraj has remarked that what is most interesting about Roy was his 'remarkable failure' as one who had all the makings of a major Indian leader, but who fell, *media res*, into obscurity. Philip Spratt, in the 1940s, spoke of a 'conspiracy to ignore a man who should be among the foremost in public life'.[7] But Roy seemed to have pursued one foredoomed cause after the next, and with combustible ferocity. He worked unreasonably hard at such abortive ventures, and seemed only to redouble his efforts the more obscure and unpopular they became. Kaviraj credited this failure to Roy's apparent 'heteronomy':[8] 'Roy ... saw Marxist theory as a set of *conclusions* which were to be transferred to another society...', thus presenting Roy as endemically out of touch with the actuality of India.[9] I propose instead that it was Roy's role as an intermediary between worlds, while not centred in any, that paradoxically contributed both to his forgetting as a political figure, and to the power and widespread influence of his ideas.

Frame Making and Frame Breaking

I locate the roots of M. N. Roy's intellectual biography in the context of responses to the colonial framing of time and history.[10] The British colonial project resolved Christian notions about redemption in history (eschatology) within a secular discourse about progress in history.[11] As both England and France began an era of colonisation and 'improvement' with evangelical zeal at the end of the eighteenth century, anti-colonial thinkers responded with attempts to drastically rupture the time frame of imperialism.[12]

I argue that exegesis — the interpretation and criticism of religious texts — as well as ascesis — practices of bodily discipline for cultivating spiritual force — constituted two major modes for creating new 'orders of time', or *chronosophies*, in nineteenth-century Bengal.[13] These two forms of anti-colonial practice, one centred on reading and criticising texts, the other on cultivating spiritual force (*shakti*) within the depth of the self, help explain why M. N. Roy, from the start, encountered Marxist texts as a coherent canon calling for criticism, and why he immediately locked on to narratives of explosive subjectivity and temporal rupture in his readings and applications of Marx.

By the 1890s, anti-colonial struggle was already an increasingly international endeavour in which activists envisioned alternative world orders from the one imposed by British imperial rule.[14] Nineteenth-century anti-colonial discourses about universal time culminated in the thought of what I call the 'Swadeshi avant-garde' — a group of philosophers and artists who wrote in the context of the Swadeshi

Movement (1903–1917), the most severe insurgency in India since the rebellion of 1857.[15] As opposed to being marked by inward-looking, territorial worldviews, Swadeshi avant-garde thinkers were remarkable for their international imagination, their anticipations of a 'new time' that would break into the present, and the deterritorial web of their political activism. Religious sentiment played an important role in creating the avant-gardist world map and the sense of universal time used by anti-colonial activists on their world travels. M. N. Roy was steeped in the discourses of comparative religion and modernist reconstructions of Hindu dharma that arose in nineteenth-century Bengal and culminated in the thought of the Swadeshi avant-garde. This had the effect, not of turning him inward, but rather of propelling him abroad. This biography calls for a shift in attention away from territorial horizons of India to its deterritorial networks of thought and travel, since a whole world of shuttling travellers, cosmopolitan thinkers, interstitial social spaces and zones of intellectual fusion are often obscured by standard, territory-fixed narratives.

Roy's intellectual and social position as a travelling intermediary comes into view as the narrative turns to consider the fifteen years Roy spent abroad. Berlin, a city in political disarray after the war, and bursting with new intellectual and artistic movements, became Roy's base of activity in the 1920s. His experimentations in political philosophy during the decade led him into contact with Futurism, German Expressionism and Hegelian Marxism, as well as Freudian psychoanalysis. Most importantly, the fusion of Roy's interpretive horizons with that of a fringe group of communists associated with the famed Spartakus Bund — the German Communist Party Opposition — created a powerful amalgam of Swadeshi–Marxism in Roy's writings. Central to my argument is the rift that developed within early communism between the Bolshevik ascendancy on one hand, and the members of the German Spartakus Bund closely associated with the thought of Rosa Luxemburg, who represented an authoritative alternate school of radical Marxism on the other. International communism was not a homogenous movement, but an unequal field of contestation in which the Soviet state eventually established its incontrovertible orthodoxy. In the period of the purges and the centralisation of the communist movement after 1928, Roy was easily marginalised within the ranks of left internationalists and labelled a traitor and 'renegade'.

Roy returned to India in the 1930s and made a significant impact on the theory and practice of the trade union movement with his advocacy of 'united front' politics. But during six years of imprisonment beginning in 1931, on charges of conspiracy against the Empire, Roy's work also took a new tack with its turn towards cultural critique. His writings on sexual politics from the prison cell constituted his entrée into Marxist cultural criticism from a standpoint beyond class analysis. This culminated in his voluminous writings about 'Indian fascism' in the 1940s, in which he argued that 'the world is in the midst of a civil war' between those advocating cultural regimentation, reactionary returns to the past, and autarchic notions of national identity, and those standing for cultural liberalisation, revolutionary anticipations of the future, and cross-cutting worldwide solidarities. Roy did not advocate a vision of strong and heroic postcolonial autonomy, but of a mediated autonomy, in which freedom would arrive within the framework of a South Asian federative union of member nations, and within a transnational federation of democratic governments worldwide. But this federative vision tended to be erased in the context of the Quit India Movement and the perceived political exigencies of mainstream Indian nationalists during the war years, and Roy quickly became a non-player on the Indian nationalist scene.

The final phase of his thought (from 1946 to 1954), what he himself termed 'Radical Humanism', tells us something about the life cycle of utopianism. Roy attempted to distil and preserve the key elements of his postcolonial hope in the context of the unwanted human devastation brought by Partition, as well as the varying degrees of 'covert and overt' authoritarianism in the postcolonial states after 1947.[16] While avant-garde anticipations of the future were once seen as revolutionary tools for rupturing the linear succession of historical time, by the late 1940s, hope was no longer a revolutionary tool but more a dispensation of 'new time' to be preserved and protected from the events of the day. The restorative, therapeutic quality of post-war humanism seemed to be at work on a global scale, and Roy joined a transnational community of scholars who insisted on universalistic keywords — 'man', 'humanity', 'reason', 'peace' — not because they were proponents of 'grand theory narratives', but because they struggled to articulate and maintain hope in a period of trauma and vulnerability.

Studying the ideas of M. N. Roy sheds light on the nexus of intellectual discourses he stood between. We glimpse a global horizon of modernism in political philosophy that already connected the Swadeshi avant-garde with Central European avant-garde movements even before Roy travelled abroad. We encounter a global ecumene of communism in the 1920s, as well as a transnational discourse on humanism in the 1950s. Indian anti-colonialism, then, looks increasingly like a philosophical discourse about value, truth and the social good that always called forth connection and comparison with philosophical debates and political struggles abroad, more than a means-end project of political calculus centred solely within Indian territory.[17]

It is useful to trace how a figure such as M. N. Roy has been cast in existing literature. He has become something of a cameo figure in South Asian history-writing, briefly brought on stage to speak about the fag end of Indian thraldom to the West, representing a form of cultural indeterminacy that was supposedly reminiscent of nineteenth-century proto-nationalism, not *en route* to Indian autonomy.[18] David Kopf, scholar extraordinaire of the 'Bengal Renaissance', wrote in 1969, 'from Derozio to M. N. Roy, there has been a highly articulate intellectual tradition of extreme Westernisation and accompanying cultural alienation'.[19] Curiously, a tendency exists within postcolonial studies to picture M. N. Roy, one of the first Marxist theoreticians of India and among the most brilliant, as heteronomous, xenophilic and Eurocentric, and as a Bengali *bhadralok* determined by that social position. Dipesh Chakrabarty remarked in his *Provincializing Europe* that M. N. Roy was entrapped in the ideologies attendant to global capital, unable to break into the temporalities and imaginary beyond Western epistemic domination. 'A long series of illustrious members of this social group [the Bengali *bhadralok*] — from Raja Rammohan Roy... to Manabendranath Roy, who argued with Lenin in the Comintern — warmly embraced the themes of rationalism, science, equality and human rights that the European Enlightenment promulgated'.[20] If an efficacious Indian anti-colonialism is understood as the construction of an inner realm of Indian selfhood against an outer realm of colonial heteronomy, as Partha Chatterjee powerfully theorised in *The Nation and its Fragments*, then Roy's thought must be considered inefficacious and out of synch with the long march of Indian anti-colonialism. The 'inner domain of national culture', Chatterjee pointed out, had to be wrested from the colonial public sphere by a return to indigenous aesthetic discourses, family life, vernacular languages and popular and peasant culture. This inner domain, the argument goes, the source of cultural autonomy, was a necessary ingredient for mature anti-colonial praxis. If anti-colonialism consists in 'symbolic contestations within a field of power', Chatterjee argued, then it is only those cultural–symbolic acts which challenged or denied Western cultural hegemony that provided the momentum for a successful twentieth-century Indian anti-colonialism.[21]

But, these important arguments by Chatterjee and Chakrabarty assume a dichotomous field of symbols and power/knowledge split between the authentic local and the heteronomous global. More recently, Andrew Sartori has proposed a way out of this dichotomisation. Contestations with colonial power/knowledge do not account for the form of Roy's thought. Rather, Sartori maintains that the determinative effect of global capital helps explain why 'parochial cosmopolitans' such as M. N. Roy arose, not only in Bengal, but also in Japan, Germany and elsewhere in the twentieth century. Roy's turn towards the 'inwardness' of humanism at the end of his life was already pre-programmed by the fact that global capitalism created the conditions for the possibility of Roy's worldview based on abstract notions of 'the human', as also on the reformulation of liberation in terms of the interiority of the bourgeois self.[22]

While these post-structuralist and neo-Marxian approaches to intellectual history offer their own important insights, I take a different, hermeneutic departure here, in order to explain global intellectual conjuncture while not losing sight of idiomatic particularity. M. N. Roy's thought, like that of colonial thinkers more generally, is best understood not within the framework of base and superstructure, however defined, but within the contexts of multiple, contingent, socially-located conversations. In a series of charged conversation zones set across the world, Roy was both the recipient and formulator of meaning. The intermediate 'third space' of conversations and the play of agency and structure it engendered provide the parameters within which to study the ideas of M. N. Roy.[23]

I suggest that Roy is actually representative of some important general features of early twentieth-century Indian anti-colonialism. He is important not for his exceptionality, but for how he serves as a heightened case of a family relation of anti-colonial cosmopolitanism. Indian intellectuals participated simultaneously in regional, transregional and global public spheres of debates, and their writings evidence this polyphony. I approach M. N. Roy, not as a stock character in the repertoire of responses to 'the West' or to 'global capital', but as a traveller and intermediary beyond the British–India axis, and a collaborator with groups abroad who were marginalised within that rather problematic and ambiguous category called 'the West'.

Fractures in the 'West' must be critically mined for their historical consequences. The international imagination of Indians was not contained within the British-India colonial axis. In fact, in the context of anti-colonialism, travels that thwarted the colonial pair-bond played a most important role. M. N. Roy's intellectual pursuits surpassed the imperial axis connecting India to Britain, taking him to the United States of America, Mexico, Germany, the Soviet Union and China along with other locales along the way. There were many termini in Roy's travels, both physical and imaginary, resulting in a complex stitching of meanings. The geopolitical tensions between nation-states such as the United States, Britain, Germany, Japan and Russia created interstitial spaces within which Indian anti-colonial thinkers could deploy their own projects. The factions and fragments *within* European and American states, and within global movements that became increasingly linked to European statecraft, such as Soviet communism, produced both possibilities for and constraints on the Indian anti-colonial struggle.

The study of cosmopolitan intermediaries, interpreters and interstitial thinkers has received much attention in recent works on South Asian intellectual history. Kapil Raj has convincingly pointed to the need for the study of mediators of knowledge within colonial zones of exchange.[24] Javed Majeed has suggestively investigated the role of travel and circulations on Indian intellectuals, while Sanjay Subrahmanyam's studies of 'conceptual contaminations' in the early modern period also enlighten this theme.[25] Leela Gandhi's work on the implications of inter-cultural friendship provides another avenue for productively studying intermediaries and their interstitial spaces of thought and life.[26] And Sugata Bose's study of the travelling imagination of Rabindranath Tagore and Subhas Chandra Bose showed how articulations of 'different universalisms' informed many anti-colonial pursuits.[27] Studying new archives that illuminate the history of in-between figures provides an important groundwork for better understanding how the play of territoriality and deterritoriality has defined the history of ideas in the modern period.

This work seeks to shift the study of South Asian cultural and intellectual history from the opposition between two mutually exclusive concepts, autonomy versus heteronomy, to the interplay between two co-existing pursuits, autonomy and solidarity, within the context of modernity.

It is with regard to the interplay between projects of autonomy and solidarity — their way of constructively building on each other — that I introduce the theme of cosmopolitanism. The term is open to many glosses, and so I must specify my usage here. Forms of cosmopolitanism, especially since the mid nineteenth century, often arose as internationalist projects of politically subordinated groups, and tended to express a strong aspirational dimension to change or destroy the existing world order, instead of preserving or affirming it. Another form of cosmopolitanism, on the other hand, was often conceived by the political elites of European nation-states as the state of benign peace within a commonwealth or concert of similarly advanced and civilised nations. From the Seven Years' War onwards, European legal theorists and philosophers wrote increasingly on themes of cosmopolitanism and internationalism, on the need for internationally recognised laws governing commerce, the high seas, the rights of exiles and refugees, and the protocols to resolve territorial disputes. These deliberations tended to peak precisely in those years of greatest inter-state conflict, whether in the 1790s with the French Revolution, or the 1810s in the aftermath of Napoleon, or the 1830s with the rise of new European competition for imperial markets.

The ethical discourse of cosmopolitanism among subordinated communities, whether inside Europe or in the colonial world, and the internationalist political and institutional pursuits that accompanied it, were qualitatively different from the projects advanced by the elites of European nation-states. The anticipatory quality of colonial cosmopolitanism, seeking both autonomy and solidarity, was a hugely important motor for anti-colonial struggle.

Besides the philosophical aspect of cosmopolitanism, Roy also demonstrated its experiential side. In this book, I depict Manabendranath Roy as an anti-colonial cosmopolitan thinker, given the way he was absorbed into multiple cultural and social horizons, and how he carried forward the impress of his past encounters almost as physiological traces informing and affecting his reactions to new circumstances. Such cosmopolitanism might indeed be seen as a feature of colonial thinkers at large, with the study of Roy offering a heightened case-study. Anti-colonial intellectuals were interested both in defining the boundaries of the nation and of national selfhood, and also in creating bonds of sympathy with foreign groups worldwide in the pursuit of broader political and ethical goals.

Quentin Skinner made the argument for the need to study the 'illocutionary force' of ideas. He envisioned authorial intent as constituting a *response* to a rich intellectual context of debate and discussion.[28] My addendum to Skinner in this work maintains that travelling intermediaries such as M. N. Roy must be set in multiple, incongruous contexts and intellectual traditions. Roy's philosophical claims developed as attempts to resolve problems within his disparate contexts, as also to build bridges and create amalgams between them. In this intellectual biography, close attention is paid to the friction of social experiences, as well as the breakdown of Roy's intellectual tools in moments of crisis. I consider the way thinking approximated a form of mental labour carried out with and against the resistance of historical events.

The diverse array of sources engaged in this book include archival materials from Russia, Germany, Britain, France, the Netherlands, the United States and India. Published and unpublished letter correspondence, press clippings and surveillance files provide views on the transnational field of Roy's thought and life. Of course, I also include a comprehensive reading of Roy's work with special attention to reorientations, crises and revisions, in order to understand the movement of his thought over the course of his life.

That figures such as Roy who upset accepted notions of national, international or cultural belonging tended to acquire a marginal status not only in Indian politics, but also within the historical narrative, does not mean that they should be understood primarily as victims of history, exiles from home, or as displaced votaries of melancholia. I resist the titillation of a narrative of exile that would represent Roy as someone alone, unprecedented, abandoned or exiled. M. N. Roy's thought was a peculiar expression of a family relation, or perhaps, the nexus between multiple family relations. Roy was not, as Nehru feelingly once wrote, 'a lonely figure, deserted by everybody'.[29] Not only did he have a chosen family of transnational dimensions comprised of like-minded thinkers, but his philosophical vision strongly resonated with many Indian thinkers generally considered more central to the South Asian historical narrative. Roy belonged to multiple social and intellectual emplotments from his position in the interstices, and in that sense, was defined by an excess of interconnection, not a condition of political loneliness.

Notes

1. The figure of the 'interstitial thinker' has received in-depth discussion by a number of scholars. See especially Dilip Menon. (forthcoming). 'A Local Cosmopolitan: "Kesari" Balakrishna Pillai and the Invention of Europe for a Modern Kerala', in Sugata Bose and Kris Manjapra (eds.), *Cosmopolitan Thought Zones: South Asia and the Global Circulation of Ideas.* London: Palgrave Macmillan. Also see the seminal work of Homi Bhabha. 1994. *Location of Culture.* London: Routledge, p. 3.
2. The Jugantar group. See Sibnarayan Ray. 1987b. *Selected Works of M. N. Roy*, vol. 1: p. 13.
3. See introduction by Robin Kelley to Aimé Césaire. 2000. *Discourse on Colonialism*, trans. Joan Pinkham. New York: Monthly Review Press.

4. James Siegel. 1997. *Fetish, Recognition, Revolution*. Princeton: Princeton University Press, p. 167. M. N. Roy does appear, under the alias of 'Professor Verma', in Mulk Raj Anand. 1941. *The Sword and the Sickle*. London: J. Cape.

5. See Vladimir Leon's 2006 Film. *M. N. Roy: Le Brahmane du Comintern*. Paris: L'Institut National de L' Audiovisuel.

6. Roy himself commented on this view, saying in a speech from 1946, 'You simply disregarded my ideas, took up a tolerant attitude: the man seems to have gone a little out of his mind...' See M. N. Roy. 1946b. *New Orientations: Lectures Delivered at the Political Study Camp held at Dehra Dun from May 8–18, 1946*. Calcutta: Renaissance Publisher, p. 6.

7. Philip Spratt, foreword to Ray, *New Orientation*, pp. vii–viii.

8. Sudipta Kaviraj. 1986. 'The Heteronomous Radicalism of M. N. Roy', in Thomas Pantham and Kenneth L. Deutsch (eds), *Political Thought in Modern India*. 1987. pp. 209–31.

9. Kaviraj, 'Heteronomous Radicalism', p. 224.

10. On the notion of 'cognitive framing' see George Lakoff. 1987. *Women, Fire, and Dangerous Things: What Categories Reveal about the Mind*. Chicago: University of Chicago Press, pp. 9–10.

11. The distinction between theoretical liberalism and political liberalism is drawn by George Lakoff. 1946. *Moral Politics*. Chicago: University of Chicago Press, pp. 19–22.

12. Sudipta Kaviraj (1995) has a number of brilliant chapters on the nineteenth century contestations of time in *The Unhappy Consciousness: Bankimchandra Chattopadhyay and the Formation of Nationalist Discourse in India*. See chapters 3 and 4.

13. Krzysztof Pomian introduces the idea of 'chronosophy'. See *L'ordre du Temps*. 1984. Paris: Gallimard, p. 26.

14. On early twentieth-century debates about 'world orders' and Western hegemony, see Cemil Aydin. 2007. *The Politics of anti-Westernism in Asia: Visions of World Order in Pan-Islamic and Pan-Asian Thought*. New York: Columbia University Press.

15. In invoking a 'Swadeshi avant-garde', I reference the convincing interpretation offered by Partha Mitter of an Indian avant-garde in art in the early twentieth century. See Partha Mitter. 2007. *Triumph of Modernism: India's Artists and the Avant-Grade, 1922-1947*. London: Reaktion Books.

16. Ayesha Jalal. 1995. *Democracy and Authoritarianism in South Asia: A Comparative Perspective*. Cambridge: Cambridge University Press, pp. 38–62.

17. This overemphasis appears in the work of Manu Goswami. 2004. *Production India: From Colonial Economy to National Space*. Chicago: University of Chicago Press, p. 201 and Sumathi Ramaswamy. 2001. 'Maps and Mother Goddesses in Modern India', *Imago Mundi*, 53(1): 97–114.

18. Ashis Nandy used psychoanalysis to describe Indian anti-colonialism as a process of 'working through' colonialism in the development of a strong, autonomous anti-colonial ego. See Ashis Nandy. 1983. *Intimate Enemy*, New Delhi: Oxford University Press.

19. David Kopf. 1969. *British Orientalism and the Bengal Renaissance: The Dynamics of Indian Modernization, 1733-1835*. Berkeley: University of California Press, p. 253.

20. Dipesh Chakrabarty. 2000. *Provincializing Europe: Postcolonial Thought and Historical Difference.* Princeton: Princeton University Press, p. 4.
21. Partha Chatterjee.1993. *Nation and its Fragments,* Princeton: Princeton University Press, p. 13.
22. Andrew Sartori. 2008. *Bengal and Global Concept History: Culturalism in the Age of Capital.* Chicago: University of Chicago Press, p. 255.
23. Hans-Georg Gadamer. 1993. *Truth and Method.* New York: Continuum, p. 105.
24. Kapil Raj. 2006. *Relocating Modern Science: Circulation and the Construction of Knowledge in South Asia.* Delhi: Permanent Black, pp. 19–21, 109–10, provides an imaginative discussion of intellectuals as 'intermediaries' and 'mediating agents'. Also see Chris Bayly on 'dubashes' and translators in C. A. Bayly. 1996. *Empire and Information: Intelligence Gathering and Social Communication in India, 1780–1870.* New York: Cambridge University Press, p. 46.
25. On 'conceptual contamination' see Sanjay Subrahmanyam. 2005. *Mughals and Franks,* Delhi: Oxford University Press, p. 12; See Javed Majeed's invocation of the 'necessarily fragile, mixed self' in Javed Majeed. 2007. *Autobiography, Travel and Postnational Identity: Gandhi, Nehru and Iqbal.* New York: Palgrave Macmillan, p. 161.
26. Leela Gandhi. 2006. *Affective Communities: Anticolonial Thought, Fin-de-Siècle Radicalism, and the Politics of Friendship.* Durham: Duke University Press, pp. 19–23; Seema Alavi. 2008. *Islam and Healing.* New York: Palgrave Macmillan; Harish Trivedi. 1993. *Colonial Transactions: English Literature and India.* Calcutta: Papyrus; Sara Suleri. 1989. *Meatless Days.* Chicago: University of Chicago Press.
27. Sugata Bose. 2006. *A Hundred Horizons: The Indian Ocean in the Age of Global Empire.* Cambridge: Howard University Press.
28. Quentin Skinner. 1974. 'Some Problems in the Analysis of Political Thought and Action', *Political Theory,* 2(3): 277–303. See also James Tully (ed.). 1988. *Meaning and Context: Quentin Skinner and His Critics.* Princeton: Princeton University Press.
29. Jawaharlal Nehru, *An Autobiography,* 1962. p. 268.

1

The Swadeshi Avant-Garde

M. N. Roy's *Memoirs* (1964) can be read as a piece of expressionist art.[1] It recounts repeated breakages of time flow, in which new ideas and new time intrude. Roy repeatedly 'discovers new meaning', announces 'lands of hope' to which he travelled in pursuit of the nationalist cause, and reports his 'rebirths' along the way.[2] The path of anti-colonial struggle and self-discovery through foreign worlds did not create a *Bildungsroman* of stadial change reaching ultimate culmination, but rather a discontinuous and fragmentary narrative of pregnant expectancy and unforeseen crisis events. Roy narrates his autobiography as a continual explosive encounter with the new, not unlike classic works of Central European literary Expressionism, such as Ernst Bloch's *The Spirit of Utopia* (1918) or Hugo Ball's *Flight Out of Time* (1927).[3] These features of Roy's autobiography — the focus on temporal rupture and on the encounter with the foreign — were standard to the Bengali avant-garde milieu in which he grew up.

Manabendranath Roy (1887–1954), born Narendranath Bhattacharya to a Brahmin family in the West Bengal village of Kseput, grew up in the context of increasingly radical anti-colonial politics. By the late nineteenth century, radical resistance movements against the British began to be organised in Calcutta. First came the enhancement of European dominance in... the Calcutta Corporation with the Amendment Act of 1899, passed to 'give the Europeans a general and adequate security' in matters of commerce and industry.[4] Then the partition of Bengal, first proposed by Viceroy Curzon in 1903 and enacted in 1905, divided Bengal between a Western Hindu and an Eastern Muslim province in the interest of a 'diminution of the power of Bengali political agitation'.[5] A violent insurgency of unprecedented proportions, the Swadeshi Movement, arose, lasting from 1903 till 1917. It marked a new era of politics and thought with implications for decades to come.[6]

From his youth, Roy was closely associated with some of the most powerful figures of radical Swadeshi politics and thought. He studied at the new Bengal Technical College with the young Swadeshi educationalist,

Benoy Kumar Sarkar, disciple of Satish Chandra Mukherjee.[7] It is likely that, as a young man, Roy undertook social work and trade union organisation in villages alongside Swadeshi labour activists. He was mentored by Barindrakumar Ghosh, the revolutionary leader and brother of Sri Aurobindo. Roy soon became a lieutenant to perhaps the greatest Bengali Swadeshi insurgent, Jatin Mukherjee.[8] For a number of years, Roy plotted heists of armouries and gun shops ('dacoities'), constructed bombs and attempted to assassinate British colonial officials.[9] From 1903 to 1915, between the ages of sixteen and twenty-eight, Roy was active in the Calcutta revolutionary underground.

The young M. N. Roy, like many of the *madhyabitta* (middle-class) high-caste Hindu youth of his day, also pursued the ascesis of dharma.

Illustration 1.1   Roy as a Swadeshi revolutionary in 1910.

Source: Sibnarayan Ray, *In Freedom's Quest: Life of M. N. Roy*, vol. 4, Part 2. Used with permission.

Practising yoga, abstaining from sexual activity and reading the Gita formed central features of the daily discipline of the Swadeshi revolutionaries.[10] The anti-colonial nationalist struggle in these years was often framed in religious terms. Swadeshi radicals believed themselves to be involved in *pracesta* (righteous striving).[11] They wanted to attain *swaswata Bharat* (eternal India).[12] They viewed the possible loss of their lives for the cause of national freedom as an aspect of *sadhana* (the spiritual journey).[13] Yet, far from simply representing the deployment of 'religion' in the pursuit of political ends, spiritual sensibilities reflected both the increasingly deterritorial social experience of the time, as well as the desire to break out of the dominant colonial framing of universal time and global space.

'Deterritoriality', as a term of art, received inconsistent glosses by Deleuze and Guattari, the very theorists who coined it.[14] My reading of 'deterritoriality' follows from their discussion in *A Thousand Plateaus* (1987), in which the 'deterritorial body' is defined as a system of 'waves and intensities' co-produced along with the formation of bounded political forms.[15] Under the conditions of a global and interconnected economy of unprecedented scale since the seventeenth century, territorial entities of the modern era are localisable in bounded space and often take the form of nation-states, while deterritorial 'bodies' are fields of waves or vectors always on the way to somewhere else, circulating across state borders and in supranational communities of value and belonging. But the 'de–' in 'deterritorial' is not privative. It does not suggest that which is antithetical to bounded national space. Deterritoriality and territoriality play together in a dialectic in the modern era, suggest Deleuze and Guattari. 'The territorial assemblage', they point out, 'implies a decoding and is inseparable from its own deterritorialisation'.[16] This has led scholars to speak of modern processes of 'de/reterritorialisation'.[17]

In the specific example of anti-colonial nationalism, the co-production of territorial politics, aimed at achieving a free Indian nation-state, and deterritorial politics, aimed at forging transnational communities of affiliation and solidarity, has received scholarly attention.[18] By invoking the deterritorial register of anti-colonial politics here, I seek to challenge the priority granted to 'home politics' and to territorial aspiration in the study of anti-colonial nationalism.[19] In fact, the nationalist system lived through the political missions and interpretive actions of globally dispersed actors as they travelled. And the objectives and anticipations of deterritorial anti-colonial nationalism often exceeded territorial frames. The inhabitation of medial spaces and interstices by Indian anti-colonial activists, travelling beyond boundaries and seeking fusions with foreign worlds, had its own ontological status, and was not simply *en route* to territorial form.

By the 1890s, in the prime colonial cosmopolis of Calcutta, it was common for individuals from diverse classes to have had some experience of foreign travel, or to know someone with stories of life abroad — whether he or she be coolie, lascar, free labourer, hajj pilgrim, student or *bhadralok* tourist. Beginning in the 1830s Calcutta was a hub port for the travel of indentured labour out of and into India.[20] The circulatory travel of Bengali elites going to Britain rose from the late 1860s onwards, especially with the rise of Indians in the colonial administration and with the increasing place of Indian professionals in the legal and higher education systems, positions that assigned great status to accreditation in the imperial metropolis.[21] From 1840s onwards, expanding greatly after the opening of the Suez Canal, Calcutta also became one of the major cities for the hajj pilgrimage by ship to Mecca, Medina and Karbala.[22] By the late nineteenth century, the polysemy of the term 'nation' in Bengali discourse, which in the writings of a nationalist author such as Bankimchandra Chattopadhyay could refer to 'all the races of India', or to 'the Hindus', or to the 'the Bengalis',[23] could also refer to a notion of a 'greater India' comprising the home population and the diaspora. An article in the Calcutta *Modern Review* of 1907, for example, blatantly declared: 'hundreds of well-to-do families, Hindu in every sense of the word, [are] found in regions as distant as South America and Oceania. It is they who in their humble way form what I call Greater India outside the limits of our motherland'.[24] Meanwhile, the celebrated Bengali editor, Ramananda Chatterjee, began publishing his journal *Prabasi* in 1897, whose title (*Prabasi* can be awkwardly translated into English as 'those Bengalis living away from home') addressed a greater Bengali community living both inside and outside the territorial bounds of Bengal.

A new kind of political thought crystallised in the context of deterritorialisation at the turn of the century in Bengal, of which M. N. Roy's writings are an expression. What may be termed the 'Swadeshi avant-garde' emphasised deterritorial notions of space and new notions of time. When Manabendranath Roy travelled abroad in 1915, initially in search of ammunition and funds to support the Swadeshi movement, first to ports in southeast Asia, then on to the United States and Mexico and then on to Germany and Russia, he had already embarked on an avant-garde project of travel, aimed not at reconfirming the extent routes of Indian voyage through the empire, but at remaking the map of the world through the agency of travel itself.

The Swadeshi Movement

Partha Chatterjee has advanced the penetrating argument that the anti-colonial era began with the turn towards an inner domain of cultural autonomy and the rejection of Western modes, a process whose roots stretch back at least to the 1860s, with the rise in stature of the tantric saint Ramakrishna, and the gradual acceptance of his mystical message by urban elites.[25] The partition of 1905 was less a cause than an occasion for the expression of long-simmering anti-colonial discontent. Secret societies in the Calcutta and Dacca undergrounds constructed bombs and hurled them at colonial officers. These *samiti* conducted raids of government munition depots, and destabilised the municipal corporations through acts of banditry. Meanwhile Swadeshi industries and storefronts were established, in which foreign goods were boycotted and locally manufactured goods sold. Urban Bengalis began wearing homespun fabrics.[26] Rabindranath Tagore and Aswini Kumar Datta started campaigns for village education, as Kshitimohan Sen and Dinesh Chandra Sen recorded the Baul folk songs of the countryside to teach city dwellers about the riches of authentic Bengali village culture. The Dawn Society under Satish Chandra Mukherji pioneered programmes for 'national education' in opposition to Viceroy Curzon's project, begun in 1899, to reassert the 'central authority and government control' over Calcutta University.[27] Meanwhile, Aurobindo Ghosh and Taraknath Palit headed the Swadeshi universities established in 1906, the Bengal National College and the Bengal Technical College.[28] And this rise of nationalist educational institutions attained culmination in 1914 with the founding of the University Science College by Ashutosh Mukherjee and P. C. Ray.[29] In the midst of these trends, Mohandas Gandhi commented in 1909 that Swadeshi marked the 'real awakening' of Indian anti-colonial nationalism.[30] So powerful was the onset, and so resonant with a global eruption of anti-colonial activity, that the British government unleashed the largest counter-insurgency measures since 1857 to meet the threats.[31]

But, I claim here that the Swadeshi movement cannot be properly configured within the dichotomous schemes of the inner versus outer, the local versus global, the spiritual versus secular or the indigenous versus the Western. Swadeshi thought went beyond 'territorial nativism'.[32] The fusion of temporalities that gave birth to twentieth-century political radicalism in Bengal and in India was not born from an 'inner national domain' alone, but arose from a re-framing of the globe and the place of Indian consciousness within global temporalities. Swadeshi avant-gardism was coded with a travelling imagination, often expressed in a register attuned to metaphysics and spirituality. Swadeshi thinkers saw their struggle as contemporaneous with other nationalist struggles worldwide, and they also envisioned the distant actions of Indian anti-colonial radicals abroad, in places such as London, Paris, New York and San Francisco, as simultaneous and connected with their own actions in Calcutta, Dacca, Lahore, Madras or Bombay.

Anti-colonial nationalism, and the Indian nation itself, was envisioned by Swadeshi thinkers as a deterritorial entity. This global system lived through the political missions and interpretive actions of its members as they travelled.[33] I suggest here that in order to begin unravelling the life-path and the intellectual project of the far-travelling Swadeshi thinker, Manabendranath Roy, anti-colonial nationalism should not be defined in terms of the 'longing for cartographic form' or the search for the 'inner boundaries of freedom' alone.[34] Apart from the modernist pursuit of form, there was also at work an equally modernist longing for the transgression of boundaries, and for alternative universal communities.

The Swadeshi movement took place in the context of growing identification by Indians with a world-wide belt of insurgencies in the first years of the twentieth century to oppose European and American imperial power: in coastal China, Japan, Egypt, the Ottoman empire, in Poland and Czechoslovakia, in German Southwest Africa and the Philippines.[35] Swadeshi radicals believed their projects to be associated with the rise of French and Russian radicalism in the 1880s, and with Czech, Irish and Chinese radicalism in the 1900s.[36] By September 1908, thirty-seven Calcutta revolutionaries were committed for trial due to their insurgent activity. Meanwhile, similar uprisings were taking place in Dacca, Bombay, Madras and Lahore. In May 1907, Lajpat Rai and Ajit Singh of Punjab were deported from India to London on sedition charges. In July 1908, Bal Gangadhar Tilak, revolutionary leader in Bombay, was sentenced to transportation in Burma where he remained until 1914. Aurobindo Ghosh was likewise tried and imprisoned at Uttarpara in 1909. In these years, a large number of prominent anti-colonial leaders departed for Europe and the United States to avoid sedition charges, including Bipin Chandra Pal, Ram Bhaj Dutt, Hardayal and G. S. Khaparda.

A number of major conspiracy cases were opened over the course of the decade.[37] The combination of deportations, imprisonments and detentions, and the 1909 promise by British authorities to reunify

Bengal, brought one phase of Swadeshi insurgency to an end by 1910. But the political vectors of the Swadeshi uprising were pointing towards the world as revolutionaries only redoubled their travels across the globe in the coming period, following paths that led to Tokyo and Nanking, to Vancouver, San Francisco and New York, and to the anarchist milieu in Paris. Swadeshi temporalities were promiscuous, continually crossing with foreign discourses and political movements. Anti-colonialism developed into an animated constellation, and not a radial hub-and-spoke system, in which all travel routes lead to the home country of territorial India.

Swadeshi thinkers imagined the political body of India to have worldwide dimensions. The idea of *antarjatik* (international) education was a central element of the syllabi at the new Swadeshi colleges established in Calcutta in 1906. For example, students at the Bengal National College and the Bengal Technical College were required to study either French or German, and by 1915, hearing German spoken in the student coffeehouse on College Street was not uncommon. For students of political science, the curriculum prescribed the study of English, French, German, Swiss, American, Japanese and Turkish societies. The history track included the study of 'Japan, China and America 1850–1900', as well as 'the historical characters of Washington, Bismarck, Mazzini, Garibaldi, Meiji Emperor Mutsuhito, Napoleon, Frederick the Great, Chengiz Khan and Abraham Lincoln'.[38] The national education movement normalised a sense that India's experience had affinities throughout the world. Recalling Bipin Pal's terminology in the *Soul of India* (1911), the curricula aimed to induct students into the 'cult of nationality as of humanity', since 'the nation [rests] eternally in Humanity'.[39]

Furthermore, the international imagination operated through an articulated plotting of global comparisons for India's anti-colonial struggle. There was a pattern to how parallels were drawn in the Swadeshi avant-garde worldview. The temporal regime of British imperialism asserted that India would gradually improve, and would become like Britain within the domain of empire, obtaining modern consciousness after passing through a gradient of apprenticeship. In opposition to this developmentalist temporal scheme, Swadeshi intellectuals collected evidence of revolutionary temporalities of revolutionary rupture and punctual change occurring throughout the world. Calcutta newspapers and journals often featured articles on the revolutionary crises in China and the Boxer Rebellion of 1900, in Japan during the Russo-Japanese war of 1905, and in the case of the Suffragists in England and Ireland.[40] Swadeshi radicals lived in a temporality of expectancy, in which the eruption of a 'new time' into the present would occur through insurgent action.[41] And yet the eruption of this mystical time would not place Indians in a solipsistic state, set apart from the world, but would reveal India as ensconced in 'the lap of Humanity'.[42]

The Swadeshi avant-garde's patently deterritorial character was itself a form of radical resistance to the way the colonial order had framed time and history.[43] One Swadeshi radical from the Punjab, Hardayal, articulated the new anti-colonial framing of 'Indianness' current in the Swadeshi years, writing in an article for the Calcutta Swadeshi press in 1913:

> The twentieth century will witness a mighty revolution in India and the world. The Time-Spirit will ring out the old and ring in the new in all civilised countries. The nineteenth century has been the period of destruction, criticism and preparation to a large extent. The twentieth century will be the era of construction and fulfillment in many respects. India is not isolated from the world.[44]

These key features of Swadeshi avant-gardism — the focus on the advent of 'the new' and the imagination of Indians as part of the world — were reiterated throughout the period. In 1917, at the instance of the Russian Revolution, Ramananda Chatterjee, editor of the *Modern Review*, wrote:

> When the popular aspirations of a country lead to an earthquake, its tremors travel far beyond its borders. They can be felt ... all over the world ... We might not be independent like the Russians and Germans but we certainly constitute a part of this world ... we are not isolated from the rest; the thoughts, emotions, aspirations and success of every country affects us. Our rightful aspirations need to be fulfilled.[45]

These kaleidoscopic mirrors in which Swadeshi avant-gardists saw their own struggle refracted throughout the world suggests that their sense of identity — their construction of selfhood — was configured in a way that was not solely based on territory, homeland and ideas about indigenous culture.

Anti-Colonial Networks

'On the outbreak of the First World War in 1914', wrote M. N. Roy in his *Memoirs*, 'Indian revolutionaries in exile looked towards Germany as the land of hope, and rushed there full of great expectation'.[46] In April 1915, Roy travelled to Dutch Indonesia as the Swadeshi insurgent deputised to organise the delivery of weapons from German consuls.[47] Roy made three trips back and forth between Jakarta and Calcutta, attempting to orchestrate the clandestine shipment of a large trove of '30,000 rifles with 400 rounds of ammunition'.[48] Ultimately, the inconstant German consul in Java stepped back from the plans and recommended that M. N. Roy travel to Berlin itself in order to plead for support. Given the Swadeshi worldview at the time, such global tours of duty were not outlandish propositions. In 1906, Hemchandra Kanungo travelled from Calcutta to Paris and back in order to learn bomb-making techniques from Russian anarchist groups.[49] Taraknath Das left Calcutta in 1903 as a Swadeshi radical, and became a leading organiser of Indian communities in Vancouver and San Francisco. Bhupendranath Datta and Abinash Bhattacharya left Calcutta in 1908 and eventually made their way to Berlin as diasporic revolutionaries, returning years later to write books on the theme of India's freedom struggle abroad.[50]

At the intersection of events in 1915, M. N. Roy, twenty-eight years old, embarked on his journey to Berlin, a destination he would eventually reach with fateful consequences some five years later. With a forged French-Indian passport provided by the German Embassy in Peking, and travelling under the alias of an Indian Christian priest named 'Father Martin', he boarded a German gunboat to Shanghai, and eventually found himself on a Japanese trans-Pacific luxury liner to San Francisco. Cushioned by German funds and by the subterfuge of an invented persona, Roy left territorial India, as many Swadeshi modernists had before him, for the promise of the foreign as experienced within the global deterritorial body of India.[51]

We must return to the nineteenth century in order to bring into view the intellectual underpinnings that made such world-travelling imaginations possible. Was the salient feature of the Swadeshi years in fact the birth of a strong, insurgent Indian selfhood, or rather the invention of avant-garde selves that continually sought to incorporate the foreign and to blur and contaminate the category of Indianness? If the latter, then our understanding of anti-colonialism must be revised. At stake was not solely a process of inventing cultural or spatial closure, but rather a dialectic between the assertion of autonomy on one hand, and the pursuit of mediation and global solidarities on the other.[52]

Schemes of Colonial Universal Time

Imperialism erected its own 'temporal architecture' — its own underlying notion of universal time and historical succession.[53] The Swadeshi modernist imagination can be seen as arising out of critiques of this temporal order of colonial universalism. Two major influences, Rammohan Roy (1774–1833) with his style of scriptural exegesis, and Vivekanada (1863–1902) with his reconstruction of Hindu ascesis and dharmic practice, provided two powerful influences on Swadeshi modernist thinkers. The intellectual giants of Swadeshi, individuals such as Aurobindo Ghosh, Satish Chandra Mukherjee, Bipin Chandra Pal and Rabindranath Tagore, fused these nineteenth-century discourses and passed them down to a younger generation of chronic world travellers, of which M. N. Roy was a major representative.

In discussing the framing of universal time introduced by the British colonisation of India beginning in the late eighteenth century, it may well seem strange to begin with a discussion of the German philosopher, G. W. F. Hegel. After all, British liberal philosophers of the nineteenth century supposedly defined themselves against the 'Idealism' of the German titan. And yet, especially in terms of the way they thought of universal time, the scions of liberal philosophy, J. S. Mill, Henry Maine, Matthew Arnold, Herbert Spencer, all commented on Hegel, and by the end of the liberal nineteenth century, Hegelian thought was perhaps the most influential force in British philosophy departments.[54] Hegel meditated upon the *Neuzeit* (new time) of European secular universalism that arose with the 'imperial meridian', as the French and British states embarked on unprecedented projects of modernisation and colonisation.[55] Hegel, greatly inspired by the French Revolution and a close reader of Scottish Enlightenment and British liberal thinkers, captured most brilliantly the framing of colonial universal time.[56] Krzyztof Pomian once commented, 'it is in the works of Hegel that a chronosophy founded on the idea of progress received its canonical form'.[57]

It should not be surprising to note that Hegel began as a young theologian, and his earliest writings were concerned with reinterpreting Christian salvation history, especially the notion of *kairos*, the 'fullness of time', that arose when God came to earth in the form of Christ, according to Christian theology.[58] This was the confessional starting point of Hegel's later discussion of the functioning of universal time as the transition from potentiality to actualisation. In some ways, one might claim that Hegel disclosed a Christian historicist sensibility within the apparently purely political or economic programme of liberalism. Through the experience of the French Revolution and the political bombshell of the Declaration of the Rights of Man, Hegel's thought moved away from theology towards political philosophy.

He developed a narrative of the World Spirit journeying through mediation and negativity, but gradually attaining self-recognition and *kairos*, in the form of the European state.[59] It was in the European state that freedom could finally be obtained, wrote Hegel, since freedom 'is the individual subjective will realising that its will is actually that of the universal will'.[60] Such a realisation was uniquely available to citizens of European states. Hegel called this the attainment of the 'concrete universal' in history, and the culmination of universal time.

Yet the problem of how the non-European, non-Christian cultures of the world would be incorporated into this universal time of the World Spirit remained. Hegel introduced a gradient of consciousness to resolve this problem, one that stretched from what he judged as the low-level sentience of Asians, to the alert, active mental capacities of Europeans. This certainly fed on a longer tradition of identifying hierarchies among human civilisations in European thought.[61] On the other hand, this does not mean that there were not other traditions native to European that contested such a hierarchical view, asserting either admiration for or conservative aloofness towards cultures outside Europe.[62]

Whereas late eighteenth-century Scottish Enlightenment discourse tended to present Europe as orderly and mannerly and Asia as licentious and rude, in Hegel's rephrasing, Europe had a plenitude of consciousness and Asia only a presentiment of it.[63] Europeans were awake and capable of self-recognition, meanwhile Asians were deficient, insentient and slumbering. For Hegel, the Asian mind was 'vegetal'. In the section on India in his *Phenomenology of Spirit* (1807), Indian spirituality is the religion of 'flowers and animals' where the 'passivity and impotence of contemplative individuality pass into destructive being-for-itself'.[64]

Hegel's gradient of consciousness, placing Asians at the far pole teetering on the vegetal, resonated with the rise of British Utilitarian scholarship on India at the time, and influenced Karl Marx's writings later on. In Hegel's *Lectures on the Philosophy of History* of 1822, his conception of the Orient seems to refer to James Mill's *History of British India*, published just two years earlier. The Utilitarians, following their intellectual patron, Jeremy Bentham (1748–1832), believed that Indian society could be salvaged only by concerted governmental measures in the realms of jurisprudence, property rights and education.[65]

In his *History of British India*, Mill made the case for drastic measures, emphasising the sheer depravity of Indian and Chinese minds. '[The Chinese and Indians] are to nearly an equal degree tainted with the vices of insincerity; dissembling, treacherous, mendacious, to an excess which surpasses even the usual measure of uncultivated society'. Mill further declared:

> Both are disposed to excessive exaggeration with regard to everything relating to themselves. Both are cowardly and unfeeling. Both are in the highest degree conceited of themselves, and full of affected contempt for others. Both are, in the physical sense, disgustingly unclean in their persons and their houses.[66]

The approach to colonialism that Mill prescribed coincided, unsurprisingly, with the rise of evangelicalism in India.[67] Utilitarianism assumed a 'world-levelling, unificatory epistemology' that was, ironically, deeply based on assumptions of hierarchy and temporal plenitude inherent in Christian universalism.[68] A hierarchisation of global space and human consciousnesses was carried out in the name of a 'world-levelling' ideal. Just as the British Utilitarians envisaged a universal temporality of modern, industrious, productive time that eventually would overcome the peculiar backward temporal flows of India, Christian missionaries believed they were interrupting the backward and profane Indian rituals and religions and raising Indians to a recognition of the one true God. The missionaries enunciated in confessional terms what British Utilitarians said in secular ones. 'That Britain is capable of becoming an extensive blessing to India is admitted by all who are thoroughly acquainted with the circumstances... That this arises chiefly from her being able to impart a knowledge of the scriptures and a love to vital godliness, is also admitted', wrote the *Friend of India*, the journal of the Serampore missionaries, in its inaugural edition of 1818.[69] The colonial project was imbued with an evangelical impulse.

Brahmo Exegesis

But from the inception of colonial universalism, Indians sought to break its frame of temporality by using religious discourse to create alternative framings of universal time. There were many trajectories for doing this, drawing on various 'great traditions' indigenous to South Asia. Brahmoism, the most influential Bengali intellectual movement of the nineteenth century, established by the cosmopolitan thinker Rammohan Roy (1774–1833), focused on excavating, through textual criticism and scriptural exegesis, a common universal time at the heart of all religious traditions across cultures in the pursuit of a more inclusive universalism. Rammohan sought to disclose a deep-lying unitary principle at the core of all religious traditions, thereby disproving colonial assertions about plenitude available only within a European order of time. Rammohan suffered the aspersion of both Christian missionaries and Brahmin traditionalists, as well as lawsuits lodged against him by his own family due to his controversial claims.[70]

Born into an elite Brahmin family of the service gentry to the Mughal court, Rammohan Roy was educated in a *madrasah*, and wrote voluminously in Persian. Assuming the canonicity of religious traditions, he made his arguments via an exegesis of the Christian New Testament, the Vedas and the Qu'ran. And his assertions of a common monotheistic principle at the core of each of these canons allowed him to make the argument for their fundamental equivalence in terms of their proximity to ultimate truth. In 1804, Rammohan published the Persian text *Tuhfatul Muwahhiddin*, 'To the Believers in One God'. His central concept, 'the monotheistic principle of God', derived primarily from the Islamic notion of *tauhid* (the existence of one God).[71]

There was a universal inner temporality, asserted Rammohan, deriving from the 'nature of the species' that was the common essence of all mankind.

> It is quite evident that all [men] are living here equally enjoying the blessings of heaven, as the light of the stars, the pleasure of the season of spring, the fall of rain ... as well as [suffering] from the same inconveniences and pain, darkness and severity of cold and mental disease and narrowness of circumstances ... without any distinction in being the follower of a particular religion.[72]

He proposed that all humans, regardless of religion, existed on an equal plane since they all experienced joy with the 'blessings of heaven' and suffered from the trials of material existence. Rammohan continued, '... in China, in Tartary, in Europe and in all other countries, where so many sects exist, all believe the object whom they adore to be the Author and Governor of the Universe; consequently, they must also acknowledge according to their own faith, that this our worship is their own'.[73] This claim that, according to each group's 'own faith', the monotheist principle could be uncovered became one of the signature assertions of Rammohan's writings, and of Brahmo exegesis. The Brahmo Samaj, started by Rammohan in 1828, made scriptural exegesis into a practice of inter-faith translation. This foreshadows the way that M. N. Roy, a century later, would look upon the exegesis of the Marxist canon as a way of disclosing the commonality at the heart of European and Asian sociological experience. Rammohan used the practice of scriptural exegesis as a form of intellectual anti-colonial resistance. Insistence on the canonicity of diverse religious traditions was a chief element of his work, whereby Rammohan aimed to destroy the gradation of human consciousness inherent in colonial universalism. The Bible itself was an Asian book, written in Asian languages with a fundamentally 'Asiatic' notion of God, he wrote. If one closely reads the Bible, he noted, one sees that 'in addressing God, the third person and also the second are constantly used in immediate sequence, and that this variation is considered a rhetorical trope in Hebrew and Arabic, as well as in almost all the Asiatic languages...'[74]

This prefigured a long succession of Brahmo exegetes in the nineteenth century who wrote on the theme of the 'oriental Christ'. Keshab Chandra Sen, the inheritor of the Brahmo mantle from Rammohan, would assert the Asian origins of Jesus in his famous sermon 'Jesus Christ, Europe and Asia' of March 1866. And in 1869, Pratap Chandra Mazumdar wrote his book *Oriental Christ*, which interpreted Jesus' actions such as bathing, praying, healing and feasting as deriving from a common fund of Asiatic culture and spirituality. Brahmos offered cosmopolitan interfaith readings of religious canons through textual practices that disclosed a universal time that cut through cultural difference.

These arguments attracted European thinkers, and spurred them to counter-cultural critiques of European exceptionalism. In 1869, the French official, Louis Jacolliot, published his *La Bible de l'Inde: vie de Iezeus Cristna*, a book that Nietzsche would later refer to in his *Laws of Manu*, as Suzanne Marchand has recently shown.[75] Jacolliot had been in Calcutta since 1865, and had no doubt been greatly influenced by Brahmo exegesis. Likewise, Rammohan's exposition of the Vedas was read by the Transcendentalists of New England, as shown in Henry David Thoreau's correspondences.[76] Pratap Chandra Mazumdar, a leading Brahmo exegete, took a celebrated tour through the United States in 1874, lecturing at Harvard and fifty Unitarian chapels.[77]

Breaking the frame of the gradient of human consciousness imagined within colonial universalism, Keshab asked in his famous sermon of 1883, 'Asia's Message to Europe': 'Is there one astronomy for the East and another for the West? Are there different anatomies in different climes and ages? Is there an Asiatic optics as distinguished from European optics? Is there such a thing as Jewish zoology and Mahometan geometry?... It is God's science, the eternal verity of things'.[78]

Brahmo textual practices were characterised throughout the nineteenth century by this sort of levelling exegesis aimed at envisioning an inclusive common temporality for all peoples worldwide.

Dharmic Asceticism

In contrast to Rammohan's universalising exegesis, a different form of frame-breaking arose in the meditations on Hindu dharma throughout the nineteenth century, which envisioned the eruption out of colonial universalism of an alternative and autonomous universal time. As opposed to proposing an 'inner realm' of Hindu authenticity as opposed to an 'outer realm' of Western culture and power, nineteenth-century discourse on dharma proposed an alternative *world* of Hindu universal time at work in both the 'canonical' texts of the Vedanta, as well as in folk traditions. This provided another source for the rise of Swadeshi avant-gardism by the turn of the century. It is worthwhile pointing out at the start that even if we might heuristically separate Brahmo exegesis and dharmic ascesis as two strategies for reframing time in nineteenth-century colonial Bengal, we must also be aware of their continual interplay. In fact, both traditions were imbricated in each other as scholars of Hindu dharma relied on the idea of a single, unified Hindu 'canon' of 'high texts' on which exegetical criticism could be applied.[79]

The notion of *Sanatanadharma*, or the 'Hindu eternal order of things', became one of the most important keyterms in the writings of Bengali Hindu intellectuals in the mid nineteenth century. Radhakant Deb, a critic of Rammohan Roy, established his Dharma Sabha in 1830 as an alternative to Roy's Brahmo Samaj. One of the aims of Deb's group was to insist, not on the fundamental identity of all religious traditions worldwide, as had Rammohan, but on the *difference* between the teachings of the Hindu canon and other bodies of scripture. Hinduism, proponents claimed, was unlike the historical religions of Christianity and Islam, founded by a prophet at a specific moment in the past. Rather, the dharma that Hindus observed was an eternal order outside the historical progression, and religious aspirants could erupt into that eternal plane through acts of individual ascesis, without the need to locate salvation (*mukti*) in a larger eschatological process of redemption through history.[80] Writers on Hindu dharma emphasised that salvation in Hinduism, that is, eruption out of the imminent realm of historical succession into the transcendent realm of the eternal present, was always available to the aspirant (*sadhak*) through the labour of spiritual practice, without the need to rely on the historical succession itself as did religions such as Christianity, Islam and even some schools of Buddhism, which variously envisioned salvation as part of a historical culmination that would occur at some point in the future.

In the years after the rebellion of 1857, this notion of *sanatana dharma or swaswata dharma* (eternal dharma), as a wholly different order of universal time *not* based on the assumption of an eschatology, or progress through history, received increasing focus among Bengali Hindu writers.[81] Writings on dharma played a major role in the late works of Bankimchandra Chattopadhyay, as well as Dayananda Saraswati and Keshab Chandra Sen. But Ramakrishna Paramahansa, the influential Hindu tantric saint, was the most powerful exponent of dharmic practice for the Bengali middle-classes. He began his twelve years of isolated ascetic pursuit (*sadhana*) in 1856. For the urban *madhyabitta* classes he would emerge as the most influential expositor of an eruptive universal time that could destroy the frame of colonial universalism, not at some point in the future, but in the eternal present of perpetual now-times available to all ascetic aspirants.[82] Vivekananda, who became the most significant interpreter and exponent of Ramakrishna's message, spoke of the coming of Ramakrishna as marking the advent of a new order of time, in which the permanence of the eternal realm, and the ever-present possibility of breaking out of the temporality of colonial universalism, finally became apparent not only to Bengali Hindus, but to people worldwide:

> The time was ripe, it was necessary that such a man [Ramakrishna] should be born, and he came... the fulfilment of the Indian sages, the sage for the time, one whose teaching is just now, in the present time, most beneficial. And mark the divine power working behind the man. The son of a poor priest, born in an out-of-the-way village, unknown and unthought of, today is worshipped literally by thousands in Europe and America, and tomorrow will be worshipped by thousands more.[83]

Ramakrishna's message of dharma arrived in a moment of *kairos*. When the 'time was ripe', as Vivekananda put it. But while Ramakrishna represented the culmination of a historical progression as 'the fulfilment of the sages', his message paradoxically aimed to free individuals from the historical progression. In Vivekananda's interpretation, Ramakrishna made tangible, accessible and *popular* the dynamic of eruption out of quotidian time that was once only available to the sages and world-renouncers. Vivekananda presented Ramakrishna as nothing less than a Hindu messiah, in that he first distributed knowledge of salvation more broadly than it had been before, but second, in that he showed that salvation lay not in fulfilment or culmination within the historical succession, but in the power of each individual, through acts of discipline and worship, to harness dharmic eternal time and rupture the linear temporal order.

Ascetic spiritual practice on the part of individual Hindu aspirants was required to achieve this goal of blasting apart the frame of colonial universalism, taught Vivekananda. The notion of world-revising spiritual force erupting out of individual subjecthoods became a central trope of the Swadeshi avant-garde. Ramakrishna spoke of spirituality as an erotic experience marked by 'anxious desire' (*vyakulata*) for universal union.[84] Meanwhile, Bankimchandra wrote of the discipline called for to pursue dharma in his *Dharmatattva* (1888). 'For the development of body culture (*anushilan*) three things are necessary: 1) time 2) energy (*shakti*) 3) determination'. Bankim went on to explain that the religious seeker, the *sadhak*, must avoid unworthy activities so as to preserve the time of good vocation in life. Time was cleaved between the quotidian and the dharmic. By 'engaging in the profane, the time of spiritual culture is spontaneously lost'.[85] Anushilan, or bodily discipline, was to create an autonomous time-experience from out of the colonial everyday.

While proponents of Brahmo exegesis focused on texts, gurus of dharmic asceticism in the last half of the nineteenth century, focused on the apparatus of the body and the self as a tool for breaking the timeframe of colonial universalism. The channelling of *atmashakti*, or spiritual force, would lead to the eruption of a wholly new order of reality. Swami Vivekananda (1863–1902) became the great expositor of politicised dharmic practice. He codified and formalised Ramakrishna's teachings into a set of systematised texts.[86] His intent was to give 'an authoritative pronouncement of Hinduism in all its phases'.[87] Perhaps the most important recurrent theme of Vivekananda's teaching was that of exploding spiritual force, channelled through the body.

The body was the conduit for both spiritual energy (*shakti*) and political change. Vivekananda was fascinated by the notion of exertion, and with the body as a working organism. 'When a man goes into deep sleep he enters a plane beneath consciousness. He works the body all the time, he breathes; he moves the body, perhaps, in his sleep, without any accompanying feeling of ego'.[88] He continued, 'one of the greatest lessons I have learned in my life is to pay as much attention to the means of work as to its end... We also read this in the Gita and learn that we have to work, constantly work with all our power; to put the whole mind in the work, whatever it be, that we are doing'.[89]

Vivekananda's vision centred around the cultivation and channelling of *shakti*, or the spiritual force, associated with worship of the mother goddess Kali.[90] Such dharmic practice generated autonomy since, '... the character of that man who has control over his motives and organs is unchangeably established. He controls his own inner forces, and nothing can draw them out against his will'.[91] But this autonomy was also socially distributive. The energy that was produced within the yogic genius (a figure of great fascination in the nineteenth century) had universal implications. 'The highest men are calm, silent and unknown. They are the men who really know the power of thought; they are sure that, even if they go into a cave and close the door and simply think five true thoughts and then pass away, these five thoughts of theirs will live through eternity'.[92] Vivekanada insisted, however, that those who think 'eternal thoughts' should not recede from the world, but should return to their people and bring about social and political change. Vivekananda did just this, of course, as he set up the Ramakrishna Mission, travelled to London, Paris and through the United States as a spokesman for modern Hinduism, just as he also stoked revolutionary unrest in Bengal.[93]

The genius, or *mahamanab*, according to Vivekananda, was capable of confecting and socially distributing a new universal time. 'Such a centre is the *real* man, the almighty, the omniscient, and he draws the whole universe towards him... The men of mighty will [that] the world has produced have all been tremendous workers — gigantic souls, with wills powerful enough to overturn worlds, wills they got by persistent work, through ages and ages'.[94] The great sage could unleash 'the power... inside every man', that would 'cause these giants [the British] to wake up'.[95]

And locating the power of salvation in the very body of individual aspirants also meant that new times could erupt throughout the world, wherever aspirants travelled. Vivekananda viewed mystical Hindu yogis as world-travelling engines of spiritual eruption for the good of the nation. For example, he himself went on two celebrated missions to Europe and America.[96] The notion of a mystic transferal of charisma, even over great distances, between the genius-saint and the people became a common trope in Swadeshi modernist thought, picked up, for example, in Benoy Kumar Sarkar's 1922 assertion that it was up to India's travelling scientists, scholars and artists to 'assimilate the new achievements of mankind in aesthetics as in the utilitarian sciences and arts... [as] one of the chief means of acquiring strength in order that the Orient may push forward the creative urge of life...'[97]

The modernist practitioner of dharma, such as Vivekananda, did not envision an eschatological history of redemption coming to Man, but more decentralised occurrences of energetic eruptions among a multitude of saints spreading throughout the world.[98] The universal time of dharmic practice would not come about in the moment of messianic fulfilment at some point in the future, but through the agency of individual aspirants in myriad, globally distributed now-times. This new time, created by dharmic practice, was not thought of as a particularity, as the etching out of an indigenous or ritual inner spirituality against the universality of secular Western public time.[99] The very fact of positing egress to a whole new order of time was based on the idea of an alternative universalism that was just as much 'everywhere' as European Christianity's Messianic history. Vivekananda, for example, went to some lengths to argue that the temporalities of Buddhism, Islam and Christianity did not contain the same plenitude as did Hinduism.[100] 'The Monistic Vedanta is the simplest form in which you can put truth. To teach Dualism was a tremendous mistake made in India and elsewhere...'[101] Dharmic ascesis asserted the autonomy and priority of Hindu universal time over other universalisms, especially the colonial variety. His claim for distinction was intended to assert an alternative universalism in the context of anti-colonial struggle.

My point in following these arguments is to show that the assertion of difference made by proponents of dharmic asceticism was not based on creating a space of interiority, or inwardness marked off from secular, political or public outer time-space. Rather the new modernist teachings about dharma, which bore the mark of hermeneutic engagement with European scholars especially in terms of asserting the canonicity of the Vedanta, involved creating an alternative englobement of time for Indian (Hindu) subjectivities. Precisely because it was universally at work, dharma provided a horizon within which some Indians could choose routes of world travel and make sense of their travels *differently* than if they presumed the timeframe of colonial universalism. The universalism of dharma was inherently opposed to notions of historical determination and the idea of stadial progress, as it was based on the perpetual potential for freedom channelled through the apparatus of the individual aspirant's body and selfhood.

In the Swadeshi period and beyond, this dharmic temporality was employed in ways that privileged the world as the appropriate milieu for the spiritual aspirant and that insisted on radical contingency — that the historical progression could be broken at any time, and that world-travelling sadhak perpetually had the potential of rupturing the course of history by their unexpected experiences abroad. Benoy Kumar Sarkar, who was M. N. Roy's teacher at the Bengal Technical University in 1907, spoke about the need for Swadeshi activists to 'digest (*hajam kara*) the atmosphere of the world', and then to transfer this novelty to their people by writing about and publishing on their experiences.[102] For the Swadeshi avant-gardist, the discipline of writing was an important element of dharmic asceticism.[103] For youth such as M. N. Roy, dharmic practice became tied up with a cult of mobile eruptive subjectivity, foreign experimentation and authorship.

Swadeshi thinkers envisioned new communities of universal belonging outside colonial universalism. Chittaranjan Das and Rabindranath Tagore imagined a Greater India associated with a 'Pan-Asian' cultural realm stretching from India through Southeast and East Asia. In the writings of Muslim Swadeshi-Khilafat writers, such as Maulana Abdul Hamid Khan Bhashani and Kazi Nazrul Islam, eruptive subjectivities were seen to populate the Islamic ecumene stretching from India to Central Asia and the Middle East.[104] And another group of Swadeshi thinkers, central among them Aurobindo Ghosh, Benoy Kumar Sarkar and his student M. N. Roy, posited a universal realm connecting Indians with the young economic juggernauts, such as Japan, Italy, America, Russia and Germany. Eventually, M. N. Roy would insist that the 'workers and labourers of the world' constituted a universal community that was ushering in a new time for all of humanity. What the 'holy man' was to dharmic aspirants of the late nineteenth century, the peasantry would become to M. N. Roy in his post-war Marxist writings. The peasant would become the collective genius through which a new revolutionary energy and a new time would be distributed throughout the world.

The Swadeshi Avant-Garde

Despite the historical tensions between the two branches of Bengali responses to colonial universalism considered above, Brahmo exegesis and dharmic asceticism, these styles of interpretation fused in the Swadeshi years at the turn of the century. Swadeshi avant-garde thought focused, on the one hand, on excavating a hidden com-monality underlying forms of cultural difference. On the other hand, practicing a new, self-conscious dharmic ascesis, Swadeshi thinkers also set out to imagine autonomous new universal communities that erupted out of the temporal linearity of colonial universalism. Needless to say, religious notions could be employed with a number of contrasting intentions. The nineteenth-century reconstructions of canonical forms of Hindu spirituality, whether in Brahmo or Shakta varieties, could be use to make exclusionary claims, or could be employed to bring an affective sensibility to projects of bridging difference and purposefully travelling the world.

How did this specifically take shape in Swadeshi avant-garde thought? Aurobindo Ghosh's writings were perhaps some of the earliest expressions. Recently returned from Cambridge where he excelled in his studies and graduated at the top of his class, (and having been embarrassingly rejected from the prestigious Indian Civil Service because of a failed horse-riding test), Aurobindo wrote a classic precursor to Swadeshi new thinking, *New Lamps for Old* (1893). It bore the marks of both the monistic and the energistic as Aurobindo argued for an alternative universalism. The author emphasised that the existential pursuit of new meanings for the modern Indian self, ones that placed Indians in an international context, went hand-in-hand with the political pursuit of struggle against British imperialism. Instead of 'eking out [a] scanty wardrobe with the cast-off rags and threadbare leavings of [the] English masters',[105] Indians had to transcend the intellectual niche that imperialism prescribed for them and associate themselves with the world. Ghosh linked India to other national cultures where humanistic universalism had been expressed: Athens, Rome and post-revolutionary France.[106] Aurobindo emphasised in 1893 that French politics, erupting in the early years of the Third Republic into bouts of anarchism and social rebellion, offered a mirror for current-day Indian anti-colonialism. Both political cultures, he claimed, aspired to nationalism and universalism simultaneously. This linking of the inner with the outer, and the national with the international, was more than a rhetorical strategy. It arose from the logic of the Swadeshi deterritorial imagination.

Leaving territorial India did not entail going into the utterly foreign; for, in distant places, Swadeshi intellectuals believed they saw reflections, or anticipations, of their own experiences. Even earlier in the nineteenth century, Calcutta intellectuals hailed the annexation of Venice by united Italy in 1866, and mourned the defeat of France in the Franco-Prussian War of 1871, maintaining that these events had an immediate bearing on Bengal's own experience.[107] The world map that Swadeshi intellectuals travelled through in the early twentieth century was informed by these earlier contestations of the centre-periphery, developmentalist framework of colonial universalism.

Another major exponent of Swadeshi avant-gardism was Bipin Chandra Pal, a thinker influenced, as so many of these figures were, by the multiple contexts of Brahmo thought, the teachings of Vivekananda, but also *Vaishnav* devotionalism and nineteenth-century Positivism.[108] Pal and Aurobindo Ghosh were the editors of the most influential Swadeshi newspaper, the *Bande Mataram*, in 1907. Bipin Chandra Pal situated universalism at the core of revolutionary nationalist politics in his haunting and evocative rumination, *The Soul of India* (1911), when he wrote, 'The Cult of the Mother among us is by no means a political cult... It is related to our highest conceptions of Humanity... The true Cult of the Mother is, therefore, with us as much a Cult of Nationality as of Humanity'.[109] This idea of the 'cult of the humanity' emanated from the Positivist notion of the 'Religion of Humanity' formulated by Auguste Comte, which had a great reception in Calcutta particularly from the 1880s onwards.[110]

The 'cult' of the Mother, Pal stated, was tantamount to the cult of humanity-wide universalism. And for Pal, this cult would best be achieved through the practice of dharma. The intellectual inspirations of Swadeshi, from Ramakrishna and Vivekananda to Aurobindo and Bipin Chandra Pal, all emphasised that anti-colonialism involved the transcendence of the spatio-temporal regimen of colonial rule through involvement in a global terrain. By the 1890s nationalists saw the *world*, however conceived, as the appropriate theatre for the cultivation of autonomous *atmashakti* or spiritual force, as well as the realm in which to discover an underlying global unitary principle. In other words, the world was the preferred object of desire of Swadeshi modernists. In 1912, Benoy Kumar Sarkar coined the term '*viswa-shakti*' or 'world-force', to describe the transformative influences that awaited Indians if they would make a discipline of travelling abroad.[111] Benoy Kumar Sarkar, like so many Swadeshi avant-garde thinkers, situated Indian subjectivity within a global frame. 'The more India advances *Swadeshi*, i.e., the indigenous industry movement, the more will she have to depend on places abroad'.[112]

Rabindranath Tagore, in his life as well as his writing, offers another example of Swadeshi avant-garde's deterrritorial imagination. In his writings, *Bharat Mata* (Mother India) is pictured as itinerant, not as fixed in place.[113] Speaking of Mother India not as a static geopolitical entity, but as a 'fugitive', a global traveller continually crossing to foreign shores, Tagore wrote in 1918:

> Darkly you swept on, Eternal Fugitive, round whose bodiless rush
> stagnant space frets into eddying bubbles of light.
> Is your heart lost for the Lover calling you across his immeasurable loneliness?
> Is the aching urgency of your haste the sole reason why your tangled tresses
> break into stormy riot and pearls of fire roll along
> Your path as from a broken necklace?
> [...]
> Leave the hoard on the shore and sail over the unfathomed dark towards limitless light.
> It was growing dark when I asked her, 'What strange land have I come to?'[114]

What characterised the Swadeshi avant-garde was the pursuit of new universal time, not enclosure within territorial frames. Swadeshi thinkers were less concerned with maintaining boundaries of cultural form, and more with rupturing the timeframe and geographic mapping of colonial universalism. In the pursuit of a retemporalisation of the world, the contingent outcomes of experiment, exploration and invention, in opposition to notions of historical determination, ensured that the ramifications of Swadeshi avant-gardism were multifarious, bridging and amalgamating the distant and familiar.

This is the framework we need to properly understand M. N. Roy's life and work as he travelled away from India in 1915, into the deterritorial system of Indian anti-colonialism in the midst of the First World War. Physical distance from Indian territory did not curtail intimate involvement in the energies of the Indian freedom struggle. Roy remained obsessively concerned with India — he would write about its economy, society and politics by Mexico City day and Berlin night. There was an alternative map to the world, a compact of solidarity and of shared consciousness, that fused India to zones abroad.

Notes

1. The memoirs first appeared as serialised articles in issues of *Independent India* beginning in 1952.
2. Germany was originally a 'land of hope' for Swadeshi activists because of its promise to provide arms for insurgency movement. Roy recalled 'finding new

meaning' while reading Marx's texts at the New York Public Library in 1916. And he reports multiple 'rebirths', in Mexico, in Germany and in Russia. See M. N. Roy. 1964. *Memoirs.* Bombay: Allied Publishers, pp. 3, 31, 81, 213, 217.

3. Hugo Ball was a leader of the Dada Movement, which peaked between 1916 and 1923.

4. Quote of Viceroy Curzon reproduced in Rajat Ray. 1979. *Urban Roots of Indian Nationalism: Pressure Groups and Conflict of Interest in Calcutta City Politics.* Delhi: Vikas Publishers, p. 60.

5. As stated by Lord Apthill, a chief administrator in Calcutta, in 1903.

6. This periodisation follows Leonard Gordon, *Bengal: The Nationalist Movement*, and not Sumit Sarkar's 1905–08 periodisation in Sumit Sarkar. 1973. *The Swadeshi Movement, in Bengal, 1903-1908.* Delhi: People's Publishing House.

7. Sarkar, *The Swadeshi Movement*, p. 248. Roy was a student of Bengal Technical College. See Sibnarayan Ray. 1998. *In Freedom's Quest: A Study of the Life and Works of M. N. Roy.* Calcutta: Minerva, vol. 1: p. 19.

8. Ray, *In Freedom's Quest*, p. 29ff.

9. According to Bhupendra Kumar Datta, a contemporary acquaintance of Roy, interviewed by Samaren Ray, in Sibnarayan Ray (ed.), *Philosopher-Revolutionary.* 1984, p. 41.

10. J. C. Ker. 1973 (1917). *Political Trouble in India, 1907-1917.* Calcutta: Superintendent Government Printing.

11. Hemchandra Kanungo. 1928. *Banglay Biplab Pracesta.* Calcutta: Kamala Book Depot.

12. Dineshranjan Das. 1924, *Kallol.* vol. 3: p. 791.

13. Abinash Bhattacharya. 1979. *Iyorope Bharatiya Biplaber Sadhana.* Calcutta: Popular Library.

14. Compare, for example, *Anti-Oedipus*, translated by Robert Hurley, 1977: pp. 9–15, with *A Thousand Plateaus*, translated by Brian Massumi, 1987: pp. 156–57.

15. Gillies Deleuze and Felix Guattari. 1987. *A Thousand Plateaus.* Minneapolis: University of Minnesota Press, p. 149.

16. Ibid., p. 336.

17. Ibid., pp. 149–66. See important applications of this concept to history by Gray Wilder in Gray Wilder. 2005. *The French Imperial Nation-State: Negritude & Colonial Humanism between the Two World Wars.* Chicago: University of Chicago Press; Rebecca Karl. 2002. *Staging the World: Chinese Nationalism at the Turn of the Twentieth Century.* Durham: Duke University Press.

18. Benedict Anderson. 1983. *Imagined Communities: Reflection on the Origin and Spread of Nationalism.* London: Verso, pp. 16–35.

19. Chris Bayly has provided a brilliant narrative of global conjunctures in the modern era in C. A. Bayly. 2004. *The Birth of the Modern World, 1780-1914: Global Connections and Comparisons.* Malden: Blackwell.

20. David Northrup. 1995. *Indentured Labor in the Age of Imperialism.* Cambridge: Cambridge University Press, pp. 65-67. Labour outflows peaked in the 1840s and 1860s but remained high throughout the late nineteenth century. See Bayly, *Birth of the Modern World*, p. 133.

21. P. N. Mathur. 1977. *The Civil Service of India*. Jodhpur: Prabhat Prakashan, pp. 91–95. Entry into the covenanted Civil Service required travel to Britain to sit in the exams.

22. Michael Low. 2008. 'British Empire and the Hajj: Pilgrims, Plagues, and Pan-Islam under British Surveillance, 1865–1908', in *International Journal of Middle East Studies*, (2008) 40(2): 269–90.

23. Tapan Raychaudhuri. 1988. 'Bankimchandra Chattopadhyay', in *Europe Reconsidered: Perceptions of the West in Nineteenth Century Bengal*. Delhi: Oxford University Press, p. 135.

24. Bhai Parmanand. 1912. 'Greater India', *Modern Review*, February, 11(2): p. 152.

25. Partha Chatterjee asserted that the 'departure' of Indian anti-colonialism occurred with the separation between an 'inner domain' of national culture from the outer domain of the colonial state. See Partha Chatterjee. 1993. *The Nation and Its Fragments*. Princeton: Princeton University Press, pp. 6, 32–45.

26. Chris Bayly. 1986. 'The Origins of Swadeshi (home industry): Cloth and Indian Society, 1700–1930', in Arjun Appadurai (ed.), *The Social Life of Things: Commodities in Cultural Perspective*, Cambridge: Cambridge University Press, pp. 285–321; Lisa Trivedi, 'A National Public in the Colonial World: Swadeshi Goods and the Making of the Indian Nation', in Dane Kennedy and Durba Ghosh (eds.), *Decentering Empire*, 2006: 150–75.

27. See quote of Curzon in Suresh Chandra Ghosh. 2005. 'The Genesis of Curzon's University Reform: 1899–1905', Minerva, 26 (4): 470. Curzon's committee drafted the Indian Universities Act of 1904, aimed at strengthening the powers of the government over higher education.

28. Haridas and Uma Mukherjee. 1957. *The Origins of the National Education Movement 1905-1910*. Calcutta: Jadavpur University, p. 48.

29. Editorial. 1943. 'University College of Science, Calcutta', in *Science and Culture*, 9(1): 19.

30. M. K. Gandhi. 1997. *Hind Swaraj and Other Writings*. Anthony Parel (ed.), Cambridge: Cambridge University Press, p. 19.

31. Between 1908 and 1910, an onslaught of repressive measures were instituted including the Arms Act, the Explosive Substances Act, the Seditious Meetings Act, the Conspiracy Law, and the Press Act. See Ker, *Political Trouble*, p. 3. In August 1908, thirty Calcutta revolutionaries were committed for trial and a further seven the following month. The following year saw the Nasik Conspiracy case and the Howrah–Sibpur Gang case in 1910. Nirode Kumar Barooah. 2004. *Chatto: The Life and Times of an Anti-Imperialist in Europe*. New Delhi: Oxford University Press, p. 50. The combination of deportations, imprisonment and detentions for trial brought one phase of Swadeshi insurgency to an end. The counter-insurgency measures of the British focused on all the theatres of revolutionary activity throughout India, not just Calcutta. In May 1907, Lajpat Rai and Ajit Singh of the Punjab were deported from India to London on sedition charges. In July 1908, Bal Gangadhar Tilak, revolutionary leader in Bombay, was sentenced to transportation in Burma where he remained until 1914. Following his sentencing, a number of prominent Indian agitators departed for London to avoid sedition charges, including Bipin Pal, Ram Bhaj Dutt, Hardayal and G. S. Khaparda. See Ker, *Political Trouble*, p. 174.

32. Manu Goswami's term. Manu Goswami. 2004. *Producing India: From Colonial Economy to National Space.* Chicago: University of Chicago Press, pp. 242–76.

33. Deleuze and Guattari, *A Thousand Plateaus*, pp. 149–66.

34. Provocatively theorised by Sumathi Ramaswamy. 2002. 'Visualizing India's Geo-body', *Contributions to Indian Sociology,* 36(1): 151–89; Thongchai Winichakul. 1994. *Siam Mapped: A History of the Geo-body of the Nation.* Honolulu: University of Hawaii Press. Manu Goswami, *Producing India*, p. 243.

35. Some important events in this period include the Boxer uprising, 1898 to 1901, the anti-American insurgency in the Philippines, 1898 to 1901, the Russo–Japanese War of 1905, the Dinshawai incident and the outbursts of nationalist sentiment in Egypt in 1906, the Boxer rebellion between 1898 and 1901, the building of the Hijaz railway in 1900.

36. On connections between Indian and Czech revolutionaries in New York around 1908 see Bhupendranath Datta.1958. *Biplaber Padacinha.* Calcutta, p. 1; On connections between Indians and Irish nationalists in the early twentieth century, see Harald Fischer-Tiné. 2006. 'Indian Nationalism and the "world forces"', *Journal of Global History*, 1(2): 325–44. Contacts with Chinese nationalists, especially Sun Yat-Sen, are explored by Cemil Aydin.2007. *The Politics of Anti-Westernism in Asia: Visions of World Order in Pan-Islamic and Pan-Asian Thought.* New York: Columbia University Press, p. 152.

37. The Nasik and the Howrah–Sibpur cases. See Ker, *Political Trouble*, pp. 3, 174.

38. Mukherjee and Mukherjee. *The Origins of the National Education Movement 1905–1910*, pp. 47–64.

39. Bipin Chandra Pal. 1958 (1911). *The Soul of India.* Calcutta: Choudhury & Choudhury, p. 138.

40. See for example, 'Japan and India' in *Bande Mataram*, 18 January 2007, a nationalist newspaper edited by Aurobindo Ghosh and Bipin Chandra Pal. See article on Ireland in 13 March 1907 issue, 'Boycotting in Ireland'. Also, 'Awakening of China', 4 April 1907, and 'Seventy-six Suffragists Arrested', 8 April 1907.

41. Discussions of 'new time' in European thought from the eighteenth century onwards are addressed in Koselleck. Reinhart Koselleck. 2002. 'The Eighteenth Century as the Beginning of Modernity', *The Practice of Conceptual History: Timing, History, Spacing, Concepts*, trans. Todd Presner. Stanford: Stanford University Press, p. 165ff.

42. Pal, *The Soul of India*, p. 138.

43. On colonial liberalism and territoriality see Uday Mehta. 1999. *Liberalism and Empire: A Study in Nineteenth-Century British Liberal Thought.* Chicago: University of Chicago Press, p. 132. Also see Matthew Edney. 2000. *Mapping an Empire: The Geographical Construction of British India, 1765–1843.* Chicago: University of Chicago Press, pp. 9–15; Goswami, *Producing India*, pp. 31–71 on the national territorialisation of India in the 1870s and 1880s; Also Partha Chatterjee on the notion of India as *Bharat* in Puranic history writing and the difference between the concept of a cultural world, and a territory, 'The Nation and its Pasts', *Nation and its Fragments*, pp. 73–94.

44. Har Dayal. 1913. 'India and the World Movement', *Modern Review*, February, 13(2): 185.

45. Ramananda Chatterjee, 'Russiai sadharantantra pratishthai amader ananda' (Our Joy at the Establishment of People's Rule in Russia), *Prabasi* 1917, quoted in Rajarshi Dasgupta. 2003. *Marxism and the Middle Class Intelligentsia: Culture and Politics in Bengal 1920s-1950s.* Ph.D. Dissertation, Oxford University Press, p. 24.
46. M. N. Roy's, *Memoirs,* p. 11.
47. *Sedition Committee Report,* 1973 [originally published in 1918]: 121.
48. Ibid.: 121, 122.
49. Sarkar, *The Swadeshi Movement in Bengal, 1903-1908,* p. 59.
50. Bhupendranath Datta. 1983. *Bharater Dvitiya Swadhinatar Samgram: Aprakasita Rajnitik Itihas.* Abinash Bhattacharya. 1979. *Iyorope Bharatiya Biplaber Sadhana.*
51. The expression is taken from the title of Vincente Rafael's excellent book on travelling Filipino anti-colonial nationalists. Vincente Rafael. 2005. *The Promise of the Foreign: Nationalism and the Technics of Transalation in the Spanish Phillippines.* Durham: Duke University Press.
52. Benoy Kumar Sarkar famously called his multivolume series of travel books in the 1920s. Benoy Kumar Sarkar. 1926. *Duniyar Abhaowa.* Calcutta: Raychaudhari.
53. Krzyszt of Pomian. 1984. *Ordre du temps.* Paris: Gallimard, p. 219.
54. On the reception of Hegel in Britain, beginning in the 1830s, and focusing mostly on his biblical criticism and his theory of history, see Kirk Willis. 1988. 'The Introduction and Critical Reception of Hegelian Thought in Britain 1830-1900' in *Victorian Studies,* 32 (1): 85-111.
55. Reinhart Koselleck. 2002. 'Remarks on the Revolutionary Calendar and *Neue Zeit*', *The Practice of Conceptual History: Timing History. Spacing Concepts,* trans. Todd Presner. Stanford: Stanford University Press. pp. 154-69; C. A. Bayly. 1989. *Imperial Meridian: The British Empire and the World.* London: Longman, pp. 100-32. Sankar Muthu has suggestively called for the need to 'pluralise' our view of the Enlightenment. Sankar Muthu. 2003. *Enlightenment against Empire.* Princeton: Princeton University Press, pp. 259-63.
56. Dipesh Chakrabarty provides an insightful discussion of Hegel's notion of time in 'Postcoloniality and the Artifice of History: Who Speaks for "Indian" Pasts?', *Representations.* 1992. 37(1): pp. 1-26.
57. Pomian, *L'order du temps,* p. 131.
58. G. W. F. Hegel. 1961. 'The Positivity of the Christian Religion' (1795-96), in T. M. Knox (trans. and ed.), *On Christianity: Early Theological Writings.* New York: Harper, p. 67ff.; See Paul Tillich. 1926. *Kairos: Ideen zur Geisteslage und Gegenwart.* Darmstadt: Otto Reichl Verlag.
59. G. W. F. Hegel. 1977 (1807). *Phenomenology of Spirit,* trans. A. V. Miller. Oxford: Oxford University Press, p. 493.
60. G. W. F. Hegel. 1952 (1821). *Philosophy of Right,* trans. T. M. Knox. London: Oxford Univeristy Press, p. 48.
61. Walter Mignolo. 1995. *The Darker Side of the Renaissance: Literacy, Territoriality, and Colonization.* Ann Arbor: University of Michigan Press.
62. See, for example, see the excellent account of deist views of Chinese religions in Peter Harrison. 1990. *'Religion' and the Religions in the English Enlightenment.* Cambridge: Cambridge University Press, pp. 61-72.

63. The interconnection between liberalism and colonialism is explored in detail by Uday Singh Mehta. 1999. *Liberalism and Empire: A Study in Nineteenth-Century British Liberal Thought*. Chicago: University of Chicago Press, p. 8.

64. Hegel, *Phenomenology*, p. 420.

65. Chris Bayly, *Birth of the Modern World*, p. 86; Javed Majeed, *Ungoverned Imaginings: James Mills' The History of British India and Orientalism*. Oxford: Oxford University Press, p. 7.

66. James Mill. 1820. *History of British India*. London: Baldwin, Cradock, and Joy, p. 137.

67. Elmer H. Cutts, 'The Background of Macaulay's Minutes', *American Historical Review* (Oct. 1952-July 1953) 58(4): 104.

68. Ernest Gellner. 1985. *Relativism and the Social Sciences*. New York: Cambridge University Press, p. 76; Majeed, *Ungoverned Imaginings*, p. 137.

69. *Friend of India*. 1818. May, 1(1): 1.

70. Sibnath Sastri. 1911. *A History of the Brahmo Samaj*. Calcutta: R. Chatterji.

71. Richard Maxwell Eaton. 1993. *The Rise of Islam and the Bengal Frontier, 1204-1760*. Berkeley: University of California, pp. 293-97. Richard Maxwell Eaton. 1974. *Sufis of Bijapur, 1300-1700: Social Roles of Sufis in Medieval India*. Princeton: Princeton University Press, pp. 45-69. Sikhism and Islam were two major forces in the expansion of exegetical and written textual practices in the pre-colonial era. Also see Romila Thapar. 2000. 'The Oral and the Written in Early India', *Cultural Pasts: Essays in Early Indian History*. New Delhi: Oxford University Press, p. 203.

72. Rammohan Roy. 1906 rpt (1804). 'A Present to the Believers in One God', in *The English Works of Raja Rammohun Roy with an English Translation of "Tuhfatul Muwahhiddin"*, (ed. and trans.) Jogendra Chunder Ghose, p. 948ff.

73. Rammohan Roy. 1906 rpt (c.1820). 'Religious Instructions founded on Sacred Authorities' *The English Works of Raja Rammohun Roy with an English Translation of "Tuhfatul Muwahhiddin"*, p. 135ff.

74. Rammohan Roy. 1906 rpt (1822). 'Final Appeal to the Christian Public' in: *The English Works of Raja Rammohun Roy with an English Translation of "Tuhfatul Muwahhiddin"*, p. 748ff.

75. Suzanne Marchand. (Forthcoming). 'On Orientalism and Iconoclasm', in Sugata Bose and Kris Manjapra (eds.), *Cosmopolitan Thought Zones of South Asia*. London: Palgrave Macmillan Press.

76. William Bysshe Stein. 1967. *Two Brahman Sources of Emerson and Thoreau* pp. x, xi.

77. David Kopf. 1969. *British Orientalism and the Bengal Renaissance: The Dynamics of Indian Modernization, 1773-1835*. Berkeley: University of California Press, p. 19.

78. Keshab Chandra Sen. 1954. *Lectures in India*. London: Cassell.

79. Rammohan Roy recorded his interest in the teachings of tantra gurus such as Pandit Sivaprasad Misrand and Hariharananda Tirthaswami. Sibnath Sastri. 1911. *A History of the Brahmo Samaj*, p. 16. In the 1870s, Keshab Chandra Sen, the doyen of the Brahmo Samaj, became a major publiciser and supporter of Ramakrishna Paramahansa. See Jeffrey Kripal. 1995. *Kali's Child: The Mystical and the Erotic in the Life and Teachings of Ramakrishna*. Chicago: Chicago University Press, p. 205. Dharma and the Brahmo movement grew so interconnectedly by the 1890s that Brahmos became increasingly uncomfortable. Bimalendu Majumdar. 1900. *Professor Max Muller on Ramakrishna and the World on the Keshub Chunder Sen*. Calcutta: Lawrence Printing Works.

80. By the end of the nineteenth century, teachers such as Ramakrishna, Vivekananda, Keshab Chandra Sen and Swami Dayananda comprised a broad group of proponents of Advaita Vedanta, the teaching of mystic universalism based on the Vedas and Upanishads. Aurobindo Ghosh represents one culmination of these nineteenth-century developments. See Aurobindo Ghosh. 'Nationalism is the Work of God', in Stephen Hay (ed.). 1988. *Sources of Indian Tradition.* New York: Columbia University Press, vol. 2: p. 151ff.
81. Wilhelm Halbfass. 1981. *Indien und Europa: Perspektiven ihrer geistigen Begenung.* Basel: Schwabe, p. 396.
82. Kripal, *Kali's Child*, p. 90.
83. Swami Vivekananda. 1970. *The Complete Works of Swami Vivekananda.* Calcutta: Advaita Ashrama, vol. 3: p. 267ff.
84. Kripal, *Kali's Child*, pp. 92–102.
85. Bankimchandra Chattopadhyay. 2004. 'Dharmatattva', in *Sahitya Samagra.* Calcutta: Tuli-Kalam, p. 599.
86. Halbfass, *Indien und Europa*, pp. 256–79. Halbfass discusses the historical processes whereby a doxa of Hinduism was developed over the nineteenth century in hermeneutic conversation with European forms. See Raychaudhuri, *Europe Reconsidered*, pp. 150–55.
87. Preface to First Edition of *The Complete Works of Swami Vivekananda,* 1970: p. ii.
88. Vivekananda, 'Raja–Yoga', *The Complete Works of Swami Vivekananda,* vol. 1: p. 180.
89. Vivekananda, 'Work and its Secret', *The Complete Works of Swami Vivekananda,* vol. 3: p. 3.
90. Vivekananda, 'Karma-Yoga', *The Complete Works of Swami Vivekananda,* vol. 1: p. 39.
91. Ibid., p. 53.
92. Vivekananda, *The Complete Works of Swami Vivekananda,* vol. 1: p. 104.
93. Vivekananda's speech at the World Congress of Religions in Chicago in *The World Congress of Religion: The Addresses and Papers, 1894.* See an interesting discussion of the interrelation between 'innerworldliness' and involvement in the world in Carolyn Bynum.1992. *Fragmentation and Redemption: Essays on Gender and the Human Body in Medieval Religion.* New York: Zone Books, pp. 66–69.
94. Vivekananda, *The Complete Works of Swami Vivekananda,* vol. 1: p. 28. Emphasis in original.
95. Ibid., p. 29.
96. Vivekananda made tours in 1893 and 1899.
97. Sarkar, *Futurism of Young Asia*, 1922: 125.
98. This energistic conception also defines Vivekananda's interpretation of Christianity's rise. 'And the [Jewish] race was forced to concentrate all its energies upon Jerusalem and Judaism. But all power when once gathered cannot remained collected... this concentrated energy amongst the Jewish race found its expression at the next period, in the rise of Christianity'. Vivekananda, 'Christ, the Messenger', *The Complete Works of Swami Vivekananda,* vol. 4: p. 139.

99.   Partha Chatterjee advanced this argument in *The Nation and its Fragments*, p. 6.
100.   He spoke of Islam as fundamentally war-like, and of Buddhism as a 'degrading' influence on ancient Hinduism. Also, Christianity had been corrupted by materialism. See Vivekananda, 'My Plan of Campaign', *The Complete Works of Swami Vivekananda*, vol. 3: p. 217.
101.   Vivekananda, 'The Freedom of the Soul', *The Complete Works of Swami Vivekananda*, vol. 2: p. 199.
102.   Benoy Kumar Sarkar. 1932. *Parajita Jarmani*. Calcutta: Oriental Book Agency, p. 39.
103.   Ibid., p. 11.
104.   Abul Kalam Azad's Khilafat journal *Al-Hilal* was being published from Calcutta in the Swadeshi years. Kazi Nazrul Islam's journal, *Dhumketu*, begun in 1922, spoke of the eruption of peasant protest out of the imperial order.
105.   Aurobindo Ghosh. 1974 (1893). *New Lamps for Old*, Pondicherry: Sri Aurobindo Ashram, pp. 37–39.
106.   Ibid., p. 39.
107.   Geraldine Forbes. 1975. *Positivism in Bengal*, Calcutta: Minerva, p. 70.
108.   Vaishnav devotionalism was also a major thread in Bankim's later works, and developed alongside his contemplation of the political importance of *shakto* devotion to the mother goddess. See Tapan Raychaudhuri, *Europe Reconsidered*, pp. 104, 154; See Sudipta Kaviraj. 1995. *The Unhappy Consciousness: Bankimchandra Chattopadhyay and the Formation of Nationalist Discourse in India*. Delhi: Oxford University Press, p. 77.
109.   Bipin Chandra Pal, *The Soul of India*, p. 193.
110.   Gorbes, *Positivism in Bengal*, p. 70.
111.   Benoy Kumar Sarkar. 1912. *The Science of History and the Hope of Mankind*. London: Longmans Green and Co.
112.   Benoy Kumar Sarkar. 1927. 'Empire Development and World-Economy: A Study in the New Foundations of National Economy for India', *Journal of the Bengal National Chamber of Commerce*, vol. 2. p. 7.
113.   Scholars have tended to emphasise the corporality, and thus, territoriality of Bharat. Manu Goswami. 2004. *Production India*, p. 201; Sumathi Ramaswamy. 2001. 'Maps and Mother Goddesses in Modern India', *Imago Mundi*, 53(1): pp. 97–114.
114.   Rabindranath Tagore. 1918. 'The Fugitive', translation of *Palataka*, reproduced in *Collected Poems and Plays of Rabindranath Tagore*, 1936: p. 327ff.

2

Marxist New Time

M. N. Roy is often presented either as the arch-pedagogue of communism in India or as a man who gingered the Communist International with a view from the East. Yet this misses the characteristic arena of his intellectual activity in the interstices between worlds. Why did Roy, who started off in the Swadeshi modernist milieu, become a communist in the first place? How, specifically, did his deterritorial nationalism come into conversation with communism? If Roy did not simply adopt a fixed set of ideas called 'communism' but invented a unique pathway within communist discourse as a thinker from the colonial world, then what was significant about that pathway? To answer these questions we must pursue a panoramic approach, seeing how structures and historical periods gave occasion to M. N. Roy as the foremost expositor of early Indian communism in the 1920s. But we must balance this with a microscopic view as well, that follows the play of ideas within his individual life experience, stretching from his arrival in the United States in 1916 to his reinvention as an elite communist cadre five years later in Tashkent.

Stops in the Journey

In June 1916, Roy arrived in San Francisco after abandoning the chase for German funds and armaments through East Asia, and made his way to the home of an old friend from Calcutta and member of the deterritorial anti-colonial nationalist network, Dhanagopal Mukherjee in Palo Alto.[1] Mukherjee, the younger brother of a leading Calcutta revolutionary, Jadugopal Mukherjee and comrade of M. N. Roy, had left Calcutta in 1908 as a Swadeshi radical youth answering the call of the national education movement to seek schooling at the best institutions abroad.[2] He began studies in engineering at Tokyo University, before soon deciding to travel across the Pacific to California. Dhanagopal completed a degree in history at Stanford by 1914, and set down strong roots in Palo Alto, befriending the president of the university, David Starr Jordan, and falling in love with Ethel Rae Dugan, another Stanford graduate.[3] Dhanagopal suggested to the then Narendranath Bhattacharya that he change his name to M. N. Roy, a more ambiguous and enigmatic name, not directly related to any specific caste.[4] Narendranath adopted his new name on 16 June 1916. Through Dhanagopal Mukherjee's girlfriend, Roy met a young graduate, Evelyn Trent, and the two soon fell in love and got married. Trent, a young West Coast progressivist, contributed to Roy's early Marxist education and played an important role in the early Indian communist movement before their divorce in 1926.[5] In addition to this Roy met David Starr Jordan, the inaugural president of the university, an ichthyologist and well-known pacifist, also a former vice-president of the American Anti-Imperialist League.[6] By the time Roy came to know him, Jordan had already been displaced from the position of university president and given the titular role of chancellor because of his controversial political views. Jordan had denounced American expansionism in the Spanish–American War of 1898, and in the context of the rampant anti-immigration debates in California at the time, he argued that race mixture would only strengthen the American people.[7] In 1909, Jordan served as Chief Director of the World Peace Foundation and in 1911 he travelled to Japan to give lectures protesting Japanese militarism in Korea. As the United States' concern about the civil war in Mexico increased in the years before the First World War, Jordan made a number of contacts among Mexican political leaders, some of them with agendas for radical social change. He befriended General Salvador Alvarado, the governor of Yucatan, and praised his anti-*haciendos* campaigns and his concern for the education of land labourers.[8] The Stanford president represented one of the most eminent voices of American pacifism in these years. He, like Woodrow Wilson before the sinking of the *Lusitania*, maintained that America should not enter the Great War. After Wilson was forced to retract this policy at the beginning of his second term, Jordan openly praised him, and hailed the Wilsonian view that a new kind of diplomacy and new international institutions were needed to ensure that the Great War would end war for good. However, Jordan was ultimately more radical than Wilson. In the 1920s, Jordan joined other liberal internationalists such as H. N. Brailsford and H. G. Wells in the call for a world government, criticising the League of Nations as a mere combination of antagonist governments instead of a 'league of men'.[9]

After his meetings with Jordan, Roy reflected upon the violent turn taken by the Swadeshi revolutionary movement. Roy recalled, 'I came in touch with new people and new ideas', and this 'marked a turning point in my life ... I resisted the temptation of arming myself with pistol, which could be purchased in the next shop... The idea of revolution, associated with the heroic deeds of individuals armed with pistols or bombs, was fading in my mind'. Roy, twenty-nine years old at the time, had grown disillusioned with 'the austere ruthlessness of revolutionary terrorism'.[10]

After his brush with American pacifism and its limitations at Stanford, Roy travelled onward to New York in early 1917 to link up with the Indian diasporic anti-colonial network. Here in the New York Public Library, Roy began reading Marx's works, long available in Calcutta libraries, with new intensity. They took on 'a new meaning' for him.[11] New York was a major hub for publications, meetings and alliances of Indian anti-colonial radicals, overseen by the celebrated nationalist leader Lajpat Rai who came there from London in 1914. The contradictions inherent in liberal internationalism were starkly drawn for Roy in 1917, as Wilson enunciated the rudiments of the Fourteen Points, officially promulgated on 8 January 1918. During that same time, American authorities were also beginning the concerted suppression of Indian anti-colonialism in cities such as New York and San Francisco. Now, as a wartime ally of Britain, Wilson authorised a number of accommodations with British imperialism. In Wilson's 14 June Flag Day speech, delivered only months after the American Declaration of War, he impugned anti-colonial activities, suggesting that India's best interest lay in peaceful acceptance of the imperial relationship.[12] Soon after, in June 1917 Roy would be forced to flee New York for Mexico City in order to escape imprisonment by American authorities.[13]

Critique of Wilsonianism

The irony of the Fourteen Points was clear. What use was there in speaking of a 'league of men', asked Roy in an open letter sent to Woodrow Wilson, when that category contained the silent acceptance of European domination of the world? He perceived that the problem at hand entailed a systematic deficiency in the foundational terms of Western liberalism. 'It is not in Europe but in the debilitated countries of Asia and Africa that the germs of war in modern times are hatched by the imperialist greed of the European nations... The panacea that can cure the evils of the world is the complete liberation of all dominated peoples and countries, not only in Europe but also in Asia and Africa'.[14] Woodrow Wilson was not a proponent of anti-colonialism. His concern was with what he termed 'small nations', intentionally differentiating them from 'colonies'. While the concluding covenant of the Fourteen Points asserted 'political independence and territorial integrity to great and small states alike', point number six introduced a crucial equivocation. 'A free, open-minded, and absolutely impartial adjustment of all colonial claims, based upon a strict observance of the principle that in determining all such questions of sovereignty the interests of the populations concerned must have *equal weight* with the equitable claims of the government whose title is to be determined'(emphasis mine).[15] Colonial universalism assumed a gradient of consciousness in which Europeans and Americans occupied a superior position. An intentional double-standard was inserted into the language of the Wilsonian blueprint for peace, in which certain imperial governments were assumed to have 'equitable claims' to their colonial territories.

The Treaty of Versailles was sure to attract anti-colonial activists from the colonial world, but they did not come with naïve hopes.[16] Lajpat Rai in February 1918, just one month after the Fourteen Points were declared, spoke skeptically of Wilson's 'New Internationalism'. 'The brotherhood of man and the brotherhood of nations can only be established on a platform of mutual respect and goodwill... None are justified in despising others. God has not given you a charter, because you are white people, to go and exploit the people of Asia and Africa', Rai announced during a speech in New York.[17]

M. N. Roy's two earliest traceable publications, the open letter to Wilson quoted above and a tract he wrote from Mexico City in 1918 entitled, *India: Her Past, Present and Future*, together constitute a critical treatise on Wilsonianism.[18] Far from praising the President, but also not carelessly lashing out against him, Roy offered a thoughtful textual criticism of the logic of Wilson's internationalism. When Roy remarked that he had grown tired of the pistol and gun, it also seems he had grown increasingly enamoured of the pen as an instrument of anti-colonial politics.

In *India: Her Past, Present and Future*, Roy pointed to the illusion of Wilsonian benevolence. 'Some Indian leaders believed that through calling on the goodwill and conscience of England's allies, the oppressed Indians would gain something from this war... To date, these patriotic Indians have been persecuted and treated humiliatingly by England's allies although they are pleading for a very natural cause'.[19] He asserted that India must not wait upon the recognition of Western Powers, and that even the pursuit of such recognition was demeaning. 'India will be free sooner or later, not through the kindness of the English rulers, but through her own energy'.[20] In conclusion, Roy returned to the Wilsonian themes of humanity and justice, using the terms of Wilson's idealism against itself. India would become a true servant of humanity, but only once the whole edifice of European domination fell. The aims of a true universal humanism would only come through the violent destruction of Europe's intransigent exploitative relationship to the world. 'The aim of this conflict will be the final termination of the arrogant rule of one part of humanity over another'.[21] Before European liberals could speak of humanity, they first had to decolonise their own understanding of that term.

At the time many Indian anti-colonial writers focused on India's civilisational grandeur — Eastern spiritual riches versus Western materialism and violence — Roy favoured destroying the assumption of civilisational difference altogether.[22] M. N. Roy's project, at this time dealing with a set of American political treatises, was informed by a Brahmo intentionality. '[Our goal] will be achieved by assuring true liberty for the whole world, putting an end to Europe's superiority complex'.[23]

Climbing the Ladder of the World

Struggling to square his insights into the impasse of Western liberal pacifism with his growing conviction that the efforts to revolutionise India through violence alone had turned into an *opera bouffe* of global proportions, Roy left New York for Mexico City to escape persecution, but also to observe social revolution first-hand. Roy recalled, 'Neighbouring Mexico, in a state of permanent revolution appeared to be the land of promise. I could not proceed further, I would settle down there and at last take active part in a revolution'.[24] It was, what Roy later called, 'the new scene of my being and becoming'.[25]

Roy arrived in Mexico City in 1917 with a letter of introduction from David Starr Jordan, in the midst of Mexico's civil war. A group of Indian anti-colonial radicals also congregated in Mexico City, but by this time Roy was seeking a way to exit the old circuit of Indian network anti-colonialism, as it still futilely pursued German funds to purchase and ship armaments to India.[26] In a relationship of mutual manipulation, Indians knew they were being used by the Germans for imperial war aims, but they also hoped they could exploit German connections in turn.

In Mexico, Roy found the perfect storm for revolution — an unmade metropolis after the fall of the Porfirian dictatorship in 1911, followed by a succession of unstable governments. Francisco Madero was the coup leader, but stepped down in 1913 in the face of American threats of invasion. The country fell into civil war. General Venustiano Carranza of Spanish–Mexican descent and an elite background became the presumptive head of government in 1915 and was in the process of consolidating his control by establishing a constituent assembly. The Queretaro Constitution was passed and took steps to limit the power of the landed aristocracy. But Carranza was opposed by Pancho Villa in the northern States and by Zapata in the environs of Mexico City, who both attempted to orchestrate revolutions of the indigenous population against the elites.[27]

With the entry of the Americans into the Great War, Mexico City became the most important outpost for German operatives in attempts to destabilise the United States from the south. This represented what Fritz Fischer famously called the German foreign policy of 'revolutionising' the colonial domains of its European enemies.[28] German imperial power sought to instrumentalise anti-Western nationalist groups to undercut and confound the Entente. Mexico City became the new satellite base for German intrigue in the Americas.[29] The fateful Zimmermann Telegram, wired from Berlin to Mexico City via Washington in January 1917, instructed the German ambassador to forge a military alliance with the Mexican government in advance of the resumption of unrestricted submarine warfare. The interception and deciphering of the telegram contributed greatly to the United States' decision to enter the war.[30]

In Mexico, Roy found himself ensconced within a community of Germans, and not by accident. He was sought out by the same German ambassadors involved in earlier efforts to funnel funds and weapons from consulates in Peking, Shanghai and Jakarta to India two years earlier.[31] At the same time, the Mexican literati were impressed by Roy's Wilsonian critiques, and the editor of *El Pueblo* invited him to write on questions of imperialism. By translating his essays with the help of a tutor, Roy began learning Spanish.[32] He made his way into the radical expatriate community of British and American war protesters and anti-imperialists that stayed at the Hotel Geneva, and he was known there as the 'melancholy philosopher from India'.[33] But the German connections were the strongest bonds for Roy. Germany was like a totem of anti-Westernism in the war years, and German officials were willing magnates of the anti-colonial flotsam and jetsam of the earth.[34] Roy met an elderly professor of Japanese philology, Dr Gramatsky, and began studying German and reading Goethe with him.[35] He would later develop near-native fluency in the language, eventually taking up prestigious editorships of German-language communist journals in his Berlin years.[36]

German officialdom in Mexico City provided the caulking that brought Roy into touch with Mexican President Carranza. Carranza held openly anti-American views, and this made for quick friendship with M. N. Roy, only boosting his status in the radical fringe communities.[37] In this anti-Western underground, social interactions and alliances seemed to take place more as Dionysian contaminations and chance infatuations, than as Apollonian elective affinities.

Through his involvement with imperial German emissaries and thanks to his intellectual acumen, Roy made friends in the Carranza government. He met the eminent leader of the Mexican socialist movement, Plutarco Elias Calles, later to become President of Mexico after Carranza's demise. In this period, between 1917 and 1918, Roy lived in the ambiguous intermediary position between anti-colonial nationalism and socialism, in which the difference between groups and ideologies was ambiguous. The first meeting of the Socialist Party of Mexico convened in December 1918. Roy played a role in the proceedings, along with other non-Mexicans, such as American communists Charles Philips, John Reed, Carleton Beals and Irwin Granwich.[38] He was elected the general secretary of the Mexican Socialist Party largely, it seems, because he was close to Carranza and to the German officials. Plutarco Calles hoped to benefit from those connections.[39] When the socialists aligned themselves with Moscow, M. N. Roy and Charles Shipman were elected as the chief representatives. Bertram Wolfe, an American radical socialist in Mexico at the time, commented on the irony that an 'assimilated Jew and an Indian Brahmin' should represent early Mexican socialism.[40] And yet given the internal power games between Calles and Carranza, as well as the larger context of metropolitan Mexican culture that identified itself as cosmopolitan and avant-garde, two foreign jewels were fitting accents for Mexican socialist modernism.[41]

In September 1919, Mikhail Borodin, born Mikhail Markovich Gruzenberg, chief Soviet envoy to the Americas, visited Mexico and met M. N. Roy.[42] Finding him to be of remarkable talent, Borodin deputised Roy to attend the Second Congress of the Communist International in Petrograd as the Mexican representative. As was part of the ritual in communist culture, the elder Borodin inducted the younger Roy into communist ideology just as Lenin had done so with Trotsky in 1902, in the course of 'long walks and talks'.[43] Borodin wrote letters to friends in Europe to prepare a network of support in Europe to ensure the easy transit of Roy and Evelyn Trent to Berlin, and then Moscow.[44] Living in interstitial zones, reacting against the futile attempts at armed struggle against British imperialism, and enjoying the experiences of transculturation, Roy was becoming a social *mestizo* and a polyglot by learning new languages, adapting new tastes and new self-stylisations.

As images of Roy from the 1915 to 1920 period attest, he doffed and donned a number of new personas, becoming a man for many occasions. According to one contemporary report, Roy in Mexico 'claimed to be an Indian prince and to have originally escaped from India under sentence of death'.[45] Roy offered a very different recollection of his self-fashioning in this Mexico period: 'still a vegetarian, I learned the European way of eating at table and dressing, so as not to feel awkward in strange company'.[46] Proud of his chameleon-like abilities in any case he wrote: 'later on, in Europe, communist friends taunted me as more European than the natives, when I criticised their bourgeois habits and

Illustration 2.1   Roy as Father Martin during his journey to California in 1915.

Source: Sibnarayan Ray, *In Freedom's Quest: Life of M. N. Roy*, vol. 4, Part 2. Used with permission.

prejudices'.[47] He did not shy away from new performances. By the time he reached Berlin in 1921, he already had a number of pseudonyms racked up, from M. N. Roy, to Father Martin, to Mr White, to Richard, to Roberto to Buddy.[48] Roy's anti-colonial practice as an intermediary between worlds did not consist in asserting a strong insurgent self, but in playing with the flexibility of the self.[49]

Borodin left Mexico for Europe in early 1919, and M. N. Roy, with his wife and colleague, Evelyn Trent, left soon after. They travelled, unsurprisingly, under pseudonyms across the Atlantic on a Spanish transatlantic liner, the *Alfonso XIII*.[50] After stopping in Zurich, they arrived in Berlin in March 1920. Upon their arrival, well-supplied with Soviet funds, they checked into a corner room of the Hotel Fürstenhof on Potsdamer Platz with a perfect vantage point on the Kapp Putsch as it broke onto the streets and threatened to dismantle the Weimar Republic. Yet again, Roy arrived just in time for revolution. He spent the next four months observing the singularly tumultuous social dynamics of Berlin, as well as making first acquaintances with the leaders of Berlin communism before travelling to Moscow for the Second Comintern Congress.

The Weimar Milieu

Berlin communist culture was astoundingly erudite. Communist presses published educational pamphlets on Marxist theory called *Elementarbücher*, and sold them at a low cost to teach workers about the writings of Marx, as well as offer interpretations of the German classics, such as Goethe and Schiller.[51] And education was mixed with leisure as communist workers' groups, such as the *Naturverein*, went on expeditions in the woods on the weekends to hear lectures on various political and cultural topics in forest cabins. The *Volksbühne*, the largest stage in the city, provided 'art for the people' with its cheap-ticket plays by the likes of Toller, Shaw, Barlach and Hauptmann.[52] Communist education usually took place in rented schoolrooms on weekends and evenings, or in the backrooms of pubs.[53] Roy found this all enthralling, and savoured the emphasis on intellectual revolution and political action for changing consciousness — so different from the blind struggle for armaments and the gun-running he remembered from the last years of the Swadeshi movement. This environment was different too, Roy would soon discover, from the climate of state communism in Moscow.

The literati of the Berlin communist world tended to collect in the salons of publishing house doyens, such as Eduard Fuchs and

Willi Münzenberg.[54] Fuchs was a publisher, a member of the original Spartakus Bund, and he wrote books on the social history of art and taste. In 1923, he was one of the founders of the *Institut für Sozialforschung* in Frankfurt. Known as *Sittenfuchs* for his book on the class history of social customs, he collected around him a group of communist intellectuals committed to Marxism as a philosophical enterprise and educational project. These were individuals such as Franz Mehring, August Thalheimer and Karl Korsch. Roy soon found inroads into the 'Old Guard' precincts of the Berlin Spartakists and became a 'regular attendant' of the Karl Korsch circle.[55]

Roy was invited to discussions at Fuchs' home in early 1920, and it was there that he first met August Thalheimer, the leader of the German Communist Party. Thalheimer would become a close friend and Roy's most important conversation partner.[56] Indeed, the first months in Berlin were characterised by a spreading social web of contacts in German communism and Social Democracy. Roy recalled meeting socialist icons such as Karl Kautsky, Rudolf Hilferding and the grand old man of the Social Democratic Party, Eduard Bernstein.[57]

Scholarship has been slow to recognise the particular cultural and intellectual force fields of German communism in Berlin that had the greatest impact on M. N. Roy, after the Swadeshi avant-garde milieu.[58] Moscow was never Roy's 'holy land', despite the fact that historiography has consistently situated him in the habitat of the fledgling Soviet state. Instead, Roy's second intellectual home after fin-de-siècle Calcutta was the fractured, amorphous, intellectual landscape of Berlin of the 1920s.

Marx's Curse

There were many vicissitudes to Marx's thinking about the East, largely due to the general unimportance of Asia to his larger philosophical and political project.[59] Marx approved of what he believed to be the introduction of commerce and social reform to the East via colonialism. He insisted in a way typical of mid-century European liberalism, and reminiscent of Hegel and James Mill, that Asia could be raised from out of its vegetal state through European colonialism. Marx wrote in 1847, 'we know that the Spanish found the *East Indies* at the same level of development as did the English, and that the Indians have nevertheless continued to live for centuries in the same manner, i.e. they have eaten, drunk and vegetated... The workers there are already migrating and through aligning with other peoples are becoming for the first time accessible to civilisation'.[60] By the early 1850s, as a London correspondent for the *New York Daily Tribune* on colonial matters, Marx began expressing views that grew out of Hegel's thought, but based themselves on the latest British colonial scholarship. Inspired by the works of demography, geography and political economy by Robert Malthus and Richard Jones, both of whom had taught at Haileybury, the college of the East India Company, and by George Campbell and Henry Maine on law and society in Indian 'village communities', Marx cobbled together his notion of the 'Asiatic Mode of Production'. Richard Jones in his lectures from the 1850s argued that vast swathes of land in temperate environments required large-scale irrigation works which could only be provided by an Oriental despot.[61] Marx adopted this view: 'Climate and the territorial conditions', he claimed, 'especially the vast tracts of desert constituted artificial irrigation by canals and waterworks [are] the basis of Oriental agriculture'.[62] The works of Henry Maine, by contrast, focused on local, instead of infrastructural, phenomena of Indian socio-economic structure. He identified Indian society with the locale of the village and the institution of the family.[63] Marx, in his *Grundrisse* of 1857, merged these two views:

> The small communities may vegetate independently side by side, and within each the individual labours independently with his family on the land allotted to him... Furthermore, the commonality within the tribal body may tend to appear either as a representation of its unity through the head of the tribal kinship group, or a relationship between the heads of families. Hence, either a more despotic or a more democratic form of the community. The communal conditions for real appropriation through labour, such as irrigation systems (very important among the Asian peoples), means of communication, and so on, will then appear as the work of the higher unity — the despotic government which is poised above the lesser communities.[64]

Marx's notion of the Asiatic Mode of Production, then, claimed that Asian societies exhibited a primitive form of democratic communism, without private property, on the micro level, and environmentally-necessitated despotism on the macro level. Put otherwise, when one zoomed in on Indian society one saw the low-level consciousness of primitive village society, and when one zoomed out, one saw despotism, a backward and stagnating form of governance. This system ensured the endless stasis of Asian society.

In Marx's writings, as had been the case in Hegel's as well, passivity was seen as the 'principle of being' of the Orient.[65] The Orient lay outside history, it was not yet a real space, and the heroic European bourgeoisie had not only brought capital to Eastern shores, but had brought History itself. As David Harvey commented, Oriental space was 'a passive recipient of a teleological historical process that [started] from the centre (Europe) and [flowed] outward to fill the entire globe'.[66] By picturing the peoples of the East as caught within the Asiatic Mode of Production, Marx positioned them on a gradient of humanity, and were said to be unable to realise the fulfilment of universal time that only industrial European society had attained. On the other hand, we must also note, as Gareth Stedman Jones has stressed, that Marx's own views on the world outside Europe were not static, and that by the time of his late writings, an enthusiasm for social revolution in the East had developed.[67] Nevertheless, given the fact that a gradient of humanity was located within that portion of Marx's corpus most read and inter- preted, it would have to be *in spite* of Marx's writings that Marxists later developed anti-colonial theories and politics in the early twentieth century. M. N. Roy, as he entered the Communist fold, found the Eurocentric assumptions of colonial epistemology alive and well.

One recent scholar has suggested that Lenin 'opened up a space in which it became possible to "think" colonial nationalism'.[68] Indeed, this view is difficult to disentangle from Soviet hagiography. It is certainly true that Lenin introduced an important reconceptualisation of colonial space with regards to the metropolis, and that his views about colonial freedom struggle were in place at least from 1907.[69] As he said at the First Congress of the Communist Third International in March 1919: 'The liberation of the colonies is only thinkable along with the liberation of the workers in the metropolis ... just as capitalist Europe has drawn the backward parts of the earth into the capitalist maelstrom, so too will socialist Europe come to the assistance of the colonies with its technology, its organization and its intellectual [*geistige*] influence...'[70] Lenin aimed his comments against Woodrow Wilson and his contem- poraneous enunciation of national 'self-determination'.[71] Still, Lenin insisted on the need for a relationship of tutelage between European communists and Asian anti-colonial movements. Furthermore, he held that the historical trajectory of India in the 1920s was fundamentally different from that of Europe. The Indian masses did not possess class consciousness, and only the Westernised Indian bourgeoisie were radicalised. Hence this colonial bourgeoisie had to be courted and co-opted by European communists in order to attain the final goal of socialist revolution.

Lenin outlined these ideas and policy suggestions in his twelve-point 'Draft Theses on the National and Colonial Question' presented at the Second Congress of the Communist International in June 1920. 'The East', he wrote, 'has definitely taken the Western path'.[72] The indigenous elites who, because of their access to Western education, had learned to crave the national ideal, were the *de facto* revolutionary force in the colonies, Lenin maintained. As opposed to Rosa Luxemburg who emphasised the role of mass action, Lenin focused his attention on the colonial bourgeois classes. Although without proper socialist goals, these indigenous elites could be instrumentalised for communist revolution.[73] Lenin insisted on the need of an avant-garde of European communist operatives who would win over and direct anti-colonial nationalism towards socialist ends.[74] The view was doggedly defended by Lenin's devotees Dimitri Manuilski and Stalin in coming years, although dissenters such as Trotsky as well as the German communists, especially August Thalheimer, believed that the colonial bourgeoisie should be side-stepped in favour of direct mass action.[75] Yet, despite the Comintern's claim of being 'international', it remained in fact quite Eurocentric. And the 'colonial question', as it was called, received all too little attention in Comintern meetings in the early 1920s.[76]

Roy's 'Supplementary Theses on the National and Colonial Questions', presented alongside Lenin's at the Congress of 1920, opposed Lenin's views with the eruptive universal time of Swadeshi modernism. It represented Roy's attempt to launch an anti-colonial exegetical struggle from within the canon of Marxism, just as much as it was a policy assertion to fight British imperialism. In his theses, Roy insisted that revolution was imminent in India, and that the Indian peasants were the force that would bring about rupture through their bodily action. Thus, the historical process of social change in India did not imitate the example of Europe, but had its own innate dynamic of total renewal. 'The supposition that, owing to economic and industrial backwardness, the peoples in the colonies are bound to go through the stage of bourgeois democracy is wrong', wrote Roy in his theses.[77] Roy opposed Lenin's colonial time with his own notion of an eruptive collective subjecthood of the peasants. Instead of reading Roy as caught in a 'misunderstanding' of the concept of the 'proletariat' as Marxist scholars in Russia and India have tended to claim, in which he believed 'the most oppressed, ill-treated and unfortunate strata of the population were synonymous with the proletariat', these supposed 'misunderstandings' were evidence of a wilful reinterpretation on Roy's part, a fusing of Marxist concepts with Swadeshi styles.[78]

Roy insisted that the demands of freedom transcended political manoeuvre, and required the development of a new consciousness. Whereas in the Swadeshi milieu, it had been the *shaktiyogin* (the ascetic seeker channelling *shakti* force) who possessed radical socially distributive agency, Roy transposed that agency in his communist writings of the 1920s onto the revolutionary masses. One of Roy's most influential brochures, which was quickly integrated into the official speeches of important political leaders such as Chittaranjan Das in India, declared, 'our task is to develop in the minds of the masses this consciousness of their own power, to awaken their interest and develop their indomitable will to conquer freedom. They will do the rest'.[79] Roy insisted on the pre-existing agency of the masses, and that unleashing this agency would surpass the political goal of national independence, and usher in a new time.

In Roy's early Berlin thought, the peasantry represented an agency of energetic eruption. 'The Moplah rising and the agrarian disturbances in northern India: these incidents show that the peasantry, which is being driven into a revolutionary channel by poverty, has not been waiting for any spiritual stimulation in order to begin the fight for their interests'.[80] In writings that riled the Moscow leadership from the very start, Roy believed, in a Luxemburgist fashion, that revolution really would move from the bottom of society upwards.[81]

Contrary to the consensus of many writers and historians, it was certainly *not* the case that after Roy left India he became estranged from the Indian political scene, dissipated by his years abroad.[82] Although conceptually contaminated to fruitful ends, Roy remained preoccupied with the pursuit of Indian anti-colonialism, and was closely tied in to the imaginative horizon of the cultural and historical background of Swadeshi modernism.[83] In the 1920s, he was a leading figure among cosmopolitan nationalists who saw national liberation and internationalism as a unified project. And upon return to India in the 1930s, despite being absent from the political scene during five years of imprisonment by the British Indian government, Roy's influence grew among Indian thinkers on the left. In the interwar period, just as in the Swadeshi period of the early twentieth century, his sense of Indian belonging was neither depleted nor put in question by travel or transnational connections. Roy's early readings of Marxism dredged a path to criticise Marxist Eurocentric assumptions from within, using the textual practices he honed in his treatises on Wilsonianism during his first years in the United States.

Indian Communist Party at Tashkent

Roy's decade in Berlin in the Weimar years was interspersed with tours of duty throughout Europe, frequent trips to Moscow, and a number of prolonged stays in the Central and East Asia. After the Second Congress of the Communist International in July 1921, Roy was deputised to found the Communist Party of India. He travelled to Tashkent from Moscow in the fall of 1920 to attain that goal. Tashkent had been a base for the German–British round of the Great Game during the First World War, as well as the Russian–British bouts that preceded it.[84] Once a city renowned for its double rows of trees along major boulevards, all the canopies and trunks had been cut down for fuel in 1919 because of the civil war.[85] Between the demise of Russian Turkistan and the establishment of Uzbekistan in 1924, Tashkent was a city in the midst of ambiguous political turf. It seemed Roy had a propensity for searching out such environments. Here in Tashkent, Roy wrote his first major book, *India in Transition*, which became a classic of Indian communist literature.

These were the threshing fields of Mahendra Pratap Mehta, Mohammed Barakatullah and Obeidullah Sindhi, who together established the 'Provisional Government of India' in Kabul in 1915, with its own federal cabinet *avant la lettre* complete with a minister of the interior (M. Obeidullah), a war minister (M. Basheer) and a foreign secretary (M. P. T. Pillai).[86] In October 1920, the Indian Communist Party was founded in Tashkent. At the Indusky Doma, the India House on Lavmentev Road, most of the major figures who worked with M. N. Roy were veterans of the global Indian anti-colonial network.[87] Obeidullah and Barakatullah were leaders of the transnational Khilafat movement linking Indian Muslim political activism with events in the Ottoman lands. M. P. T. Acharya, a Tamil radical, came to Tashkent from Madras, and travelled through Swadeshi and Khilafat channels to London, Constantinople and Kabul to reach the destination.[88] Bam Roy and Abani Mukherjee, Swadeshi radicals from Calcutta, made a similar global tour to Tashkent during the war years.[89]

The Khilafat network proved particularly important in peopling the space of emerging Indian communism. In the intermediary cities through which *muhajjirin* travelled, young Indian Muslim youth with strong anti-British sentiment were recruited as communist emissaries.[90] Tashkent was a major city on the overland pilgrimage route from India to the Ottoman and Arab lands, and M. N. Roy's objective was to convert these travellers to the communist cause. About 80 per cent of the young men who served as the main colporteurs of communist literature to India, such as Shaukat Usmani, were Muslim. By March 1921, there were about 110 Indians studying with Roy at Indusky Dom.[91] And out of the Khilafat Movement came some of the most significant Indian communist intellectuals, such as Mushir Hosain Kidwai, Obeidullah Sindhi, Feroz-ud-Din Mansoor, Mir Abdul Majid and Fazal Ilahi Qurban.[92] The Ghadar Movement led by Sikh revolutionaries was another source of Indian radicals for the fledging communist ecumene.[93]

The Tashkent School, while nominally a Soviet institution, was far from a priority for the leaders in Moscow, and was left generally unregulated and under-provisioned. M. N. Roy, who established himself as the school's director, wrote letters of complaint about the lack of necessary equipment and uniforms, the poor quality of the food, and the poor state of the library.[94] In May 1921, the school closed down and the operations were relocated to Moscow, where Roy was enlisted as Soviet instructor on Marxism and colonialism at the new Communist University for the Toilers of the East.[95] He did not enjoy staying in the power centre of Moscow, and soon moved back to fallen imperial capital of Berlin, still reeling with political instability and social unrest.[96]

Communist New Time

In the same era as the rise of the Swadeshi avant-garde, Europeans were also engaged in their own avant-gardist experiments in aesthetics and politics. In Germany, this took shape with movements in artistic, literary and philosophical Expressionism.[97] A founding myth of communism, as it broke away from the Social Democrats in 1917, asserted that while the Second International subscribed to a progressive, developmentalist framing of temporal flow, the communist Third International envisioned a temporality of rupture. The Bolsheviks, when declaring the advent of Soviet Russia in October 1917, said that a 'leap from the realm of necessity to the realm of freedom' had taken place.[98] In November 1919, Kurt Eisner declared a short-lived Bavarian Soviet Republic centred in Munich.[99] But outside the realm of political action, youthful German philosophers, such as Ernst Bloch, summoned a mood of pregnant expectation for impending eruptions within the realm of culture and ideas. Bloch wrote in his 1918 *Geist der Utopie* of the need to envision the future as the 'not-yet' (*Noch Nicht*), and as the 'wholly-other' (*Ganz Andere*) from the present. He wanted historical breakage instead of chronological continuity:

> It must be noted that of essential importance is the future, the trope of the unknown, within which alone we enter, in which alone, newfangled and deep, the functions of hope are sparked without the empty reprisal of Anamnesis — it is no different from an expanded darkness, as a darkness that gives birth from its womb, and increases its latent potential.[100]

Bloch had a different view of the future than Marxist philosophers of an earlier generation, such as Karl Kautsky, who spoke of the role of the utopian imagination. In his *Thomas More and his Utopia* (1890), Kautsky, informed by his neo-Kantian context, proposed that utopia was a regulative idea alone, a theoretical *summum bonum* used to measure the need for progress in the present. The dualism between 'what is' and 'what ought to be' was assumed. Bloch wrote something of a response to Kautsky in *Thomas Münzer als Theologe der Revolution* in 1921.[101] Here, utopia is not a regulative idea, but had its own ontological status as a force born from within the present, breaking it apart.[102] Bloch would eventually abandon the word 'utopia', calling it abstract and idealist, and instead speak of a 'processive-concrete utopia' and 'concrete anticipation' that sought to activate the 'not yet realised objective-real possibilities in the world'.[103] This notion of time punctuated by rupture — the time of the new breaking out of the old and parturition — was the central temporal dynamic championed by the communist world and by artistic movements, such as futurism and expressionism of the same period.

In Germany, after 1923, a reaction against expressionism began to set in, as the political and economic stabilisation of the Weimar Republic introduced a 'new sobriety' to art and philosophy.[104] In Russia, futurist poets such as Alexander Blok and Vladimir Mayakovski proclaimed that the Soviet notion of time had no precedent, and that technology and industry materialised the forms of the future.[105] Lenin's death in 1924 marked a downturn in the giddy optimism, and a new programme of 'socialist realism' was formally promulgated by the Soviet Union in 1934. But at the peak of the movement in the early 1920s, Mayakovski celebrated the new Third International by already calling for the advent of the 'fourth revolution':

> Making heads start by its explosions of thought,
> Booming away with its artillery of the heart,

There rises from the depth of time
A different revolution,
The fourth revolution
Of the spirit.[106]

In Italy, Filippo Marinetti, the Egyptian-born, Sorbonne education, Italian artist and intellectual, wrote his famous Futurist Manifesto in 1909, which served as a major inspiration to Russian and German artists.[107] He founded the Italian Futurist Party, and wrote often on the theme of creative destruction. The future could only be built on the rubble of the past, he exclaimed. 'This is a gay manner of fertilising the earth! Because the Earth, believe me, will soon be pregnant. She will grow big — until she bursts! — From a sublime start to illuminating explosions'.[108] Italian futurism expanded through the 1920s, as it was intertwined with the rise of fascism. The Italian Fascist Party also proposed the eruption of a new time that would destroy the mundane linear succession of history. This fascist new time would allow for the regeneration of a national people and renewal of its great civilisation. Both fascism and communism, while having divergent historical implications, nonetheless were early twentieth century political movements sharing a similar avant-gardist view of temporal rupture.

The styles of thought associated with Italian futurism and German expressionism bore a resemblance to Swadeshi avant-gardism, especially in terms of the *topoi* of eruptive change and destructive pregnancy. A global modernist thought zone concerned with the eruption of new time out of the mundane present developed not genealogically, but conjuncturally in the early twentieth century. M. N. Roy's *India in Transition* was published simultaneously in four language from Berlin in 1922, right at the peak of the German Expressionist, Italian futurist, and Russian futurist movements.[109]

Transition in India

The terms 'future' and 'revolution' were keywords of Roy's first major communist text entitled, *India in Transition* (1922). The book would become a classic of colonial Marxist literature. It developed the Swadeshi-inspired narrative of eruptive new time, but through Marxist concepts. Roy wrote in an optative or anticipatory mode, eliding how things *would be* with the way things are. He insisted, as did Ernst Bloch and other Expressionist communist thinkers, that envisioning the future was inseparably tied up with actualising it. By doing this,

M. N. Roy challenged the line of colonial difference that ran through European Marxist thought. Indian agricultural workers were *already* a 'land proletariat, in every sense of the word' in Roy's writing. Along with this, Roy insisted that 'feudalism as a hereditary element in social economics had already been irretrievably undermined' in India, as early at the late eighteenth century. 'The Land had been freed from feudal fetters'.[110] Given the news of agrarian revolts in 1920, Roy insisted that class consciousness among peasants *had already* developed and that revolt was on the way. In addition, the urban proletariat, 'a recent group to develop in India', would lead this revolt. 'The first stage of the proletariat struggle [in India], which was marked by a mad wave of spontaneous strikes, followed invariably by riots and disturbances, seems to have terminated by the end of the last year. Since then, the proletarian movement has apparently entered the period of organisation and preparation for continuing the struggle with renewed vigour in the near future'.[111]

Roy's major claim in *India in Transition* of 1922, the argument from which the title derived, was that a wholly different future was already blasting apart the chronosophy of colonial universalism. 'To [the 'extreme nationalists'] it is not so much a transition, but a revivalist period, through which India is passing. Because they think that the Indian people are struggling to liberate themselves ... not to begin a new life with a new vision, but to revive the old. But the past is doomed by history, one of whose most important chapters is the present transition'.[112] India would be born anew, and the eruption would transcend the mundane chronological continuity of past and present. Through the revolutionary agency of 'the progressive forces latent in the Indian society', inherent in the 'masses of India ... the future of the Indian nation is going to be shaped'.[113]

These pronouncements provided grist for the subsequent common view that Roy wilfully disregarded the specificities of Indian culture and social realities, or that he exuberantly imposed European categories where they did not belong.[114] And yet, this misses the avant-gardist and optative mode of Roy's work — his claims were intended to speak of the 'what ought to be' as the 'what is'. By speaking of a future India as if it had already come, an 'eruptive new time' could be interjected into the present. Like Walter Benjamin who insisted that writing history should not simply involve recalling facts as with the 'counting of beads in a rosary', but should critically reconstruct the past in the light of current-day revolutionary potential, so too Roy, in 1921, wrote that

Indians did not need history in order to know 'exactly how many sacks of *kishmish* the great Aurangzeb had consumed in his illustrious life'.[115] The past was rather a great skein in which new patterns useful for blasting out of the present moment were selected by the 'searchlight of Historical Materialism'.[116]

Avant-gardism in Indian thought was a growing movement in the early 1920s. In fact, Roy's former teacher at the Bengal Technical College, Benoy Kumar Sarkar, published his *Futurism of Young India* from Berlin in 1922. In it, Sarkar emphasised that the temporalities of Indian progress aimed not at the local liberation of the Indian polity, but at the attainment of a whole new universal temporality for the world. 'There must be a psychological revolution in Eur-America... The futurists of Young Asia are looking forward to the spiritual re-birth of the world'.[117] A new world order entailed a new order of time. There was a growing interest in dreams and visions of the future in Bengali literary modernism in the 1920s. Nripendrakrishna Chattopadhyay, in a 1924 article in the Calcutta-based avant-garde literary journal, *Kallol*, wrote of the Soviet gift for 'luxuriating in dreams' (*swapna bilasi*) in poetry and politics.[118] Dineshranjan Das said it was necessary to erect a 'dream India' (*swapna Bharat*) through literary creation that would inevitably dismantle the oppression in 'actual India' (*bastab Bharat*) and help give rise to 'eternal India' (*swaswata Bharat*).[119] There was a longer history of this political use of 'imaginary histories' in Bengali thought.[120] Bhudev Mukhopadhyay, in his *History of India as seen through Dreams* (*Swapnalabdha bharater itihas*) of 1862, provided the archetype for this emphasis on dreams and hope in social and political thought, just as similar themes were expounded in the novels of Bankimchandra Chattopadhyay.[121] Bhudev, writing in mid nineteenth-century Bengal, proposed a utopian history of hope that looked to the past with an optative intent.[122]

The critical anticipatory starting point of Roy's *India in Transition,* with its utopian narrative, sought to disclose a strong class-conscious peasantry already present in Indian history in the interest of radically changing the present social order. M. N. Roy would go on to write a series of 'dream histories' of India, including his *Revolution and Counter-revolution in China* (1930), *Historical Role of Islam* (1939), and *Reason, Romanticism and Revolution* (1952). In each case, the return to the past is carried out as a project to redeem the shards of revolutionary time as called forth by the revolutionary needs of the present. Just as the 'ought' had ontological status and could infuse and transform the 'is', so too the past, if deployed properly by the practitioner of historical materialism, could also play a revolutionary function.

Much later, Roy recalled of *Transition*, the book that earned him entrance into the highest precincts of the Communist International, 'You may be interested to know that I wrote *India in Transition* in 1922, which was celebrated by the accepted authorities of the time, including Lenin, as the first Marxist interpretation of Indian history. By that time I had not read anything of Marx. What I mean to say is that my Marxism was derived from my own philosophical convictions'.[123] Far from an artefact of Roy's appropriation of codes or modules of Marxist thought or Western 'conclusions' to Indian problems, the conceptual brilliance of *India in Transition* derives from the impressive powers of bridging and amalgamating Russian, German and Bengali discourses about temporal progression and eruptive change within a global context of post-war avant-gardism.

Marxist Canon, Indian Exegete

The writings of Marx and his major interpreters were not merely occasional or dispersed treatises of political philosophy for M. N. Roy. Rather, he saw them collectively as comprising a canon. The canonicity of Marxism as a coherent body of authoritative texts was a framework Roy imposed on the dispersed and scattered writings and debates he encountered within the early communist world, and he carried this framework over from the Swadeshi milieu. Roy approached Marxism as an exegete approaches a canon of scripture not because of something necessary or innate to 'Marxism', but because of Roy's historically effected style of interpretation greatly informed by the Brahmo tradition. He maintained that the economic logic of dialectical materialism was a universal principle that inhered in all human societies. Human societies were equal and translatable to one another on sociological grounds. For M. N. Roy, there was a common deep rationality to all social unrest worldwide. 'The present situation in India is not unique in history. It is a stage of social development marked by a sudden and rapid introduction of modern means of production, resulting in a dislocation of the status quo, economic as well as territorial, of the population'.[124]

Roy proposed that the 1857 Rebellion and the protest against the Bengal partition in 1905, while episodes of nationalist struggles, also represented the class interests of social elites. He portrayed the late nineteenth century as one of financial aggrandisement by the Indian business classes. Yet the Swadeshi uprising marked the 'swelling by the lower strata of middle-class intellectuals', and the development of a 'declassed' group of radicals.

Roy's discussion of Indian society was not only aimed at understanding Indian society futuristically, but was also *en route* to the project of challenging Eurocentric assumptions of the West's civilisational exceptionalism, or Asia's supposed endemic social stagnancy. This view of a native, eruptive agency found in India's peasants was seen as heterodox among European communists. Yet, it also became a great inspiration to non-European colonial intellectuals.[125] From 1921 onwards, Roy assumed the role in the Comintern of a master exegete of Marxism on topics relating to the colonial world. He read the Marxist canon to criticise, reinterpret and renovate claims about the social revolution outside Europe.

Roy observed at the 1921 Congress of the Communist International, 'when we debate the conditions of world economy and the crisis of contemporary capitalism, we should not limit ourselves to Europe and America'.[126] Two years later, he was arguing the same point, only now with added exasperation: 'Comrades! The question of the Orient should have been discussed many times already. It should have arisen in relation to debates about the offensives of capital ... and when the question is finally brought up there is always so little time remaining that it is practically impossible to coherently discuss it'.[127] In 1925 he published his article 'Europe is not the World' in *Inprecor*, the major journal of the Communist International, in which he again admonished: 'It should not be forgotten that, to be effective, our unity should not be European unity, but truly international unity — world unity'.[128] These same years saw Roy's meteoric rise within the Comintern organisation. The early communist world offered a space for such exegetical criticism.

Swadeshi's Future, Gandhi's Past

Manabendranath Roy clearly saw communism as a way of renewing and vindicating the deterritoriality and insurgent temporalities of the Swadeshi avant-garde. 'All hold that a "New India", — "Young India" is in the process of birth', he wrote at the introduction of *India in Transition*.[129] Roy explicitly likened Swadeshi radicals to Bolshevik revolutionaries — both groups had launched their first revolutionary assaults in 1905. Furthermore, Roy associated the liberally-oriented Swarajya Party, established by C. R. Das and Motilal Nehru in 1922, with the reformist Russian Cadets who refused to accept the exigency of revolution:

> Lenin compared the Cadets with worms born out of the decayed carcass of [the] Revolution of 1905 … Lenin said that the Party of the Cadets was the growth on the dead body of the Revolution of 1905. Similarly, the Swaraj Party rose out of the ruins of a great movement which did not reach such a definite revolutionary climax as the Russian Revolution of 1905, but which was undoubtedly the nearest approach to a revolutionary crisis in India.[130]

The 'great movement' that Roy did not name, that 'nearest approach to a revolutionary crisis in India', was the Swadeshi movement in which he had played an important role. The fact that he did not actually mention the name 'Swadeshi' directly, rather employing a circumlocution, suggests the trauma that followed in the aftermath of the exhausted Swadeshi movement after 1917.

In Roy's lifelong attempt to come to terms with the great failure of his original revolutionary experiences as a Calcutta youth, he preserved a sense of the magnitude and singularity of the Swadeshi moment by contrasting it with Gandhism and mainstream nationalist politics that had already begun to champion territorial closure by the early 1920s. For Roy, the desire for a territorial Indian nation, like the states of Western Europe, represented a rot of the imagination — 'worms' that festered in the 'ruins of a great movement'. In Roy's 1920s writings, 'Gandhism' and the Swarajya leaders after they distanced themselves from communism, represented movements that sought to betray the deterritorial dimensions of Swadeshi insurrection, and the radical eruption of a new universalism.[131] Comparing Gandhi with Lenin, Roy said that while Bolshevism 'forged ahead, breaking one link after another of the mighty chain of time-honoured servitude', Gandhism 'gropes in the dark, spinning out ethical and religious dogmas'.[132] Gandhi, for Roy, was the quintessence of the anti-colonial leader who lacked a 'programme'. Gandhi could not 'countenance the spirit which spells revolution', and substituted 'spiritual patriotism' for true revolutionary thought.[133] Roy saw in Gandhi's politics a threat to the deterritorial body of India, especially given Gandhi's radically local and territorialising politics, in which one dwelled amidst *khaddar*, *charkha*, village imaginaries and swadeshi goods.[134]

It was Gandhi's critical reinterpretation of 'swadeshi' in the movement's fag-end years that reframed the term as relating to patriotic physical labour, such as cotton spinning, and the cultivation of a territorialised nation–body. Of course, Gandhi was himself a deterritorial politician in terms of his view of the Indian nation as including its worldwide diaspora. The very origins of his politics lay especially in efforts to protect the right of Indian indentured and free labour in South Africa, but also worldwide.[135] But, in the realm of culture his was certainly a territorialising imagination. Even for Indians abroad, Gandhi insisted on the intimate practice of Indian body culture, and the preservation of Indian cultural continence against Western influence. It was the cultural body of India that Gandhi primarily sought to territorialise and to make autonomous, even as the Indian population body was scattered across the globe.[136]

Already in *Hind Swaraj* of 1910, Gandhi had many critical words for the deterritoriality of Bengal radicalism. 'The sons of India were found wanting, its civilisation has been placed in jeopardy', Gandhi wrote. 'But its strength is to be seen in its ability to survive the shock'.[137] He protested against what he saw as the heteronomy of Bengali Swadeshi movement, with its recourse to violence, an ill of 'Western' civilisation, and its tendency to posit the equivalence between the Indian struggle, and that of the Italian, French and Irish revolutionaries.[138] Gandhi critically reinterpreted the term 'swadeshi' to refer specifically to practices of body hygiene and home industry that helped define the boundaries of Indian cultural autonomy vis-à-vis the West. This was a very different notion of 'swadeshi' from the deterritorial horizons of Bengali Swadeshi avant-garde thought. Swaraj is achieved, maintained Gandhi, 'when we learn to rule ourselves'.[139] In Gandhi's powerful articulations of a new path of political and ethical struggle in the 1920s, the Indian nation–body as a cultural entity, both in India and in diaspora, was asked to shore up its boundaries and purify itself — to reterritorialise itself — by returning to inherited customs, village-scapes and locally made swadeshi goods. This represented a clear shift, almost an inversion, in the significance of the original term, and heralded the move of the mainstream Congress increasingly away from the deterritorial imaginaries of the pre-War years to an increasing preoccupation with the continence of national form.

As opposed to Gandhi's way of defining the boundaries of cultural autonomy, M. N. Roy, like other Swadeshi thinkers such as C. R. Das, Subhas Chandra Bose and Rabindranath Tagore, vigorously opposed his view with the call for a politics of boundary transgression not boundary assertion, and of solidarity building not ascetic solipsism. Roy's writings of the 1920s continually spoke of 'a new India' that lay beyond the horizon. 'The nationalist movement is the expression of that striving [for indispensable changes] ... its basic task is to build a modern India on the ruins of the old'.[140] Furthermore, this new India would be 'constitutionally' different from the one that presently existed.

> What is revolution? A very wrong notion about it obtains in Indian nationalist circles... The forces that go into the making of the new epoch are originally conceived and go on gathering strength within the framework of the old that eventually must burst if the germs of the new contained therein are to fully fructify. This process is to be noticed throughout all the physical existence. Revolution, therefore, is in the very nature of things; it is quite constitutional.[141]

Roy here adopted an obstetric language to describe the workings of revolutionary time, in which the *novum* would germinate, fructify and ultimately erupt from the old structure of the world. Such change was not merely political, Roy insisted, it was structural and constitutional as well. 'The organism of society, subjugated and exploited for centuries, is surcharged with inflammable materials which once ignited by a revolutionary leadership, will shatter the chain of slavery'.[142]

In Roy's attempt to assert the inadequacy of contemporary Indian politics in the homeland in the 1920s, he suggested that the Gandhian nationalist ideology lacked an understanding of the fundamentally global, universal and futuristic dimensions of India's path to independence. India would be freed not as an exceptional territory–body, but as a particular expression of the universal struggle of the workers and peasants. If Gandhi mined the symbolic resources of place and home, Roy heralded Swadeshi globalism and a modernist commitment to 'new time' and to the 'Not-Yet', not as farce but as actualised history.

Notes

1. Sibnarayan Ray. 1998. *In Freedom's Quest: A Study of the Life and works of M. N. Roy.* Calcutta: Minerva, vol. 1: p. 47.
2. Dhanagopal was the younger brother of Jadugopal Mukherjee. A number of articles in the *Modern Review* (Calcutta) from 1907 to 1911 argued for the benefits of sending Indian students to Japan and America for studies. For example: Nihal Singh, 'A message that Japan gave me', *Modern Review* February 1909, and also Har Dayal, 'India in America', *Modern Review* July 1911, 10(1): 1–11.
3. N. Innaiah. 1995. *Evelyn Trent alias Shanti Devi: Founder Member of the Exile Indian Communist Party.* Hyderabad: Booklinks Corp, p. 9. See Dhanagopal Mukerji's autobiography. Dhan Gopal Mukerjee (Dhanagopal Mukherjee). 1923. *Caste and Outcaste.* New York: E. P. Dutton & Company. I thank Dilip Menon for pointing

out to me that Dhanagopal Mukherjee went on to become a celebrated author in the United States, and won the prestigious John Newbery Medal for children's fiction in 1928.

4.   M. N. Roy. *M. N. Roy's Memoirs.* Bombay: Allied Publishers, p. 22.

5.   Innaiah, *Evelyn Trent alias Shanti Devi,* p. 9.

6.   See David Starr Jordan. 1922. *The Days of a Man.* Yonkers-on-Hudson: World Book Company vol. 2: p. 445. On Dhanagopal Mukherjee see Ray, *In Freedom's Quest,* vol. 1: pp. 46–49.

7.   Edward McNall Burns.1953. *David Starr Jordan: Prophet of Freedom,* Stanford: Stanford University Press, p. 217.

8.   M. N. Roy's *Memoirs,* pp. 43–44.

9.   H. G. Wells. 1929. *The Outline of History.* Garden City: Doubleday, p. 579ff. The culmination of history would result in 'man's coming of age', and so would follow the 'unification of the world into one community of knowledge and will'.

10.   M. N. Roy. 1953d. 'In the Land of Revolutions', *Radical Humanist,* 8 March, vol. 17: p. 114.

11.   Roy, M. N. Roy's *Memoirs,* pp. 28, 29.

12.   Woodrow Wilson, 'Flag-Day Address', 14 June 1917. Reproduced in Woodrow Wilson. 1918. *In Our First Year of War.* New York: Harper & Bros., p. 64.

13.   Roy *Memoirs,* p. 43; Ker. 1973 (1917). *Political Trouble in India 1907–1917.* Calcutta: Superintendent Government Printing, p. 259.

14.   Roy, 'Open Letter to His Excellency Woodrow Wilson', reproduced in Sibnarayan Ray. 1987b (1917). *Selected Works of M. N. Roy.* Delhi: Oxford University Press, vol. 1: pp. 67–83.

15.   Woodrow Wilson. 2005. 'Fourteen Points', in Ronald Pestritto (ed.), *Woodrow Wilson: The Essential Political Writings.* Lanham: Lexington Books, p. 262.

16.   Erez Manela makes this point too. For this reason, Wilson held that colonies should be administered by the small nations, but also that the resources of the colonies should be made available to all members of the League. Ray Stannard Baker. 1927. *Woodrow Wilson: Life and Letters.* Garden City: Doubleday, vol.1: p. 10.

17.   Lajpat Rai, 'New Internationalism', Speech at the International Dinner organised by the People's Council of America, 16 February 1918. Reproduced in Lajpat Rai. 2003. *The Collected Works of Lajpat Rai,* B. R. Nanda (ed.). New Delhi: Manohar, vol. 7: p. 23.

18.   'Open Letter to His Excellency Woodrow Wilson' (1917) and *India, Her Past, Present and Future* [originally published in 1918] in Ray (ed.), *Selected Works,* vol. 1: pp. 64ff. M. N. Roy spoke of articles he published in the Swadeshi press before leaving Calcutta, but these have not survived.

19.   Ibid., p. 148.

20.   Ibid., p. 153.

21.   Ibid., p. 153.

22.   On civilisational discourse in Indian anti-colonialism, see Ashis Nandy. 1987. 'Outside the Imperium: Gandhi's Critique of the West', in *Traditions, Tyranny, Utopias,* Delhi: Oxford University Press, pp. 127–62.

23.   Roy, *India: Her Past, Present and Future,* 1918: 153.

24. M. N. Roy. 1953b. 'In the Land of Liberty', *Radical Humanist*, 15 February vol. 17: p. 80.
25. Ibid., p. 127.
26. There were at least four other prominent Indians anti-colonial activists in Mexico City at this time. See Bertram David Wolfe. 1981. *A Life in Two Centuries*. New York: Stein and Day, p. 317; Friedrich Katz. 1981. *The Secret War in Mexico: Europe, the United States, and the Mexican Revolution.* Chicago: University of Chicago Press, p. 424.
27. Roy, *Radical Humanist*, 15 March 1953, 17: 127.
28. Fritz Fischer. 1962. *Griff nach der Weltmacht: die Kriegzielpolitik des Kaiserlichen Deutschland 1914-1918.* Dusseldorf: Droste, pp. 109-31.
29. Katz, *The Secret War in Mexico*, p. 415. Mexico became the headquarters of the German secret service in North America after the United States entered the war in 1917.
30. Deutscher Reichstag. 1919-20. *Untersuchungsausschuss über die Weltkriegsveran twortlichkeit.* Berlin: Deutsche Verlagsgesellschaft Fur Politik und Geschichte, p. 355.
31. The Germans attempted to ship a large trove of guns from the coast of Mexico to Peking in 1915. See German Foreign Office Archive, Berlin (AA).1915. 21079-2, 11 February, p. 167.
32. M. N. Roy. 1918. *La India, Su Pasado, Su Presente y Su Porvenir*. Reproduced in Sibnarayan Ray (ed.), *Selected Works of M. N. Roy*, vol. 1, pp. 89-158.
33. M. N. Roy. 1953a. 'The City of the Sleeping Woman', *Radical Humanist*, 22 March. vol. 17: p. 138.
34. Kris Manjapra. 2006. 'The Illusions of Encounter: Muslim "minds" and Hindu revolutionaries', *Journal of Global History*, 1(3): pp. 363-82.
35. Roy, *Memoirs*, p. 81.
36. Roy wrote essays directly in German by the mid-1920s, and his English writings, even after return to India, were occasionally marked by 'Germanisms'. In a letter from 1939, he wrote that he 'made many experiences in prison' and in a letter to Ellen Gottschalk from prison in 1935, he wrote that his work 'is not interbroken'. See M. N. Roy, 'Letter from M. N. Roy to Gandhi', *Independent India*, 18 November 1939, vol. 3: pp. 341-43. In his late years, friends remember that Roy spoke German with his wife at home. Oral history interview with R. M. Pal, 19 January 2005.
37. Charles Shipman. 1993. *It had to be Revolution.* Ithaca: Cornell University Press, p. 76.
38. Theodore Draper, *Roots of American Communism*, 1957: 11; Charles Shipman, *It Had to be Revolution*, p. 119; Carleton Beals. 1938. *Glass Houses: Ten Years of Free-lancing.* Philadelphia: Lippincott Company, pp. 43-51.
39. Friedrich Katz, *The Secret War in Mexico*, pp. 423-24.
40. Wolfe, *A Life in Two Centuries*, p. 285.
41. On the Mexican construction of modernist identity see Mauricio Tenorio-Trillo. 1996. *Mexico at the World's Fair: Crafting a Modern Nation.* Berkeley: University of California Press, pp. 28-47.

42. Ray, *In Freedom's Quest*, vol 1: pp. 50–54.
43. Isaac Deutscher. 2003 (1954). *The Prophet Armed: Trotsky, 1879–1921*. New York: Oxford University Press, p. 58.
44. Roy, M. N. Roy's *Memoirs*, p. 217; See Borodin to Wijnkoop, International Social History Museum, Amsterdam (IISG), 'Letter of Introduction by Borodin', Fond 581, Nr. 62, dated 1919.
45. Beals, *Glass Houses*, p. 43.
46. Roy, M. N. Roy's *Memoirs*, p. 19.
47. Roy, M. N. Roy's *Memoirs*, p. 165.
48. Roy, M. N. Roy's *Memoirs*, p. 18; 'Buddy' comes up often in secret correspondence. See Evelyn Trent to Henk Sneevliet, 7 July 1924, IISG: Sneevliet Papers, 362.
49. On self-performance and self-fashioning see Thomas Greene. 1968. 'The Flexibility of the Self in Renaissance Literature', in Peter Demetz (ed.), *The Disciplines of Criticism*, pp. 241–64; Stephen Greenblatt on play, Stephen Greenblatt. 1984. *Renaissance Self-fashioning*. Chicago: University of Chicago Press, p. 193ff.; Marjorie Garber. 1992. *Vested Interests*. New York: Routledge, pp. 21–40.
50. Roy, M. N. Roy's *Memoirs*, p. 223.
51. Henry Maximilian Pachter. 1982. *Weimar Etudes*. New York: Columbia University Press, p. 89ff; Wolfgang Abendroth. 1978. *Sozialgeschichte der europäischen Arbeiterbewegung*. Frankfurt: Suhrkamp, pp. 1–75; Theodor Bergmann. 2001. *Gegen den Strom: Die Geschichte der Kommunistischen-Partei-Opposition*. Hamburg: VSA-Verlag, pp. 14–17.
52. Cecil Davies. 2000. *The Volksbühne Movement: A History*. Amsterdam: Harwood Academic, pp. 80–96, 99–113.
53. See Abelshauer et al. 1985. *Deutsche Sozialgeschichte 1914-1945: ein historiches Lesebeuch*. Munich: C. H. Beck, pp. 327–47.
54. Ulrich Weitz. 1991. *Salonkultur und Proletariat: Eduard Fuchs*. Stuggart: Stoffler & Schutz, pp. 409–13.
55. Pachter, *Weimar Etudes*, p. 54.
56. Bergmann, *Die Thalheimers*, p. 215.
57. Roy, M. N. Roy's *Memoirs*, p. 267.
58. Roy, M. N. Roy's *Memoirs*, p. 213.
59. See introductory comments by Shlomo Avineri to *Karl Marx*. Karl Marx et al. 1968. *Karl Marx on Colonization and Modernization*. Garden City: Doubleday, p. 5. 'Yet time and again (Marx) warns his disciples not to overlook the basically *European* horizons of his discussions of historical development'.
60. *Marx-Engels Gesamtausgabe*, edited by Institute for Marxism-Leminism, 1972, 1: 637.
61. Richard Jones wrote: 'The history of the eastern powers, as we can read or see, shows an almost constant effort on the part of then active rulers to force these physical barriers against the excesses of their exaction'. See Richard Jones. 1859. *Literary Remains, Consisting of Lectures and Tracts on Political Economy, of the Late Rev. Richard Jones*, William Whewell (ed.). London: J. Murray, p. 123. On Marx's reading of Jones and Malthus, see Perry Anderson. 1979. *Lineages of the Absolutist state*. London: Verso, pp. 471–73. See Marian Sawer. 1977. *Marxism and the Question of the Asiatic Mode of Production*. The Hague: Nijhoff, pp. 47–48.

62. Article by Marx, 25 June 1853, *New York Daily Tribune*, reproduced in Avineri (ed.), *Karl Marx on Colonialism and Modernization*, p. 84.
63. Henry Summer Maine. 1966. *Lectures on the Early History of Institutions*, 7th ed., New York: Kennikat Press, p. 39.
64. 'Pre-Capitalist Economic Formations', *Grundrisse der Kritik der politischen Ökonomie 1857–1858*, 1939: 70–1.
65. Sanjay Seth. 1995. *Marxist Theory and Colonial Politics: The Case of Colonial India.* New Delhi: Sage Publications, p. 33.
66. David Harvey. 2000. *Spaces of Hope*, Berkeley: University of California Press, p. 65.
67. See Gareth Stedman Jones. 2007. 'Radicalism and the extra-European World', in Duncan Bell, (ed.), *Victorian Visions of Global Order*, pp. 7–12.
68. Seth, *Marxist Theory*, p. 67; See Sobhanlal Datta Gupta. 1980. *Comintern India and the Colonial Question.* Calcutta: Centre for Studies in Social Sciences, p. 12, 'Lenin ... opened up an almost hitherto unknown perspective to the question of application of Marxism to colonies...'
69. Sobhanlal Datta Gupta, *Comintern India*, pp. 7–12.
70. Communist International. 1919. *Bibliothek der kommunistischen Internationale I. Manifest, Richtlinien, Beschlüsse des ersten Kongresses.* Hamburg: Hoym, p. 11.
71. Statement by Lenin: 'Das Programm Wilsons bezweckt im besten Fall nur eine Änderung des Firmenschildes der Kolonialsklaverei', (Wilson's programme intends to bring about at most a change in company sign for colonial slavery). *Bibliothek der Komintern*, 13.
72. Lenin, *Democracy and Narodism in China.* Reproduced in *Collected Works*, 1927, 18: 163–69.
73. Communist International. 1920. Lenin's speech, *Theses and Statutes of the Third International: Adopted by the Second Congress 1920.* Moscow: Publishing Office of the Communist International, p. 20.
74. Thesis eleven reads: '(All) Communist parties must assist the bourgeois-democratic liberation movement in these countries, and that the duty of rendering the most active assistance rests primarily with the workers of the country the backward nation is colonially or financially dependent on'.
75. See the comments by Manuilski at the Fifth Congress, *Protokoll des V. Weltkongresses der Kommunistischen Internationale*, 1924, 2: 620: '... die Richtigkeit der auf dem 2. Internationalen Kongress gefassten Richtlinien ist durch den gesamten Entwicklungsgang in Europa und den Kolonien bestätigt' (The correctness of the guidelines formulated at the Second International Congress is confirmed by the whole course of development in Europe and the colonies...).
76. Henk Sneevliet, another member present at the Second Communist International also commented on the lack of interest among the delegates, '... I have the impression that, with a few exceptions, even this Congress of the Communist International has not fully understood the significance of the oriental question'. In *Second Congress of the Communist International*, 1977: 170–71. See also Tony Saich. 1991. *The Origins of the First United Front in China: The Role of Sneevliet (alias Maring).* Leiden: E. J. Brill, p. 14.
77. M. N. Roy, 'Oriental Draft of Supplementary Theses'. Reproduced in Ray (ed.), *Selected Works of M. N. Roy*, vol. 1: p. 168.

78. This standard view of Roy's supposed misunderstanding is articulated in Gupta, *Comintern India and the Colonial Question*, p. 29. On the other hand, Charles McLane locates M. N. Roy within the heteroglossia of debates about communist colonial policy, and does not posit the framework of orthodoxy and misunderstanding. See Charles McLane. 1966. *Soviet Strategies in Southeast Asia*. Princeton: Princeton University Press, p. 22.

79. M. N. Roy. 1971b. *What Do We Want?*. Bombay: Nachiketa Publications reprinted in Ray (ed.), *Selected Works*, vol. 1: p. 531.

80. M. N. Roy. 1922. *Vanguard*, 'Our Immediate Task', 1 March vol. 1: p. 4.

81. On Gandhi's strategy of marking a new form of anti-colonial politics through the repudiation of undisciplined direct action, see Shahid Amin. 1995. *Event, Metaphor, Memory: Chauri Chaura, 1922-1992*. Berkeley: University of California Press, pp. 13,14.

82. Roy has traditionally been portrayed as a political figure who fell out of touch with the political realities of India. The view was partially the result of writings against him by Indian Communists after his break from the Comintern.

83. The phrase is from Sanjay Subrahmanyam. 2005. *Explorations in Connected History. Moghuls and Franks*, Delhi: Oxford University Press, p. 12.

84. F. M. Bailey. 1946. *Mission to Tashkent*. London: Travel Book Club.

85. Ibid.

86. Report on Raja Kumar Mahendra Pratap. AA: 21078-4, 1915; Sohan Singh Josh. 1978. *Hindustan Gadar Party*, New Delhi: People's Publishing House, p. 234. Also see the evocative fictional account of frontier communism and Indian revolutionaries in Mulk Raj Anand. 1942. *The Sword and the Sickle*. London: J. Cape, pp. 8-79.

87. A. C. Bose. 2002. *Indian Revolutionaries Abroad*, Delhi: Northern Book Centre, p. 204.

88. See 'Notes on Acharya', Zentrum Moderner Orient, Krüger Nachlass (ZMO): File 138, 4 January 1968.

89. 'Protokol über Gründung der KP Indien in Tashkent 1920', Russian States Archive of Social and Political History, Moscow (RGASPI): Fond 495, Opus. 68, File 4.

90. 'Communism in India', OIOC, L/PJ/12/48, 2 November 1923, p. 163; Muzaffar Ahmad. 1962. *Communist Party in India and its Formation Abroad*. Calcutta: National Book Agency.

91. Other original members who came out of the Khilafat movement were Muhammad Ali, Muhammad Shafiq and Amin Farooq. RGASPI: Fond 495, Opus 68, File 36.

92. Ahmad, *Communist Party in India and its Formation Abroad*. Also see a contemporaneous British surveillance report, 'Communism in India', Oriental and India Office Collection (OIOC): L/PJ/12/48, 2 November 1923, p. 163; Ayesha Jalal. 2000. *Self and Sovereignty: Individual and Community in South Asian Islam since 1850*. New York: Routledge, p. 239ff.

93. Ghadar leaders were in communication with M. N. Roy particularly after his return to Berlin in 1921. See OIOC: L/PJ/12/178, report from 25 April 1922.

94. Gangadhar Adhikari. 1971. *Documents of the History of the Communist Party of India*. Delhi: People's Publishing House, vol. 1: pp. 230-33. Also see 'Protokol über Organisation der Kursen', RGASPI: Fond 495, Opus 68, File 20.

95. Bhupendranath Datta. 1983. *Bharater Dvitiya Swadhinatar Samgram: Aprakasita rajnitik itihas*, Calcutta: Navbharat Publishing, p. 484.
96. On the notion of 'non-places' see Marc Augé. 1995. *Non-places*, trans. John House. London: Verso.
97. While typically a term referring to art, Peter Gordon has considered form of 'Philosophical Expressionism' that arose during the Weimar period. See Peter Gordon. 2003. *Rosenzweig and Heidegger: Between Judaism and German Philosophy.* Berkeley: University of California Press.
98. Isaac Deutscher, *The Prophet Unarmed*, p. 250.
99. Eisner was assassinated in February 1919. The leaders of the more established and well-organised group of German communists, Karl Liebknecht and Rosa Luxemburg, had been assassinated about one month earlier in Berlin.
100. Ernst Bloch. 1918. *Geist der Utopie*. Munich: Dunker & Humblot, p. 253.
101. On 'Modern Jewish messianism', see Anson Rabinbach. 1997. *In the Shadow of Catastrophe: German Intellectuals between Apocalypse and Enlightenment, Weimar and Now;* 14. Berkeley: University of California Press, p. 30.
102. On Weimar discussions of temporality, see the study by Rüdiger Graf. 2008. *Die Zukunft der Weimarer Republik*. Munich: Aldenbourg.
103. Ernst Bloch.1986. *Principle of Hope*, trans. Neville Plaice et al. Oxford: Oxford University Press, vol. 2: p. 623.
104. Anton Kaes et al. (eds.). 1994. *Weimar Republic Sourcebook*, Berkeley: University of California Press, pp. 474–76.
105. Bengt Jangfeldt. 1976. *Majakovskij and Futurism: 1917-1921*. Stockholm: Almqvist & Wiksell International.
106. Mayakovksy's 'The Fourth International', written in 1922, is reproduced in Victor Terras, *Vladimir Mayakovsky*, p. 40.
107. Berghaus. 1996. *Futurism and Politics: Between Anarchist Rebellion and Fascist Reaction, 1909-1944*. Providence: Berghahn Books, p. 18.
108. Marinetti, *Scritti francesi*, quoted in Günther Berghaus, *Futurism and Politics*, p. 21.
109. Juliette Stapanian. 1986. *Mayakovsky's Cubo-Futurist Vision*. Houston: Rice University Press, p. 7.
110. Roy, *India in Transition*, reproduced in Sibnarayan Ray (ed.), *Selected Works*, vol. 1: p. 225.
111. Ibid., p. 218.
112. Ibid., p. 185.
113. Ibid., p. 186.
114. Muzaffar Ahmed, *The Communist Party*.
115. Walter Benjamin. 2003 rpt (1940). 'On the Concept of History', Addendum A in: Marcus Bullock et al. (eds.), *Walter Benjamin Selected Writings*, p. 397; Roy, *India in Transition*, p. 186; Sudipta Kaviraj, *The Unhappy Consciousness*, p. 125.
116. Roy, *India in Transition*, p.187.
117. Benoy Kumar Sarkar, *Futurism of Young Asia*, p. 22.
118. Nripendrankrishna Chattopadhay. 1924. 'Russahitya o tarun bangali', *Kallol*, vol. 3: p. 59ff.
119. Dineshranjan Das. 1925. 'Rolland o tarun Bangla', *Kallol*, vol. 4: p. 789ff. Note the resonance with the notion of *swaswatadharma* discussed in chapter one.

120. Kaviraj, *Unhappy Consciousness*, pp. 124–26.

121. Tapan Raychaudhuri. 2002. *Europe Reconsidered: Perceptions of the West in Nineteenth Century Bengal*. Delhi: Oxford University Press, pp. 27–104; See Sudipta Kaviraj's discussion of writing 'imaginary history' in Bengal, *The Unhappy Consciousness*, p. 109.

122. Bhudev Mukhopadhyay. 1862. *Swapnalabdha bharater itihas*. Calcutta: n.p. 'Our name is hope. I have met the dawn', he wrote at the conclusion to his work.

123. Roy to Sushil Dey, 5 July 1946 , Nehru Memorial Museum and Library (NMML): List 70, 'Correspondences', Sushil Dey file.

124. Roy, *India in Transition*, p. 118.

125. Claude McKay. 1922. 'Report on the Negro Question' in: *International Press Correspondence*, vol. 3, 5 January 1923, pp. 16–17. Also see, Bill Mullen. 2003. 'Du Bois, *Dark Princess*, and the Afro-Asian International', *Positions*, 11(1): 217–39.

126. Communist International. 1921. *Protokol des III. Kongresses der Kommunistischen Internationale*. Hamburg: Verlag der Kommunistichen Internationale, p. 120.

127. *Protokoll des IV. Weltkongresses der Kommunistichen Internationale*, 2: 297.

128. M. N. Roy. 1924b. 'Europe is not the World', *Inprecor*, 31 December, 4(90): 1045–46. The statement was picked up by Zinoviev during the famous Fifth ECCI meeting in 1925. 'Germany is not the whole of Europe ... Europe is not the world'. See quote in E. H. Carr. 1964. *Socialism in One Country*. New York: Macmillan Carr, vol. 3: p. 289.

129. Roy, *India in Transition*, p. 185.

130. M. N. Roy. 1924-25. 'Who Will Lead', *Inprecor*, 9(11): 55–65.

131. Originally, Roy was a proponent of the Swaraj Party and courted its major leader, Chittaranjan Das.

132. M. N. Roy. 1924c. 'Mahatma and Bolshevism' in *Vanguard*, 15 October, 5 (2), reproduced in Sibnarayan Ray, *Selected Works of M. N. Roy*, vol. 2, pp. 311–16.

133. M. N. Roy. 1922. 'The Political Situation', *Vanguard*, 15 October, vol. 1: p. 7. M. N. Roy. 1923c. 'The Uses of Patriotism', *Vanguard*, 1 June, vol. 2: p. 8.

134. M. K. Gandhi to Rabindranath Tagore, 1 June 1921, in S. Bhattacharya (ed.). 1997. *The Mahatma and the Poet: Letters and Debates between Gandhi and Tagore, 1915-1941*. Delhi: National Book Trust India, pp. 63–69.

135. Peter Van der Veer. 1995. *Nation and Migration: The Politics of Space in the South Asian Diaspora*. Philadelphia: University of Pennsylvania Press, p. 5.

136. Gandhi's *Young India* (1919–32) was filled with articles about the experiences of diasporic Indian populations, as well as the habitual sense that the Indian diaspora belonged to the Indian national struggle. See Claude Markovits. 2004. *The Un-Gandhian Gandhi*. London: Anthem Press.

137. M. K. Gandhi. 1997. *Hind Swaraj and Other Writings*. Cambridge: Cambridge University Press, p. 73.

138. Ibid., pp. 49–50.

139. Ibid., p. 74.

140. Roy, 'Lessons of the Lahore Congress', quoted in Ray, *In Freedom's Quest*, vol. 3: p. 376.

141. M. N. Roy. 1924a. 'Appeal to the nationalists', 15 December, *Vanguard*, vol. 5, Supplement. Reproduced in Sibnarayan Ray, *Selected Works of M. N. Roy*, vol. 2, p. 316–24.

142. Roy, 'Appeal to the Nationalists'.

3

The Transformations of M. N. Roy

Territorial and deterritorial notions of anti-colonial liberation converged in Roy's thinking. Resonating with claims quite standard in the Swadeshi milieu, Roy wrote in 1919, 'the struggle for Indian independence is not a local affair, having for its end and purpose the creation of another egoistic nationalism; the liberty of the Indian people is a factor in world politics, for India is the keystone of British Imperialism which constitutes the greatest and most powerful enemy of the Social and Economic Revolution that exists today'.[1] What distinguished Roy from other Swadeshi modernist intellectuals, however, was the extent to which he took the notion of India's deterritoriality. If Indian independence really was not a 'local affair', and if the body of India really extended into global space, then an appropriate Indian anti-colonial politics could focus on upsetting imperialism in any particular location worldwide. This radical notion of solidarity that aimed at a radical identification — not just affiliation — with other liberation projects worldwide was a distinguishing feature of Roy's thought.

Roy began to articulate a politics of solidarity and mediation across the bounds of identity that arose from his lived experience of travel, transculturation and in-betweenness. Solidarity was something continually to be reconstructed, something that belonged to the 'new time' breaking into the present.[2] The plenitude of international solidarity belonged to the future and was anticipated, not fully realised. M. N. Roy can be heard from his first days in the Comintern demanding the end to prejudices about gradients of humanity among members of the International.

German Fringe Communism

Roy's interactions in Europe were more subtle than a mere transaction between an 'indigenous' Swadeshi avant-gardism and a 'Western' Marxism. Roy was not mediating between two fixed nodes of the East and the West, nor between 'Indian' knowledge and 'Western' episteme. Rather there were fractures and circuits within global zones of interaction creating intellectual fusions and amalgam forms. As Roy's thought developed in the 1920s, he came to associate specifically with German fringe communists who had been the original leaders of the Spartakus Bund, instead of with the dominant group of the Bolsheviks. In the 1920s these German fringe communists tended to celebrate the recently deceased Rosa Luxemburg instead of Vladimir Lenin, and they saw themselves as inheritors of theoretical discussions about Marxism from outside the Bolshevik camp. I wish to differentiate my argument here from a classic post-World War II polemic, most ardently articulated by John Plamenatz, that Marxism was a progressive philosophy when still in its 'original' German context, before the theory was 'taken over by a revolutionary party in the most backward of the great European countries'.[3] Rather, I will argue that the way Marxism was thought of in different cultural locations — whether enfranchised within a powerful state or on the margins of state power — made a difference in the illocutionary force of the theory articulated. It is not German Marxism, *in toto*, that I speak about here, as if it were a undifferentiated entity, but rather a specific group of German and Polish intellectuals who constituted a fringe group within German communism and within Weimar society.[4]

A significant number of prominent Polish Jewish intellectuals counted among this group, including Rosa Luxemburg, Leo Jogiches and Karl Radek. Other German-Jewish intellectuals included August Thalheimer, Jakob Walcher, Rosie Wolfstein and Heinz Möller.[5] They influenced mainstream communist discourse in its early years through the transmission belt of the Berlin Communist Party, but they soon faced the suppression of the Soviet centre beginning in earnest already in 1924. German Marxism provided an important channel for cultural outsiders to affect the mainstream at the start of the communist experiment, but such groups were soon peripheralised and vilified. M. N. Roy's fortunes in the Communist International were tied up with the fate of this fringe group.

There were two major features of German communist thought that formed a countervailing tradition to Bolshevism during the early Comintern, before the era of regimentation and authoritarianism set in under Stalin. The first was the importance assigned to soldarity-building and worker education by the German Sparakists. The second was their critique of rule by a party elite, and the call for radical democracy. What I call German fringe communism grew out of the politics of the German Spartakus Bund, as well as the philosophical tendency to read Marx as part of the Continental philosophical tradition. This foreshadowed the discovery and publication of the *Economic and Philosophical Manuscripts* in 1929.[6] In the very period of the October Revolution, Luxemburg hailed Lenin's achievement while also trenchantly criticising the violence of land redistribution and the role of the small Bolshevik vanguard in making decisions. Luxemburg wrote, 'when the proletariat seizes power...it must exercise a dictatorship, but a dictatorship *of the class*, not of a party or of a clique — and dictatorship of the class means: in full view of the broadest public, with the most active, uninhibited participation of the popular masses in an unlimited democracy'.[7]

Rosa Luxemburg laid the basis for a distinctive trajectory of 1920s communism. Her ability to provide an alternative communist route outside of Leninism was already seen as somewhat of a danger to the establishment of the Communist International in 1917, and her name was omitted from the 1918 Column of the Revolution that commemorated the intellectual leaders and precursors of communism just outside the Red Square. Luxemburg insisted on the work of building solidarity versus a politics of centrally-planned insurgency. She insisted that bonds of empathy had to be built through communicative action among disparate groups of the labouring and working classes, peasants and industrial workers alike.[8] Revolution had to swell up from below, and from the building of bridges between groups — the proletariat, the peasants, the artisans, and the colonised. The proletariat must be won over to 'listen to the voices and appreciate the situation' of the 'broadest circle of non-organized groups'.[9] Luxemburg maintained that the work of transcending identitarian divides would take place through discussion and education, and not through the catharsis of group violence.

Luxemburg, of Polish Jewish decent, arrived in Berlin in 1898 and immediately entered the leading circles of the socialist Left, arguing against what many radicals viewed as Eduard Bernstein's revisionist politics of compromise. She helped found the Polish Social Democratic Party two years earlier along with other leading figures, Julian Marchlewski (Karski) and Leo Jogiches. Editor of the important *Leipziger Volkszeitung* with Franz Mehring by 1901, her writings already demonstrated a fascination with the psychology of the working class, and with questions of consciousness. Her emphasis on the pursuit of solidarity required a theory of how to convert minds and create a revolutionary consensus.[10]

The context of German neo-Kantianism in the late nineteenth century with its focus on cognition — how structures of mind determine the knowledge of the world — provided the field in which Luxemburg's concerns developed. Neo-Kantianism also brought a renewed interest in practical reason and social rationality.[11] Yet this led to a response among young intellectuals, concerned not with the deduction of static universal principles of action, but with the central trope of social *change* in history. Presaging the return of Hegelian Marxism by the late 1920s, young thinkers such as Karl Korsch, Georg Lukács, Ernst Bloch and August Thalheimer in the years after the Russian Revolution proposed that changing the world really did involve interpreting it anew — entailing mental operations that could not be achieved by insurgent political strategy alone. They meditated on Marx's eleventh Thesis on Feuerbach: 'philosophers have only *interpreted* the world, in various ways; the point, however, is to *change* it'.[12] Thinkers increasingly responded to this injunction by probing the ways that interpretation and social actuality were intrinsically linked and inseparable. German communists were fundamentally interested in the role of subjective mental processes in bringing about revolutionary social change.

Karl Korsch's *Marx and Philosophy* (1923) inquired into the cognitive process whereby revolutionary consciousness was produced.[13] Rethinking the relationship between consciousness and objective reality was crucial to his work. Korsch argued that ideas do not exist in dualism with reality. Consciousness and objective conditions co-create each other. This was particularly the case when it came to social conditions. Revolutionary praxis should not focus on changing material conditions through political economy or strategy alone, which he called a vulgarisation of Marxism. Instead, a praxis was needed that changed consciousness. The work of changing minds was a necessary dimension of the process by which social reality would be fully transformed.

Georg Lukács' famous *History and Consciousness*, published in 1923 soon after Korsch's work appeared, made a resonant argument. Lukács, a Hungarian thinker, had studied with the neo-Kantian philosopher Heinrich Rickert in Heidelberg, and his *History and Class Consciousness* can partly be read as a Marxist critique of neo-Kantianism through recourse to Hegel. In Lukács' rendition, Marx's thought represents the salvaging of the revolutionary aspects of Hegel's philosophy from the reactionary 'exploitation' of the young Hegelians who were 'reverting back to Kant'.[14] 'This movement exploited Hegel's obscurities and inner uncertainties in order to eradicate the revolutionary elements from his method', Lukács continued.

While Korsch proposed the intrinsic link between revolutionary consciousness and social change, Lukács was concerned with the role of consciousness in history. Marx argued for the world-historical significance of proletarian consciousness. The journey of the proletariat from the status of class-in-itself to class-for-itself was humanity's journey. Lukács took this further. He argued that the proletariat was the sole revolutionary class because it alone was able to grasp the totality of human social experience through time. As both the subject and object of history, by coming to awareness of its own condition, by attaining the highest degree of self-consciousness, it grasped the human condition at large leading to a humanisation of the world.[15] And through this ultimate recognition the historical progression came to fulfilment. In other words, the proletariat did not win social freedom only for itself, in a merely subjective mode; rather, it obtained objective freedom for human society as a totality. The transformation of the world entailed first and foremost a change in states of mind.[16]

Whereas in Moscow, the world political centre of communism, political protocols were established and institutions erected, German communists were suspicious and antagonistic towards the Weimar State. The abortive final attempt at a German communist revolution in Thuringia in October 1923 followed after a series of previous abortive revolutionary uprisings.[17] A section of German communists thus positioned themselves as members of a fringe tradition providing a critical perspective on Bolshevik political muscularity. Of course, philosophical divides and party politics did not all cleave the same way. Lukács, who, although Hungarian, participated in German Marxist discourse, became a champion of the Stalinist regime. Korsch, on the other hand, was expelled from the Comintern for his insubordination in 1926, and a large number of individuals among the German fringe, many of them German Jews, were 'excommunicated' from the Communist International in 1928. August Thalheimer was another intellectual leader of one group of those expelled.

August Thalheimer, as an intellectual of the German fringe, valued the work of education and developing consciousness over the pursuit of means–ends political calculation. The intimate friendship between Thalheimer and M. N. Roy would have significant effects on both men's thought, especially as Thalheimer had long been interested in the comparative study of European and Asian societies.[18] Thalheimer, leader of the German Communist Party until 1923, also a German

Illustration 3.1   Roy in Weimar Germany, c. 1923.
Source: Author's private collection.

Jewish intellectual and perhaps the greatest champion of Luxemburg's thought throughout the 1920s, was uncomfortable with the positivist assumptions of Bolshevism. Revolution should not be envisioned as a social algebra that would necessarily occur at a predictable time and place once all historical conditions had been satisfied.[19] Thalheimer applied this further to an argument about how Marxism should be taught to the peoples of Asia. In his *Introduction to Dialectical Materialism* originally delivered as a lecture series at the Sun Yat Sen University in Moscow from 1924–28 and then published as a book, Thalheimer argued for the gradual development of revolutionary consciousness.

The Chinese and Indians could return to their own traditions, to Taoism, Buddhism and Sanskrit philosophies, and find the needed sparks for a revolutionary conversion of consciousness. These traditions too maintained that 'everything was unfinished, but developing, and going to be changed' and that 'things always develop out of their

Illustration 3.2   Roy, Member of the Comintern Presidium, Soviet Envoy
to China, c. 1926.

Source: Author's private collection.

opposite'.[20] Marxism was the modern expression that 'incorporated
and developed the results of two thousand years of natural and
social science'.[21] Thalheimer's approach involved first discussing the
materialist philosophies of India and China in an appreciative tone,
and then slowly showing how these modes of thought were improved
upon and completed by Marx. He attempted to show that Marx, in fact,
belonged to the native philosophical traditions of India and China, that
his thought was not foreign to, but a natural outgrowth of, the logic
already native to Eastern philosophical traditions. Yet, Thalheimer
concluded his lectures with the clear admonition: 'dialectical materialism
is on a much higher level than the primitive materialism [of China and
India]. It has *incorporated* and developed the results of two thousand
years of natural and social science. We cannot turn back; our prospect
must be ahead'.[22]

Indian Communists and the Comintern

M. N. Roy's intellectual encounters in the crucible of Weimar Germany in the 1920s must be situated specifically within the circle of the German communist fringe. These German conversations most inspired and affected Roy, not the debates at the Moscow centre. To bring this specificity to light, we must give up the telescope that pictures a nebula of communism gathered around the Soviet star, and take out a finer lens to explore the fissures and critical distinctions of the communist ecumene. Roy's closest associates and interlocutors in the early years of the Comintern were figures on the fringe. In 1920, Thalheimer, as member of the colonial committee, helped choose Roy as the chief Indian communist, and since then the two remained very close. Roy published his journal, the *Vanguard*, through Thalheimer's *Rote Fahne* press, and he initially received funding through Thalheimer.[23] Roy founded the Indian Labour Bureau in January 1923 in Berlin with Thalheimer's assistance. Acquaintances reported that both of them could often be observed during social gatherings nestled in the corner of meeting halls engaged in hushed conversation.[24] Thalheimer even named his son after Roy.[25] Occasionally, M. N. Roy frequented the Karl Korsch circle and conversed with Lukács, discussing topics such as the art of Rabindranath Tagore.[26] And through his connection with Felix Weil and Eduard Fuchs, Roy gained affiliation to the Frankfurt School of Social Inquiry in 1930, during which time he wrote his major historical work, *Revolution and Counter-revolution in China*.[27] The communist ecumene was a perfect place for Indian deterritorial politics to unfold in ways that supported, but also transcended, ideas about cultural autonomy and national difference.

In terms of the different camps of early Indian communism, on one hand there was Roy's group situated between Berlin and Moscow, including students and envoys trained at Tashkent as well as colleagues inspired by his radical Swadeshi-inspired Marxism. On the other hand, another group of Indian communists in Berlin was organised around Vivendranath Chattopadhyay and Bhupendranath Datta. Chattopadhyay was a veteran of the London and Paris Indian anti-colonial hubs during the previous two decades, and brother of the celebrated Indian poet and Congress member, Sarojini Naidu. Bhupendranath Datta was a Swadeshi revolutionary from Calcutta, and younger brother of Vivekananda. Bhupendranath left in 1908 to travel through the global Indian anti-colonial network, to New York, Chicago and eventually Berlin during the

First World War.[28] There was also the Indian section of the Communist Party of Great Britain led by Clemens and Rajani Palme Dutt, Shapurji Saklatvala, as well as a number of British communist envoys to India such as Charles Ashley and Philip Spratt. And, finally, there were the early communist leaders in major Indian cities: S. A. Dange in Bombay, Singaravelu Chettiar in Madras, Ghulam Hussain in Lahore, Muzaffar Ahmed and Nazrul Islam in Bengal.

These different groups represented contrasting opinions about the meaning of Indian communism and its relation to nationalist struggle, especially before the consolidation of international communism under Stalin beginning in 1924 onwards. Roy's work came increasingly in line with that of German fringe communism especially after the China crisis of 1927. Up until that time, he took a radical Swadeshi-inspired stance attacking the Indian Congress, the Swarajya Party and Gandhian politics as bourgeois obstacles to true Indian social revolution. After 1927, he adopted a much different perspective in his writings, now arguing for collaborative 'united front' politics. The 'masses of India' were the sole bearers of an eruptive agency in Roy's view up until 1927, not the 'Indian bourgeoisie'. But after 1927, Roy transferred the locus of revolutionary agency again, this time to an even broader group — the Indian peasants, proletariat and petty bourgeoisie.[29] This ongoing march of imagining an increasingly more general collective agency for the channelling of eruptive universal time was matched by Roy's move away from violent politics towards a more educational, Luxemburgist, humanist project by the late 1920s. Partly a response to failed revolutionary attempts, but more importantly representing an engagement with different philosophical principles specific to the German communist fringe, Roy began thinking of social change differently by the late 1920s thanks to the fusion of horizons he was experiencing in Berlin.

Vivendranath Chattopadhyay's group, following Lenin's colonial thesis, asserted from the start that the Indian bourgeoisie would lead the revolution in colonial lands. Chattopadhyay's group proposed a national consortium of diverse anti-colonial parties in India led by the Congress that would both force the end of colonial rule and bring about social revolution.[30] In addition to the Berlin Indian communists, leaders on the ground in India in the early 1920s, such as S. A. Dange, argued for the possibility of combining communist radicalism with Gandhian politics. In fact, the fusion of Gandhian non-violence with a communist social agenda represented a perfected acculturation of communism to India, Dange maintained. 'Gandhism suffers from too much and unwarranted faith in the natural goodness of human nature, while Bolshevism suffers from too much neglect of human interests and sentiments', said Dange.[31] But the two projects were ultimately compatible. 'Gandhism aims at curing Society of modern industrialisation and modern civilisation. At the same time, Bolshevism is working with the same view in Russia and in European Society'.[32] But this collaborationist policy did not last into the late 1920s, as Indian communists were increasingly subordinated to the more militant 'ultra-leftist' stance announced at the Sixth Congress of the Comintern in 1928. After that point, and lasting until 1935, the official communist stance entailed opposition to 'bourgeois' nationalist parties such as the Congress.

The relationship between M. N. Roy, who was rooted from the start in the German fringe, and Indian communists linked with the Moscow centre, was chiasmatic. Roy's group began with a radical 'anti-bourgeois' stance and moved towards collaborationist 'united front' politics during the 1920s, while Indians more closely associated with Soviet politics, the group that would be institutionalised as *the* Indian Communist Party, moved from the collaborationist stance to a more entrenched oppositional approach by 1928. The disagreements between Roy and Moscow-centred communism were dynamic but persistent.

Throughout the 1920s, there was significant competition and ideological differences between the Roy and Chattopadhyaya groups. Roy was in touch with groups situated in India, and he directed a number of envoys who shuttled back and forth between India and Central Europe.[33] Roy built up networks with leaders in India, but vied for pride of place as the master interpreter of Indian communism. He even approached the *dadas* (senior comrades) of the Bengali revolutionary underground for their support. One of Roy's first orders of business was to reestablish contact with the former leaders of the Calcutta and Dacca of Swadeshi movement. However, as he rose in stature in Berlin and Moscow in the 1920s, those in Bengal sensed that he had changed — he even changed his name after all. Rumours spread of his supposed misuse of Soviet funds, and his high-handed approach to his former Swadeshi colleagues.[34] When Roy wrote to the old leaders of the Swadeshi underground, Pulin Das, Upendranath Bhattacharya, Sachin Sanyal, Bipin Ganguly — many of whom had spent difficult years in jail after the Rowlatt Act — he received slow reply.[35] The period from 1919 onwards also represented a new rise in revolutionary politics in Bengal and India, and these Swadeshi veterans still sought to resuscitate the older politics of insurgency against the British, not necessarily the new ideology of communism.[36] Roy's letters to the old Calcutta base were quickly filled with tension. 'I wonder if you consider me still entitled to call you "friends". Well, having failed to get any reply from you about our political goals, I decided it wise to keep quiet and work in my own way'.[37] And yet even broken friendships were a kind of bond. Despite their suspicion of Roy's changes in bearing and demeanour, and the seeming gulf of experience that separated them, Pulin Das, Jogesh Chandra Chatterjee, and others in the Calcutta underground, eventually agreed to collaborate with Roy's Berlin group.[38] British imperialism interrupted these global relays, however, through massive imprisonment of communist operatives in 1924 and 1925.[39]

Imperial Vertigo

In the 1920s the British Empire was still in its phase of what one historian called 'superpower' status.[40] However, this period of triumphant Empire was coming to an end, as attested to by the intensification of imperial paranoia, as surveillance officers chased Indians across the globe, particularly to counter the communist and the 'Pan-Islamic' threats.[41] The 1914–32 period was a peak era of British counter-insurgency. It was one in which battles within Europe gave way to the threat of anti-imperialist contagions spreading through the colonies. In this period came the revolt in Egypt (1919) leading to flag independence in 1922, the Somaliland uprising (1919), the Iraq revolt in 1920, the Irish Civil War (1921–24), the Khilafat movement (1917–24), Gandhi's first civil disobedience movement (1919–21), the Moplah Uprising in Southern India (1921) and the Palestine uprising (1929) to name just some of the major sites of unrest within the British Empire. New transportation and information technologies, especially the use of air power both in bombing missions and in logistics supply, gave the British new powers of coercion.[42] In addition, the rhetoric of 'trusteeship' after the Paris Peace Conference allowed the empire increased legitimacy at home, as well as among other coloniser nations.

But despite its apparent strength, British officials were worried in the 1920s. The contagions of communist ideology and propaganda were viewed with alarm.[43] British intelligence determined in 1923 that 'the importance of Berlin as a centre of Indian intrigue [had] increased considerably'.[44] The city was of such concern for two main reasons: first, it had a porous boundary to the East, with envoys from Moscow using the city as the Western Europe base of operations. And second, Berlin attracted a large number of Indian students because of the reputation of the German university system.[45] The simultaneous presence of communists and Indian students in the mixing zone of Berlin was seen as a threat to imperial stability.

The first meeting of the Anti-Imperialist League, organised by communists in Berlin and held in Brussels in February 1927, brought together many leaders of anti-colonial movements worldwide, including Jawaharlal Nehru along with famous European anti-colonial sympathisers, including Albert Einstein and Henri Barbusse.[46] It was supposed to have taken place in Berlin, but was banned due to British pressure on the German state. M. N. Roy was involved in organising the League meeting, which served as the archetype for the Asian Relations Conference of 1947 and the Bandung Conference of 1954.[47] While M. N. Roy and Ho Chi Minh were slotted to attend, they were both sent to China in late 1926 as envoys to the Chinese communists during the civil war.[48]

Already in 1922, with the number of Indian students in Germany rising, the British Government began to raise concerns about the revolutionary leanings of the colonial community in Berlin. And since December 1922, there were discussions taking place at the highest level of the India Office, and involving the Chief of Special Branch for Intelligence in India, Charles Tegart, about finding ways to have Roy expelled from Berlin.[49] In 1923, the British explicitly requested the extradition of M. N. Roy of the German government, and black-listed twenty other Indian revolutionaries who lived in the city, including Vivendranath Chattopadhyaya and Bhupendranath Datta, as well as M. N. Roy's wife, Evelyn Trent.[50] In India, the Cawnpore conspiracy trial of 1924 locked up four main communist leaders and temporarily arrested the development of a communist party on Indian soil.[51] By October 1924, British concern over the Berlin hub of Indian anti-colonialism reached its crescendo as the government successfully delegated the Weimar government to destroy the anti-colonial bases in Berlin.[52] If the Germans cooperated in stamping out the anti-colonial offices, the British promised them access to Indian markets.[53] In October of the same year, the French Ministry of Foreign Affairs also promised the British embassy in Paris that Roy, who had just fled there, would be expelled from Paris, and that his journal, *The Vanguard* would be suppressed.[54] Frustrated, Roy wrote to his friend Henk Sneevliet in Amsterdam:

> Now, I don't know where to go. They will not tolerate me here for long (in Berlin). The same influence operates here perhaps with more effect. It seems that there is no room for me in Europe. It is so annoying. We built

up a very good centre in France... it was precisely for this that the English were determined to break it up... Damn it all. If it keeps on this way, I will do something rash.[55]

The subsequent assault on Indian political activities in Berlin in late 1924, with M. N. Roy and Bhupendranath Datta fleeing the city, and Virendranath Chattopadhyaya falling into inactivity and depression, caused anti-colonial energies to temporarily scatter throughout Europe before returning to Berlin two years later.[56] In 1928 the British unleashed their largest offensive against communism to date in the Meerut Conspiracy Case. More than thirty communist leaders were put behind bars.[57] Yet even in 1933, after many prisoners were released, the director of the Indian Intelligence Bureau wrote, 'the star of Communism has risen and waned ... we are now entering a third cycle wherein Communist emissaries, wiser by the experience of their comrades of yesterday, will work in India with sharper tools and greater circumspection...'[58] Suppression begot only more anxiety and paranoia on the part of the British colonial administration.

In 1924, Roy was sentenced in absentia to twelve years in prison in the Cawnpore Conspiracy Case. This was the same year in which he attained the vertiginous heights of the Communist International, was elected to the Comintern Executive in Moscow and made a candidate member of the Presidium. He soon was named a full member of the Presidium, the high command of the Communist International, as well as to two other supreme organisations, the Secretariat and the Orgbureau — posts otherwise reserved for Europeans.[59] Roy was appointed to the editorial staff of the *Communist International*, while he also joined the British Commission and the Agrarian Commission, and assumed the chairmanship of the Chinese Commission and the Eastern Commission.[60] These positions afforded him access to unmatched status within an alternative cultural-symbolic order from that of British colonialism, and in 1924 the British correspondingly labelled him the 'arch-conspirator' against the British Empire.[61]

But the acclaim did not entail security. During these years, Roy was 'hunted by the police'.[62] From Berlin to Paris to Amsterdam, Roy and his wife, Evelyn, fled from one city to another. They were both arrested in Paris in January 1925, and while Evelyn was released, Roy was expelled from France. Evelyn Trent remembered the almost daemonic fixation of M. N. Roy on the Indian cause. 'I have given my whole self to India', wrote Trent, 'because I must if we were to live together, that being [Roy's] whole life'.[63] The relationship between Roy and Evelyn became increasingly strained.[64] Evelyn wrote to Sneevliet that she was 'weary of being hunted from place to place, country to country, of having to hide and always to be rewarded by a thick fog of suspicion and fear'.[65] Fleeing Berlin with Roy in 1924, and now threatened with a second imprisonment in Paris, Evelyn asked in a farewell letter to Roy:

> ... did you ever stop to think what it meant to a person of my type to leave home, family, friends, environment, country and traditions, to sail out upon an utterly unknown sea with only faith in one man to steer my course and chart the compass? Then to be deprived of that — nothing was left.[66]

In 1926, she eventually decided to return home to the United States. Many have remarked that Roy never spoke directly of Evelyn Trent again. Her name does not even appear in his *Memoirs*. Yet, during his six-year imprisonment in India, between 1931 and 1936, Evelyn Trent, now settled again in California, helped organise a campaign for Roy's release, and sent reading materials, magazines and books to him.[67]

World Comparisons

Roy wrote at a Stakhanovian pace in these years, and would continue to do so throughout his life. In the early years of the Comintern, he rose to such high ranks partly because he was an intermediary between intellectual camps, and bridged them in novel ways. Roy was now a 'gray-suited Marxist', and known as one of Stalin's 'young men'.[68] It was precisely Roy's cosmopolitan creativity and his ability to don new personas that comprised part of his avant-garde politics. It represented an alternative approach to anti-colonial liberation played out through mediations and crossings of cultural domains, as opposed to the insistence on indigenous cultural forms.

Roy proposed a different spatialisation of the world, in which the 'vertical lines' of 'sects, races, castes, religions' in both India and Europe would give way to a clear-sighted appreciation of the way the world was 'split horizontally into great classes, those owning the means of production (including land), distribution (trade) and exchange (banking and usury); and those living on wages. The more prominent the horizontal line becomes, the less becomes the significance of the vertical lines'.[69]

The globe was ruled by an underlying 'horizontal' universal time. Roy compared 'India, Ireland and Egypt' and saw them all engaged in a contemporaneous effort of freedom-struggle against British rule.[70] Like many Indian intellectuals of the 1920s, he equated the conditions in India with those in the Soviet Union: 'Nor is India a solitary instance. Russia in broad outlines belonged to the same category ... it was left for the proletariat to carry through the bourgeois revolution — to lead the peasantry in the final struggle against the landed aristocracy'.[71] Throughout the 1920s, Roy continually suggested new equivalences: of Indian revolutionaries with Americans before their Independence,[72] with Chartists of England in the early nineteenth century,[73] with the Bolsheviks, with the Germans after the war, and with the Chinese during the civil war of 1926–27.

Of particular interest to Roy in the early 1920s were the events occurring in Germany in the years of civil instability. He read the unrest of his German context as sharing a common temporality with Indian anti-colonialism. Especially in 1923, the year the German communists organised the largest and most ambitious attempt to orchestrate revolution, Germans and Indians were linked as comrades. 'The mass-strike and demonstration in Berlin on July 4th was but another symptom of the conflict that rends world today, the conflict of class against class, which grows every day sharper as the contrast between rich and poor increases, as the exploitation of man by man continues.'[74] Roy observed Heinrich Brandler and August Thalheimer at close quarters as they planned the revolutionary attempt in Berlin and Thuringia in October 1923.[75] The events in Berlin were a particular expression of the same general 'conflict' that also existed in India. Given the French occupation of the Ruhr in 1923, Roy likened the workers of Germany to the position of a colonised people, asserting that the '[German] workers are throwing up a new challenge to French Imperialism.'[76] The temporality of German worker radicalisation in the Ruhr was perceived by Roy as equivalent to that of rising protest against British rule in India. In 1923, as Roy hailed the potential for growing unrest in the Western Germany, his concerns were also with the Indian peasant at Chauri Chaura who faced death sentences for their violent uprising the previous year. In an open letter to the British Labour Party, Roy implored its members to prevent the executions, or suffer the retribution of the British workers and proletariat who stood in solidarity with the 'toilers and labourers' of the world.[77] Two years later, China became the country of anticipated revolution within the communist world. And it became Roy's most favoured site to search for revolutionary equivalencies with India.[78]

Crisis and Crossing

By 1926 the influence of Roy's involvement in the communism of the German fringe was becoming apparent. A temporary aphasia developed in his writings between the advocacy of eruptive insurgency that marked his early Marxist views, and a contrasting argument for the tempered politics of critique, education, and solidarity that came to mark his thought from the late 1920s onwards.

The project of forging the united front with the Social Democrats was developed by groups of the German fringe after 1921 as a moderating alternative to the growing inveterate Soviet insistence on revolutionary insurgency, especially in the context of Stalin's rise to power after Lenin's death.[79] The Fifth Congress of 1924 asserted a policy of 'Russification' of the communist movement. German leaders with ties to the Spartakus Bund were reprimanded for their 'opportunistic' Marxist interpretations. Moscow leaders insisted that attempts to build a broad solidarity with groups outside the party could lead to collaboration with socialists and 'socio-fascists', thus compromising the communist movement. Stalin upped the ante by speaking of 'socio-fascism' as the new threat to communism, insisting that the Social Democrats were the greatest enemy due to their supposed complicity with the capitalist order. The Social Democratic Party was the major party in power in Germany in the Weimar years. A militant communist programme was inaugurated to extirpate party moderates who sought collaboration with the SDP.[80]

In contrast to the insistence on muscular party discipline and militancy by the Moscow centre, August Thalheimer became the major spokesman for a politics of collaboration with all groups on the German left, including the Social Democrats, in a broad anti-fascist 'united front'.[81] He insisted that, especially given the rise of Nazism, the German Communist Party had to work towards the 'sympathy of the majority of the working classes' at large.[82] Through the practical experience of cooperation between political parties, consciousness of a broader solidarity that traversed party lines would be built up. 'Revolution from below' would be a slow process, but offered the only true safeguard against the spectre of Nazi rise.[83]

The theoretical agon between German communists associated with the Spartakus Bund and the Bolshevik orthodoxy created fractures within the Communist International from early on. The Moscow metropole charged Thalheimer and his colleague Heinrich Brandler with insubordination for their united front initiatives, removed them from their posts as leaders of the German Communist Party, and summoned them to Moscow for the *auto da fe* before the internal Comintern court. Thalheimer and Brandler, erstwhile members of the old Spartakus Bund, and leaders of the German Communist Party from 1920 to 1923, were placed in 'honourable exile' — forced stay in Moscow from 1924 to 1928 — as punishment for their heretical views. After 1925, the Soviets installed a group of young, and supposedly untainted, party members as the new leaders of the German Communist Party.[84] Stalin advanced his 'blank sheet' policy that leaders in Germany had to be free from any taint of the German Spartakus Old Guard.[85]

Already by 1926, before the climacteric of Roy's experience in China, the influence of the German communist fringe on his thought was already beginning to show through. He adopted a united front line in his *Future of Indian Politics*, published in October, before leaving for Shanghai in January 1927 as an envoy to the anticipated Chinese communist revolution. 'The People's fight for freedom must be led by the party of the people — a party organisation which will be broad enough for all the forces of national revolution. The proletariat will be in it, but it will not be a proletarian party, *nominally or essentially*. In this party the proletariat will stand side by side with the petty bourgeois and peasant masses, as the most advanced democratic class.'[86] Roy was no longer thinking solely in terms of insurgency, but contemplating the possibilities of building solidarity in the Indian context.[87] The ambiguity in his writings from this year points to the conceptual crossings Roy had embarked on. His expedition to China as a Soviet envoy in Canton and Shanghai during the 1927 civil war would seal his transition to a new political approach.

Trusting in Roy's commitment to the violent revolutionary upheaval in Asian societies, Stalin sent Roy to Canton in January 1927 with a group of Comintern leaders.[88] In the context of a great chess game between the Chinese Communist Party and the Kuomintang under Chiang Kai-Shek, Mikhail Borodin, the chief communist envoy in China, already active in Shanghai for four years, viewed the nationalist Kuomintang Party as the most important organ for revolution. Borodin proposed that the communists should assist the Kuomintang to consolidate power, with the expectation that it would maintain allegiance to the Communist International.

Roy on the other hand, in articles written for the Moscow press and in addresses in Shanghai, insisted on the insurgent agency of the Chinese peasants, not the nationalist bourgeoisie. Roy opposed Borodin's plan to woo the Kuomintang, and instead proposed that the revolutionary stirrings among peasant groups in southern China should be supported in the first instance. If the Swadeshi revolution in Bengal, or the German uprising in Thuringia, had not managed to unleash revolutionary force to spontaneously change the social order, then the peasants in China would make amends for this, Roy seemed to think. Roy repeated the claim that the basis of revolution would be 'agrarian revolution' on multiple occasions during this period. Rural self-government should be established after the destruction of the feudal lords.[89] 'The petty-bourgeois Left (of the Kuomintang), on to whose wagon Comrade Borodin wants to harness the Communist Party, has neither the daring, nor simply the desire to start an agrarian revolution'.[90] By April 1927, the antagonism between Roy and his erstwhile mentor from the Mexico days burst into open conflict. 'I do not intend to explain in detail here the advantageousness of a radical agrarian reform to both the petty bourgeoisie and the peasantry', Roy exclaimed during a speech to the Chinese communists.[91] It was, at root, a contest between Borodin's views about the weak agency of the Asian peasantry and the need to ally with the Chinese Kuomintang 'bourgeoisie', and Roy's insistence on the peasants' eruptive and heroic world-transcending agency. There was a certain indiscretion inherent in both perspectives — a certain assumption that revolution could be engineered by temporary envoys of the Comintern. Both Borodin's and Roy's attempts to 'scientifically' orchestrate upheaval in China failed to have any effect. In fact, some Chinese communists viewed them both with disdain. Mao recalled that Borodin 'stood a little to the right', and Roy 'stood a little to the left', but they both 'only stood'.[92]

At least in one mundane sense, Mao's evaluation was not accurate. In fact, Roy travelled quite extensively through villages around Canton and Hankow (Wuhan), trying to rally peasants with pamphlets, translating speeches through the use of an interpreter.[93] He also made contact with the Sikh community in Hankow, and distributed anti-British literature in Shanghai among the sizeable number of British India troops stationed there. An 'Indian Brigade' travelled to Shanghai with support from members of the Indian National Congress.[94] Roy's internationalism did not mean that he was rootless, exiled or distanced from the Indian anti-colonial struggle. The sheer fact that he embarked on Indian propaganda work while in China, in addition to his travels through villages, shows that his actions were interwoven with questions of Indian politics.

Nevertheless, neither Borodin's nor Roy's strategy led to a communist revolution in China. The ascendant Kuomintang soon asserted its opposition to the Soviet Union and succeeded in suppressing the communist party of China. The so-called 'right' group of the Kuomintang under Chiang Kai-Shek commenced a violent campaign against the communists. In the months subsequent to Roy's departure from China in July 1927, the Chinese communists were routed by Kuomintang forces. A Soviet myth developed of an 'abortive revolution' in China caused by Kuomintang 'betrayal', and this complemented the other myth of the failed communist revolution in Germany in 1923. Roy's third attempt at unleashing revolution failed miserably. In this context, he decisively, or perhaps desperately, turned towards the German fringe upon his return to Europe to find a path out of failure.

Transformation of Thought

No longer declaring the indigenous radical agency of the peasantry after the China fiasco but asserting the need to build consciousness and solidarity among the large coalition of actors, Roy reflected upon the limitations of his pre-China thought. The Chinese campaign, he reflected, had become 'a purely peasant movement... but they were certainly not fighting for Communism'.[95] On a clear note of self-criticism, Roy remarked, 'the revolution... could not succeed until it embraced the urban areas also. In other words, the peasants could not free themselves exclusively by their own action, however powerful that might be... And the peasantry could not carry the revolution to the cities. That should have been known beforehand. However, it was proved by experience'.[96] Roy concluded in a self-searching tone, throwing the crossings in his thinking into relief: 'the utopian experiment of making a proletarian revolution with village paupers had already gone too far'.[97]

Roy now felt, after his return from China, that mass consciousness had to be *cultivated* through the ongoing work of building social solidarity and that outright violent revolution was no longer a worthwhile pursuit. This viewpoint took on practical, strategic expression in 1927, when Roy sent his 'Assembly Letter' to the communist groups in Bengal, outlining his suggestion for a change of programme. Roy now prescribed the formation of Workers and Peasants Parties (WPP) in India, which would be legal organisations, clandestinely run under communist patronage. These parties would have as their goal the development of a united front from below, linking workers, peasants and the petty bourgeoisie, thus creating a broader franchise for future social revolution. '[The Workers and Peasants Party] should be the rallying ground of the exploited social elements (proletariat, peasantry and petty-bourgeois) which must unite themselves in a revolutionary struggle against foreign imperialism and native reaction'.[98] Roy included the 'petty bourgeoisie' in the list of those who could enter into a community of collective action with the peasants and workers. 'The social elements ready to fight for this programme are not all necessarily communists and never will be communists; but organized in the WPP they will be under the influence of the proletariat and be led by the communist party without subscribing to the programme of socialism', he continued, effectively breaking with his earlier view by broadening the definition of the revolutionary classes.[99] Roy's position as an intermediary between intellectual positions meant that Roy often broke the frame of his own way of thinking.

But the most brazen proclamation of his turn away from revolutionary voluntarism to a politics of coalition came with Roy's 'Draft Resolution on the Indian Question' presented in July 1928. This document, with its so-called 'decolonisation thesis' would provide the official grounds for Roy's expulsion from the Comintern. The fundamental issue at hand was Roy's new outspoken support for the more moderate stance of the German opposition against the Soviet juggernaut.

Now transferring revolutionary will to an even broader group — no longer the Swadeshi revolutionary, no longer the peasant masses — Roy spoke of a consortium of 'oppressed groups' whose solidarity had to be built up. He wrote that violent attempts to instigate revolution were foolhardy. Following the logic of dialectical materialism, Roy insisted that the expansion of global capital was ineluctable, but it would also produce, in time, the seeds of its own demise and the possibility of transcendence to a higher order of social organisation. Change would come through altered structures not through abrupt acts of individual agency. 'The compromise between imperialism and the native bourgeoisie does not weaken the struggle for national freedom. On the contrary, it enters a revolutionary stage', Roy wrote. In classic Luxemburgist fashion, Roy asserted that a new order of redoubled native capitalist exploitation would lead disparate groups to grow in solidarity with one another: the proletariat exploited in the cities, the peasants exploited on the land, the artisans facing the destruction of the handicrafts industry, the 'teachers, students, employees, small traders' looking for relief.[100] He made the telling remark that 'the revolution will reach the final victory through successive stages of development', and not through an ecstatic moment of eruption. Roy's 'decolonisation thesis' had implications for anti-colonial national struggle. In effect, he now asserted that British imperialism was on its last legs and would naturally end without the need for violent revolution. The eruption of the future into the present would come only by cultivating the consciousness of the broad camp of exploited groups in India to recognise the universality of their struggle.

> By advocating revolutionary democratic freedom *for all the oppressed classes*; by putting forward demands to safeguard and further the interests of the peasants and petty bourgeois masses; and by placing itself in the forefront of the entire national revolutionary struggle the proletariat will conquer the leadership of the national revolution.[101]

A united front party should be created step by step through acts of solidarity, led by the proletariat. Roy now placed great emphasis on trade unions for educating workers and building the consciousness of solidarity. 'The millions and millions of transport workers, plantation coolies and handicraft workers are not yet organized... The Communist party must explain this [the proletariat's historic role] to the proletariat in popular literature, public meetings, trade union, clubs, etc.'[102] This turn towards education and building consciousness had an immediate impact on his activities in the years after return from China.

The Communist Party in Germany was organised into local *Ortsgruppe* in which workers would gather to hear lectures, attend rallies, go on hikes, and generally build a sense of solidarity.[103] On weekends, lecturers were held for party members where attendees could hear talks such as 'Sun Yat Sen, Gandhi or Lenin' or 'Imperialism', for example.[104] The German Communist Party Opposition circle (KPD-O), one of the many fringe groups that protested Bolshevik radicalism, had its own dedicated experts on colonial topics who gave weekend lectures to local groups from 1928 to 1931. M. N. Roy presented regularly on imperialism and anti-colonialism in India and China for this group to German audiences.[105] Furthermore, he joined August Thalheimer as the co-editor of the Opposition's journal, *Internationalen Nachrichten der kommunistischen Opposition*, and commissioned articles to cultivate new consciousness.[106] And this same united front stance, derived from an amalgam of experiences in China and Germany, would inform the most significant features of his politics once he returned to India.

By 1929, Roy came to the conclusion that the pursuit of united front politics in India had to take place through the vehicle of the Indian

National Congress, and not in opposition to it. This stance differed drastically from that of the official Indian Communist Party at the time, which was locked into direct opposition to the Congress after the Sixth Comintern Conference of 1928 when Stalin declared the end of collaborative politics and the start of an era of communist retrenchment worldwide 'communism in one country'.

Revolution and Counter-Revolution

These intellectual crossings occasioned by Roy's place as an intermediary provided the material for his Weimar masterpiece, *Revolution und Konterrevolution in China*, written in German at the Frankfurt School and published in 1930. The text became a classic of communist literature among Central European communists in its time, but was only translated into English in 1946. It was both a treatise on Marxist historiography of Asian societies, as well as a 'dream history' with futuristic intent.[107] If revolutions were dependent upon a change of consciousness, Roy proposed, revolutions of the mind already had a long history in Asian cultures. This element of the argument was reminiscent of August Thalheimer's *Dialectical Materialism* (1924). Here Roy insisted that changing consciousness was not only attainable through adoption of European or Marxist philosophy. Revolution was an endemic aspect of Asian societies and was brought about not through violent struggle, but through the outcomes of philosophical and ethical debates.

Far more than just an account of the 'failed' Chinese communist revolution of 1926–27, *Revolution* also exhibited a new approach to political praxis that defined all of Roy's subsequent work. Roy wrote as an affiliate of the Institute of Social Research in Frankfurt. Eduard Fuchs, one of the Institute's founders wrote to Marx Horkheimer in its inaugural year of 1924 that the Institute's research should also deal with the study of 'the national independence movements of the Irish, Turks, Egyptians, Indians, etc...'[108] Roy's temporary position as an affiliate of the Frankfurt School represented a contribution towards that goal. He wrote much of the manuscript in a Berlin office provided by Felix Weil, another founder of the Institute. But he visited Frankfurt occasionally during 1929 and met and corresponded with Max Horkheimer.[109]

Roy's *Revolution und Konterrevolution in China* marked an important milestone in his preoccupation with Marxist theory. It asserted that ideas and debate have a determinative effect on the material world. In this respect, his thought coincided with the broader shift within mid-century Marxism from debates about political manoeuvre, to works of cultural critique. *Revolution und Konterrevolution* provided the opening for the next two decades of Roy's writings.

In the work, Roy proposed that contrary to the picture of China produced by the Orientalist assumption of Marxist scholarship, such as the writing of contemporary Frankfurt School member, Karl Wittfogel, there was no such 'Asiatic Mode of Production' existent in China as Marx had asserted.[110] But Roy's critique of Eurocentric assumptions followed different lines from his early 1920s oeuvre. It is not that Chinese society was filled with an eruptive energy that would rip apart the old in a violent revolution. Rather, the focus was now on the lively ethical debates and class-based ideological battles native to Asian societies, and the contingency of their outcomes.

Roy began his book by asserting that the course of Chinese history was contingent upon the contest between ideologies during specific moments of social crisis in its past. According to Roy, in the time of Confucius, Chinese society experienced a crisis of production due to the lack of sufficient means for production, such as livestock. This commenced an ancient period of class-war in China giving rise to a war among opposed ideologies. Confucius supposedly represented the class-interests of the dominant classes, while Lao Tse spoke for the exploited'.[111] Lao-Tse's followers, especially Yang and Mu, were successful organisers of social movements. Yet, due to the strong charismatic personality of the Confucian leader Menzius, the proponents of social revolution lost the contingent war of ideology.[112]

According to Marx's Asiatic Mode of Production, Chinese society had never developed the concept of private property, and for this reason, China missed the train of history and progress. And current Marxist thinking on the 'Asiatic Mode of Production' as promulgated by the prominent scholar, Karl Wittfogel, revised and extended this view with the assertion that Oriental stagnation was due to the impact of infelicitous environmental conditions, especially an 'unmasterable geographic terrain' and large semi-arid climatic zones.[113] The crucial point to take from Roy's rehearsal of a mythic history of failed revolution in ancient China was an argument for possibility as opposed to determination. The outcome of the battles between warring ideologies was unpredictable and not determinable by socio-economic or environmental conditions.

Roy sardonically commented on this mainstream deterministic view of an Asian time different from the capitalist time of progress: 'The

Communist Manifesto had proclaimed that human history was to begin with the triumph of the proletarian revolution. Until then, there was only "pre-history", man having, through the ages, lived in the bondage of class-ridden society'.[114] Given the intellectual dynamism of ancient Chinese society, long before the encounter with Europe, Roy argued that there had long been history outside the West. Perhaps he saw himself as the Lao Tse of India — an ethical philosopher embarked on a mission to convert minds.

Renegade

In the era of 'Bolshevisation' and Comintern centralisation, what opponents called 'Russification', there was increasingly less space for debate and discussion within the Comintern, and dissenting views came to be seen first as 'opportunistic' and then later as renegade. From Lenin's passing in 1924 up until 1928, communism underwent a transition from a worldwide institution of ecumenism to one of increased authoritarianism. Early communism was a mélange of diverse opinions and charged debate precisely because the consolidation of Soviet state power had yet to fully emerge.

The group that formed Roy's social and intellectual circle in Berlin since his first days in the city in 1920, the circle around August Thalheimer and Heinrich Brandler, officially organised themselves into the 'German Communist Party — Opposition' (KPD-O) in 1928. They were ousted from the Comintern officially in July 1928, and labelled 'Luxemburgists'. Roy was expelled along with them in that same year after the Sixth Comintern Congress. The disgrace experienced by Roy in 1928 grew out of his intellectual crossings of 1927. 'Roy, by contributing to the Brandler press and by supporting the Brandler organization, has placed himself outside the ranks of the Communist International', the Comintern condemnation pronounced.[115] Fringe thinkers of all types, thinkers who did not ascribe to the Comintern orthodoxy, were increasingly seen with suspicion and expelled. Stalin used the pretext of disciplining and centralising communist activities, and the pursuit of 'socialism in one country', to eliminate and purge threats to Soviet authority.[116]

Roy, during this period, began publishing articles on the need for a communist path out of authoritarianism in *Gegen den Strom* [Against the Current], the most influential communist opposition journal of the 1930s, edited by August Thalheimer.[117] The journal decried Roy's expulsion from the Comintern as a 'scandal of the first order'.[118] 'Roy has belonged to the Communist International since its founding', said the announcement. 'Here again we have a comedy of expulsion carried out by the Comintern'. Soon afterwards, Roy wrote a major twelve-part treatise critiquing the Communist International published over two years, entitled 'The Crisis of the Communist International'.[119] With it, Roy became one of the most vocal and acerbic critics of the Soviet Union in Europe from within the communist fold. 'The reason [for the weakness of the communist movement] is a lack of leadership. The current leadership of the communist international is weak, untalented and has little authority'.[120] Roy argued that the 'ultraleft' line of the Soviet Union had led to a 'despairing politics of putsch-like sectarianism, and a deviation from Marxism towards anarchism'.[121]

On May Day 1929, the German Communist Party under Soviet directives organised another revolutionary attempt. Roy lambasted the move as inopportune and intemperate, especially when a united front politics with the Social Democrats was most needed.[122] He criticised the failed structure of Soviet politics, which had almost totally deformed the culture of internationalism to one of long-distance puppetry by Stalin's iron hand.[123] The way to rejuvenate the international movement, Roy wrote in 1929, was the necessary 'integration of non-Russian perspectives'. 'In fact, we have experienced over the past two years the elimination of the very best forces of the revolution through indiscriminate expulsions...'[124] The only option was disaggregation and decentralising of power. 'The reigns of power must no longer be held by a Russian monopoly alone... The coming forward involves the development of independent sites of leadership in various sections of the international ... which will lead to the breaking up of the official apparatus'.[125] The crisis of the International became 'crass' in 1928, observed Roy, when Stalin carried out a 'violent surgery' on almost all leading segments of the International, using the excuse of the fight against 'Right deviationism' and 'Luxemburgism'.[126] In his article of July 1930, sarcastically entitled 'Stalin triumphs', Roy called the Comintern a mere notional organisation, now caught up in Stalin's personal rule.[127]

For this outspokenness, Roy was paid back with one of state communism's favourite terms in this era: 'renegade'. By the end of 1930, he was labelled a 'traitor'.[128] Kuusinen indicted him for his united front stance, saying that as a member of the 'Brandler renegade press he was urging co-operation with the Swarajists'.[129] He was thus chastised and condemned in the main Comintern journal, *Inprecor*, by the likes of

Safaroff, Eugen Varga and Piatnitksy, as a 'bourgeois liberal' and a 'lackey of imperialism' not only for his criticism of the Soviet Union, but for his insistence that political strategy should include collaboration from inside the Indian National Congress.[130] As with the excommunication from a church, it was officially decreed by Moscow that Roy should no longer be referred to as 'comrade', and there were immediate ramifications in India, as Indian communists began speaking of 'ex-comrade Roy'.[131]

Responses of Indians

Beginning in 1928, with his ouster from the Comintern, Roy became a figure of derision within the official Indian Communist Party, while also finding praise among a broad group of Indian thinkers inspired by Marxism but outside the regimen of the party, such as Jawaharlal Nehru and Jayaprakash Narayan. In 1926 while in Moscow, Motilal and Jawaharlal Nehru met with Roy.[132] Roy made a strong impression especially on the young Nehru and earned his respect.[133] Jayaprakash Narayan likewise recorded his deep admiration for Roy's writings as a student in the United States since 1922.[134] Narayan recalled, 'naturally, [Roy] had a great hand in moulding my thought and leading me to Communism, which was still a revolutionary doctrine. That Roy was a colleague of Lenin and was a big personality in the Communist International, made him in my young eyes a hero and a great Indian ... In the States I was drawn towards him as a disciple to the master'.[135] Gangadhar Adhikari, who went on to become one of the most influential theorists of the Indian Communist Party, came to Berlin as a chemistry student in 1925 and received mentorship from Roy. He broke with Roy in the context of his 1928 'excommunication'.[136]

Shapurji Saklatvala, on the other hand, an Indian member of the Communist Party of Great Britain, said of Roy, 'I have been telling the communist international repeatedly that M. N. Roy is an agent of the English government, but the leaders have refused to listen to me. Thankfully Roy was expelled from the International in 1929...'[137] A forty-two-page anti-Roy pamphlet prepared by the Communist Party of India in 1932 amounted to an extensive syllabus of errors. It declared Roy a representative of the 'bourgeois intelligentsia', whose 'treachery was not accidental' but represented an intensification of class warfare in India.[138] He had a 'bourgeois programme', desiring to 'fight for small demands only', and proposing that the natural death of British imperialism would be followed by the rise of a reactionary Indian bourgeoisie — all heretical views.

Rajani Palme Dutt, a leading theorist of the Communist Party of Great Britain and a specialist in Indian matters had been a great admirer of Roy until his expulsion. After the 1928 Congress, and his official expulsion in November 1929, Dutt repudiated the Indian renegade. Writing to Bengali communist leader Muzaffar Ahmad, Dutt recorded, 'Roy was severely criticised for his theory of "decolonisation"... After the Congress, Roy visited me in Brussels. He was furious with the criticism he had received ... I informed him that the criticism and line of the sixth Congress to be correct ... I wish to have no further dealings with him. This was the last time that I saw Roy, with whom I had previously worked closely'.[139] A major attacker of M. N. Roy was Saumyendranath Tagore, a Bengali student and nephew of Rabindranath Tagore, closely associated with Saklatvala. Saumyendranath travelled to the Lenin School in Moscow in 1928, and launched a number of diatribes against M. N. Roy, calling him a failed theorist and a betrayer of the Indian communist movement.[140] The 'expulsion of renegades and traitors of the sort of M. N. Roy has led to the improvement in the Indian section', Tagore commented.[141] After 1928, virulent criticism of Roy became a standard feature of the Comintern colonial politics as well as of the Indian Communist Party. The taboo of M. N. Roy stemmed precisely from the fact that he interfered with the cultural–symbolic regime of Soviet communism, and fashioned himself as an intermediary, not fully assimilable into the Soviet order of power and knowledge. His close affiliation with German fringe communism meant that his intellectual trajectory in the 1920s formed a chiasm with those Indians who remained linked to shifts in the Bolshevik programme. Eventually, with the rise of Stalin, there was precious little room for debate. If Roy had sought egress from the prison of British colonial liberalism, he found that communist discourse of the late 1920s had transformed itself into a new kind of conceptual and cultural prison.

Notes

1. Roy, 'Hunger and Revolution in India', in Sibnarayan Ray (ed.). 1987a. *Selected Works of M. N. Roy*, vol. 1: p.158.
2. See Ernst Bloch on the 'not yet'. Ernst Bloch. 1986. *The Principle of Hope*, trans. Neville Plaice et al. Oxford: Oxford University Press, vol. 1: pp. 306–13.
3. John Petrov Plamenatz. 1954. *German Marxism and Russian Communism*. London: Longmans Green, p. xxiii.
4. Intellectual histories based on assertions of trans-historical civilisational or cultural qualities were very common in the 1950s. See also Hans Kohn. 1960. *The Mind of Germany*, New York: Scribner.

5. Theodor Bergman. 1987. *'Gegen den Strom*: die Geschichte der Kommunistischer-Partei-Opposition.

6. Alexandre Kojève. 1969. *Introduction to the Reading of Hegel: Lectures on the Phenomenology of Spirit.* New York: Basic Books, Mark Poster. 1975. *Existential Marxism in Postwar France: From Sartre to Althusser.* Princeton: Princeton University Press.

7. Rosa Luxemburg. 1922. *Die Russische Revolution, Eine kritische Würdigung aus dem Nachlass vom Rosa Luxemburg.* Verlag: Gesselchaft und Erziehung, p. 77. See discussion in Paul Frölich. 1972. *Rosa Luxemburg: Her Life and Work*, 1928: 253–83.

8. See, for example Rosa Luxemburg. 1906. *Massenstreik, Partei und Gewerkschaften.* Hamburg: E. Dubber, p. 137, where she carried out an analysis of recent mass action in Russia and concluded that successful revolution would take place only when various labouring groups, each with their own specific experience of 'suffering', could find mutual recognition of each other's plight.

9. Luxemburg, *Massenstreik*, Partis und Gewerkschaften, p. 144.

10. J. P. Nettl. 1966. *Rosa Luxemburg*, London: Oxford University Press, pp. 130–87.

11. Klaus Christian Köhnke. 1991. *The Rise of Neo-Kantianism.* Cambridge: Cambridge University Press, p. 151ff, provides a discussion of the ascent of neo-Kantianism in Germany from the 1860s onwards. The rise partly stemmed from scholars such as Friedrich Albert Lange returning to Kant in order to find the philosophical ground for a new ethics, in the context of the 'Social Question' of that period.

12. This same comment would become a focus of meditation for Althusser. See Louis Althusser. 1969. *For Marx.* New York: Pantheon, p. 28.

13. Karl Korsch, 'Indiens Erwachen' in International Institute of Social History, Amsterdam (IISG): Korsch Papers 62. On Roy's participation in the Korsch circle in Berlin, see Henry Maximilian Pachter. 1982. *Weimar Etudes,* New York: Columbia University Press, p. 54; On Korsch's ties to Luxemburgism, especially in terms of the insistence on the 'spontaneity' of revolution, and the de-emphasis of party organisation see Otto Langels. 1984. *Die Ultralinke Opposition der KPD in der Weimarer Republik.* Frankfurt am Main: Lang, pp. 37–45.

14. Georg Lukács. 1971. 'What is Orthodox Marxism?', 1984. in *History and Class Consciousness,* trans. Rodney Livingstone. Cambridge: Cambridge University Press, p. 17.

15. Lukács, *History and Class Consciousness*, pp. 165–72.

16. Anson Rabinbach. 1997. *In the Shadow of Catastrophe: German Intellectuals between Apocalypse and Enlightenment,* Weimar and Now; 14. Berkeley: University of California Press, p. 63.

17. In Munich, Hamburg and Leipzig and in other cities.

18. He wrote his dissertation of 1908 in linguistics on the language of 'Micronesia' and showed a sustained interest in questions of cognition and language in cross-cultural perspectives. See August Thalheimer. 1908. *Beitrag zur Kenntnis der pronominal personalia und possessiva der Sprachen Mikronesien.* Stuttgart. See Jürgen Kaestner. 1982. *Die politische Theorie August Thalheimers.* Frankfurt: Campus-Verlag, p. 17.

19. Hermann Weber. 1969. *Die Wandlung des deutschen Kommunismus; die Stalinisierung der KPD in der Weimarer Republik*. Frankfurt an Main: Europäische Verlagsanstalt, p. 89.

20. August Thalheimer. 1935. *Introduction to Dialectical Materialism*, trans. George Simpson and George Weltner. New York: Covici Friede, p. 11.

21. Ibid., p. 239.

22. Ibid., p. 239.

23. A commission composed of August Thalheimer, Borodin, James Bell, Troyanski and Rakosi, established Roy as the chief Indian representative to the Comintern. See Bhupendranath Datta. 1983. *Bharater Dvitiya Swadhinatar Samgram: Aprakasita rajnitik itihas*. Calcutta: Nababharat Publishing, p. 285. Jens Becker. 1923. *Heinrich Brandler*, p. 192; Purabi Roy et al. *Indo-Russian Relations*, 1997: p. 144.

24. Reminiscence of Claire Thalheimer in oral history interview with Ray, *In Freedom's Quest*, vol. 3: p. 38n.

25. Interview with Dr Theodor Bergmann, 3 October 2004, Stuttgart.

26. Georg Lukács's review of Tagore's *Gora*, 'Tagore's Gandhi Novel', published in the *Rote Fahne* newspaper, 1922, reprinted in *Reviews and Articles*, 1983.

27. On the fact that the *Institut für Sozialforschung* published the original German edition of Roy's 1930 *Revolution und Konterrevolution in China*, see Ellen Gottschalk to Max Horkheimer, 30 April 1956, Frankfurt University, Horkheimer Archive: III-11-298-301.

28. Peel to CID, 'Memorandum on Bhupendranath Datta', OIOC: L/PJ/12/221, 10 July 1924.

29. Roy, 'Draft Resolution on the Indian Question' (1928) reprinted in Ray (ed.), *Selected Works of M. N. Roy*, vol. 3: pp. 77–112.

30. John Haithcox. 1971. *Communism and Nationalism in India: M. N. Roy and Comintern Policy*. Princeton: Princeton University Press, p. 31.

31. S. A. Dange, *Lenin and Gandhi* (originally published in 1921) reproduced in Bani Deshpande (ed.), *Selected Writings of S.A. Dange*, 1974: p. 96.

32. Dange, *Lenin and Gandhi*, p. 73.

33. The main envoys were Usmani, Nalini Gupta, Jotindranath Mitra. See OIOC: L/PJ/1/117.

34. Muzaffar Ahmad. 1962. *The Communist Party of India and its Formation Abroad*. Calcutta: National Book Agency, pp. 88, 89.

35. On the jail experience of the Swadeshi fighters, see Barindrakumar Ghosh. 1922. *The Tale of My Exile*. Pondicherry: Arya Office.

36. David Laushey. 1975. *Bengal Terrorism and the Marxist Left*. Calcutta: Firma Mukhopadhyay, p. 21.

37. See letter by M. N. Roy to 'Friends', OIOC: L/PJ/12/47.

38. 'Indian Communist Party', OIOC: L/PJ/12/14.

39. A total of 183 persons were imprisoned under the Bengal Criminal Law Amendment Act of 1925. See Laushey, *Bengal Terrorism and the Marxist Left*, p. 29.

40. Anthony Clayton. 1986. *The British Empire as a Superpower, 1919-39*. Hampshire: Macmillan.

41. See Charles William Gwynn. 1934. *Imperial Policing*. London: Macmillan Martin Thomas, *Empires of Intelligence*, 2008: 73–106. See a fictional account of the malarkey of surveillance penned by Somerset Maugham, who served as a British intelligence officer during First World War, *Ashenden: Or the British Agent*, 1928.

42. Italy bombed its colonies in 1911. In 1915, the British bombed Arab towns in Egypt, Iran, Afghanistan and elsewhere. Bombing was 'perfected' in the Iraqi rebellions of 1920. See Sven Lindqvist. 2000. *A History of Bombing*. New York: New Press.

43. David Petrie. 1972 rpt (1927). *Communism in India*. Calcutta: Editions Indian.

44. Anonymous, 'Indian Communists', Reports from 21 November 1922 to 10 May 1923 in: Zentrum Moderner Orient, Krüger Nachlass Annex, Berlin (ZMO-A): Item 41.

45. The Indian Information Bureau was set up by Vivendranath Chattopadhyay and A. C. Nambiar in Berlin during the 1920s to facilitate the enrolment of Indians in German universities. See 'Indian Information Bureau and Chattopadhyaya', 15 May 1930, OIOC: L/PJ/12/223, pp. 79–81; Compare with Chinese and Japanese excitement for German education in this same time. Thomas Harnisch. 1999. *Chinesische Studenten in Deutschland*. Hamburg: Institut Fur Asienkunde, p. 155; Christian Spang et al.(eds). 2006. *Japanese-German Relations*, London: Routledge, pp. 131–33.

46. Contemporary report on conference proceedings was published as *Das Flammenzeichen vom Palais Egmont*, 1927, pp. 55–61.

47. See 'Intelligence Report of I. P. I', 31 January 1927, OIOC: L/PJ/12/226, p. 3.

48. On Roy's involvement with the planning of the League against Imperialism see 'IAH: Liga gegen Imperialism', 1927, RGASPI: Fond 536, Opus 2, File 20. Roy is referred to by his alias, 'Robert', in this file.

49. See Letter to Hose. OIOC: L/PJ/12/55, p. 6.

50. India Office List of Indians living abroad who should not be granted passports, 8 July 22 1923, OIOC: L/PJ/12/69.

51. Those charged in the case were M. N. Roy, Nalini Gupta, Muzaffar Ahmad, Shaukat Usmani, S. A. Dange, Ghulam Hussain, R. C. L. Sharma, and Singaravelu Chettiar. Only four were imprisoned, since Roy and Sharma were not residing in the jurisdiction of the British, Hussain became a witness for the State, and Singaravelu fell ill. See Laushey, *Bengal Terrorism and the Marxist Left*, p. 89.

52. Letter of Joseph Addison to J. Ramsay MacDonald, 16 October 24, OIOC: L/PH/12/223, pp. 6, 7.

53. See the comments by Baron von Richthofer in German surveillance files. 'Aus politischen Gründen, insbesondere im Interesse unserer auf Wiederzulassung Deutscher nach Indien gerichteten Bestrebungen, empfiehlt es sich dringend, dem Anschein entgegenzutreten...' (On the basis of our political interests, especially our interests in the readmission of German ambitions in India, it is recommended that we give the impression (of cooperating) without delay...) See Richthofen report, 17 October 1924, Bundesarchiv, Berlin: 'Reichskommissariat für Überwachung der öffentlichen Ordnung', R1507/67299/650, pp. 11–12.

Meanwhile in India, von Collenberg was also busy trying to obtain new permissions for German traders. In an interview for the Industrie und Handels Zeitung of May 1925, no. 1, pp. 245–46, the German consul general of India said that Germany's trade aims must take pride of place.

54. Ministry of Foreign Affairs to Embassy of Great Britain, 10 October 1924, OIOC: L/PJ/12/99, p. 14.
55. Roy to Sneevliet, 6 February 1925, Berlin, IISG: Sneevliet Files.
56. This was ordered by Ministry of Foreign Affairs on 11 December 1924. See Hose to the Undersecretary of State, Foreign Affairs, United Kingdom, 4 May 1925, OIOC: L/PJ/12/99, p. 43. The Berlin centre was re-established in 1929, especially due to the efforts of Virendranath Chattopadhyaya and A. -C. Nambiar. 'Indian Information Bureau and Chattopadhyay', 15 May 1930, OIOC: L/PJ/12/223, pp. 79–81.
57. Laushey, *Bengal Terrorism and the Marxist Left*.
58. Horace Williamson. 1933. *Communism in India*, Calcutta: Editions India, p. 19.
59. Ray, *In Freedom's Quest*, vol. 2: p. 93.
60. Haithcox, *Communism and Nationalism*, p. 62.
61. Petrie. 1972. rpt (1927) *Communism in India*, 67.
62. M. N. Roy to J. Horner, Berlin, 11 September 1923, IISG, Sneevliet 362.
63. Trent to Sneevlieg, 17 August 1925, IISG: Sneevliet Files 362.
64. That an affair broke the relationship between M. N. Roy and Evelyn Trent is suggested in the following passage from her letter to Henk Sneevliet: 'So painful was the shock and disillusionment of the last two weeks I spent in Europe … I am trying so very hard to understand how it could ever be possible for the man I worshipped so, and whom I thought loved me very greatly, to so betray every finer thought and feeling without a scruple, apparently without even a regret… What is it that he could toss all, all that I tried to be to him, so lightly and scornfully away,… and for what? For really nothing — for a momentary whim, an imprudence, of this I am sure'. Evelyn Trent to Henk Sneevliet, 17 August 1925, IISG: Sneevliet Files 362.
65. Evelyn Trent to Henk Sneevliet, 13 March 1927, IISG, Sneevliet Files 362.
66. Evelyn Trent to M. N. Roy, 25 December 1926, IISG, Sneevliet 362.
67. Ray, *In Freedom's Quest*, vol. 3: p. 283.
68. M. N. Roy. 1964. *M. N. Roy's Memoirs*. Bombay: Allied Publishers, p. 532.
69. Roy, *Vanguard*, 1 May 1923, 2: 6.
70. *Inprecor*, 1924, 8(4): 123–27.
71. *Inprecor*, November 1924, 8(6): 83–93.
72. M. N. Roy. 1925. 'Foundation of Democracy: The American Experience', *Masses of India*, September, vol. 1: p. 9.
73. Also see Santi Devi (a.k.a. Evelyn Trent) published a long serial article on 'Some Historical Parallels: Chartism and the Nationalist Struggle in India', in which the comparability of the progression of history in Indian and British politics was argued. See *Vanguard*, 15 March 1923.
74. Ibid.

75. M. N. Roy. 1923b. ' Revolution versus Reaction in Germany', *Vanguard*, 12 January, vol. 2: p. 4.
76. M. N. Roy. 1923b. 'Struggle of the German Proletariat', *Vanguard*, 15 July, vol. 2: p. 11.
77. See Roy to British Labour Party, Zurich, Switzerland, 1 February 1923. West Bengal State Archives: File No. 100/23, p. 45. My thanks to Subhas Chakrabarty for showing this file to me.
78. For example, at the League Against Imperialism conference held in Feburary 1926 in Brussels, anti-colonial nationalists from Egypt, South Africa, Senegal and India all spoke of Chinese communists as the leaders of a worldwide revolution of 'colonial and semi-colonial lands'. *Das Flammenzeichen vom Palais Egmont*, 1927, pp. 55–61.
79. See August Thalheimer, *Einheitsfront gegen Faschismus*, Bremen: 1932a. Jürgen Kaestner. 1982. *Die politische Theorie August Thalheimers*. Frankfurt: Campus, pp. 53–55. E. H. Carr. 1954. *The Interregnum*. London: St. Martin's Press, vol. 3: pp. 293–308. Carr explores the astounding rhetoric of 1920s communism, in which coining new mottos or slogans and labelling enemies with newfangled epithets brought about the continual thrust and parry between competing groups. 'Bolshevisation' became a keyword in 1925, and was presented as the proper strategy against ' Trotskyism', but also against 'Socio-fascism'. Uncatalogued document in the Forschungsstelle für Zeitgeschichte in Hamburg (FZH): 'Skizze der Geschichte der Einheitsfront in Deutschland'. See Wolfgang Abendroth, *Ein Leben in der Arbeiterbewegung*, 1976: 43.
80. The policy of battling 'socio-fascism', and of declaring the Social Democratic Party as the mortal enemy of communists became *modus operandi* after 1925. Historians have commented on the ill-fated results of this policy in terms of disabling resistance to the rise of the Nazis. See Hermann Weber. 1963. *Der deutsche Kommunismus*. Cologne: Kiepenheuer & Witsch, pp. 187–91.
81. Kaestner, *Die politische Theorie August Thalheimers*, pp. 53–68.
82. August Thalheimer, 'Das Kampffeld', *Rote Fahne*, vol. 5: p. 373.
83. Thalheimer, *Inprekorr*, vol. 2: p. 194.
84. The new leaders were Ruth Fischer, Arkadij Maslow and Heinz Neumann.
85. E. H. Carr, *Socialism in One Country*, 1958, 3: 295.
86. My emphasis; M. N. Roy. 1927. *The Future of Indian Politics*. London: R. Bishop, p. 86.
87. My interpretation runs counter to the standard understanding of the significance of this text, particularly in Indian Marxist literature. Gangadhar Adhikari identified the importance of *Future of Indian Politics* to lie in its supposed incorrect assertion that the Indian bourgeoisie would betray the nationalist movement. See Gangadhar Adhikari. 1971. *Documents of the History of the Communist Party of India*, vol. III-B. Delhi: People's Publishing, 1979: 33, 79. But this view does not allow us to explain how Roy was expelled from the Comintern the following year on precisely the opposite charges, that is, he was too enthusiastic to work with the Swarajist Congress. See Jane Degras. 1956. *The Communist International: Documents, 1919–1943*, vol. 3: p. 28. In fact, this text

represented a less militant stance, given that Roy wanted to differentiate a 'petty bourgeoisie' from a treacherous 'bourgeoisie', and claim that the latter, and not just the workers alone, would work towards social revolution.

88. Sibnarayan Ray's discussion of the circumstances of Roy's travel to China is the most authoritative account available. In *Freedom's Quest*, vol. 2: pp. 259–318. Haithcox, *Communism and Nationalism in India*, pp. 64–68.

89. Robert C. North and Xenia J. Eudin. 1963. *M. N. Roy's Mission to China: The Communist-Kuomintang Split of 1927*. Berkeley: University of California Press, p. 66.

90. M. N. Roy, 'The Base and the Social Forces of the Revolution', speech to the CCP leadership, 13–15 April 1927, included in *Kitaiskaia revoluiotsiia*. See Ray (ed.), *Selected Works of M. N. Roy*, vol. 2: p. 610.

91. Roy's second speech at the Fifth Congress of the Chinese Communist Party, 3 May 1927, Ray (ed.), *Selected Works of M. N. Roy*, vol. 2: p. 643.

92. Edgar Snow. 1937. *Red Star Over China*, London: Gollancz, p. 161.

93. North and Eudin, *M. N. Roy's Mission to China*, p. 67.

94. 'Statement Exhibiting the Moral and Material Program and Condition of India During the Year 1926, 1927', OIOC: L/PJ/12/62.

95. From the new comments added to the 1946 edition of M. N. Roy. 1973 (1946) *Revolution and Counter-revolution in China.* Westport: Hyperion Press, p. 639.

96. Ibid., p. 641.

97. Ibid., p. 643.

98. Roy, 'Assembly Letter' (1927), in Ray (ed.), *Selected Works of M. N. Roy*, vol. 2: pp. 300–25.

99. The 'Assembly Letter' was infamous because it was intercepted by the British authorities and became a central exhibit in the Meerut Conspiracy Case of 1929–33 that resulted in the arrest of many Indian communists, as well as the long-term imprisonment of M. N. Roy himself. See Overstreet and Windmiller, *Communism in India*, pp. 104–05; A Workers and Peasants Party was already established in Bengal in 1925, independent of Roy, and under the leadership of Kazi Nazrul Islam, Muzaffar Ahmad and Nalini Gupta. Laushey, *Bengal Terrorism and the Marxist Left*, p. 90.

100. M. N. Roy, 'Draft Resolution on the Indian Question', Ray (ed.), *Selected Works*, vol. 3: p. 95.

101. Ibid., p. 97.

102. Ibid., p. 107.

103. 'Listen und Kurse Angabe über indische Studenten, 1924–28, KUTV', RGASPI: Fond 532, Opus 1, File 375, p. 173.

104. Willi Münzenberg. 1931. *Solidarität: Zehn Jahre Internationale Arbeiterhilfe, 1921–1931*. Berlin: Neuer Deutscher Verlag, p. 100. These are examples from the weekend course held for an Ortsgruppe in Essen in 1930.

105. Theodor Bergmann. 1987. *Gegen den Strom: die Geschichte der Kommunistischen Partei Opposition*. Hamburg: VSA Verlag, p. 173.

106. Hans Piazza, 'M. N. Roy', in Theodor Bergmann and Mario Kessler (eds.). 2000. *Ketzer in Kommunismus: 23 biographische Essays*. Hamburg: VSA-Verlag, p. 176.

107. Sudipta Kaviraj. 1995. 'Imaginary History', in, *The Unhappy Consciousness: Bankimchandra Chattopadhyay and the Formation of Nationlist Discourse in India.* Delhi: Oxford University Press, pp. 124–26; Interview with Dr Theodor Bergmann, 3 October 2004, Stuttgart.
108. See Fuchs to Horkheimer, 12 February 1924, quoted in Ulrich Weitz. 1991. *Salonkultur und Proletariat.* Stuttgart: Stoffler & Schutz, p. 413.
109. The association of M. N. Roy with the Frankfurt School is particularly interesting given the general lack of discussion among Frankfurt School scholars of colonial domination. On the absence of discussion of colonial questions among Frankfurt School thinkers, see Keya Ganguly. 2002. 'Adorno, Authenticity, Critique' in: Crystal Bartolovich and Neil Lazarus (eds), *Marxism, Modernity, and Postcolonial Studies.* Cambridge: Cambridge University Press, pp. 240–57.
110. Karl August Wittfogel. 1926. *Das Erwachende China.* Wien: Agis; *Wirtschaft und Gesellschaft Chinas*, 1931: vii–ix; and Karl Wittfogel. 1957. *Oriental Despotism.* New Haven: Yale University Press, all make a diametrically opposite argument to that of Roy, insisting that Asian backwardness and lack of revolutionary potential could be traced to its climatic and environmental conditions.
111. M. N. Roy. 1930. *Revolution und Konterrevolution in China.* Berlin: Soziologische Verlagsanstalt, p. 30.
112. Ibid., p. 41.
113. Wittfogel, *Oriental Despotism*, p. 129.
114. M. N. Roy. 1981. *New Humanism: A Manifesto*, Calcutta: Renaissance Publishers, pp. 2–3.
115. *Inprecor*, 13 December 1929.
116. Carr, *Socialism in One Country*, p. 3. See chapter 31. Carr systematically explores the impact of the 1925 policies on communist parties worldwide, especially the German, French, British and Italian.
117. Overstreet and Windmiller, *Communism in India*, p. 142.
118. 'Genossen Roy ausgeschlossen', *Gegen den Strom*, 2(36): 681.
119. These were spread over two years, published under the pseudonym 'Richard', and appeared in volume one and two of *Gegen den Strom*, 1929–30.
120. Roy, 'Die Krisis der Kommunistischen Internationale', *Gegen den Strom*, 2(39): 8.
121. Ibid., p. 7.
122. S. M. Ganguly. 1984. *Leftism in India: M. N. Roy and Indian Politics, 1920–1948.* Calcutta: Minerva, p. 98.
123. Isaac Deutscher. 1959. *The Prophet Unarmed: Trotsky, 1929–1940.* New York: Oxford University Press, p. 289.
124. Roy, 'Die Krisis', *Gegen den Strom*, 2(40): 9.
125. Ibid., p. 9.
126. Ibid., p. 7.
127. Roy, 'Stalin triumphiert', *Gegen den Strom*, 3(30): 46.
128. The same was true for Jay Lovestone in the United States and many others. See Theodore Draper. 1957. *The Roots of American Communism, Communism in American Life*, New York: Viking Press, p. 7.

129. Jane Degras, commenting on March 1929 ECCI Manifesto, Jane Degras. 1956. *The Communist International, 1919–1943: Documents*. London: Oxford University Press. vol. 3: p. 21.
130. Roy collates epithets used against him in the communist press, M. N. Roy. 1938c. *Our Differences*. Calcutta: Saraswaty Library, p. 27.
131. Adhikari, *Documents of the Indian Communist Party*, p. 79; It was noted that the accused at the Meerut Conspiracy Case in 1928 spoke of 'ex-comrade Roy', see Williamson, *Communism in India*, p. 163.
132. Jawaharlal Nehru. 1962. *Autobiography, With Musings on Recent Events in India*. Bombay: Allied Publishers, p. 161.
133. Ibid., p. 154.
134. Jayaprakash Narayan, *Socialism to Sarvodaya, 1956*. See also letter written to Roy by Manuel Gomez (alias Charles Philips) from the USA, presenting Jayaprakash Narayan as a promising student interested in Roy's work. Purabi Ray et al. (eds.), *Indo-Russian Relations*, 1999: 227–36. See discussion in Sibnarayan Ray (ed.), *In Freedom's Quest*, vol. 2: pp. 299–300; See Bhola Singh. 1985. *The Political Ideas of M. N. Roy and Jayaprakash Narayan: A Comparative Study*. New Delhi: Ashish Publishing House, pp. 49–51.
135. J. P. Narayan on M. N. Roy, *The Radical Humanist*, March 1978, 41:12: p. 8; Also see Narayan, *Socialism to Sarvodaya*, p. 10.
136. 'Gangadhar Adhikari', Humboldt Universität Archiv, Phil. Fak. 637. On his association with Roy see Haithcox, *Communism and Nationalism in India: M. N. Roy and Comintern Policy*, p. 175.
137. See 'Memorandum on V. Chattopadhyaya', by Peel, January 1929, OIOC: L/PJ/12/280, 29–36.
138. 'An Anti-Roy Pamphlet', 1932, in P. C. Joshi Archives, Jawaharlal Nehru University.
139. Muzaffar Ahmad.1970. *Myself and the Communist Party of India, 1920–1929*. Calcutta: National Book Agency, pp. 479–80.
140. Saumyendranath Tagore. 1944. *Historical Development of Communist Movement in India*. Calcutta: Red Front, p. 10; Ray (ed.), *In Freedom's Quest*, vol. 2: p. 323; Saumyendranath Tagore, *Against the Stream*, 1975, 1: xiii.
141. Roy, 'Probleme der indischen Revolution', *Gegen den Strom*, 3(4): 37.

4

Criticism and Incarceration

By the middle of 1930, Roy decided to return to India, after having considered an invitation by the communists in New York to join them there.[1] Given the rising intimidation campaigns carried out against the Left by the Nazi party in Berlin, Roy knew Germany was not a good place for an excommunicated member of the Communist International.[2] Stalin's proroguing of the Comintern in 1929 and the commencement of his purges had begun transforming the Communist International into a militant international order. In this context, Roy chose Bombay as his destination, the major centre of Indian labour unrest. Despite being almost assured of imprisonment by the British if he returned to India, Roy felt it was a 'stage that must be gone through' in order to remain involved in Marxist theory and praxis outside the official communist organisation.[3]

More than half a million workers participated in over 200 strikes in India between 1928 and 1931.[4] India seemed to be blowing up with social unrest, with the South Indian Railway strike, the Jamshedpur steel strike and the numerous Bombay textile mill strikes of 1928 and 1929.[5] Gandhi soon inaugurated his civil disobedience campaign with the Salt March in hopes of disciplining and harnessing labour and peasant uprisings to press for constitutional reform. The period from 1928 to 1937 also witnessed the rise of the left within the Congress. Jawaharlal Nehru and Subhas Chandra Bose stridently expressed their support of labour internationalism, Tagore published his *Letters from Russia* (1930), students in Calcutta began yearly celebrations of May Day, Lenin Day, and November Day on the streets.[6]

Roy's 'return' to India in this context is not to be understood as the repatriation of an exile. Rather, given how global and porous the boundaries of the political body of India were throughout this period, the idea of taking up political action in India after a long stay abroad was common practice among some of the most eminent Indian anti-colonial figures of the era, including M. K. Gandhi, Lajpat Rai, Mohammad Obeidullah, Mohammad Barakatullah and Subhas Chandra Bose. The irony is that M. N. Roy spent most of this 1930–37 in a colonial prison. Yet, the political party he started in India during his brief stint of activity in Bombay played an important role in Indian politics during this time, especially in the trade union movement. Meanwhile, a difference developed between the writings he smuggled out of prison to guide his political organisation, and those essays he authored in his prison journals, which addressed themes of sexual politics and cultural criticism.

The continuity of Roy's political action between Berlin and Bombay is striking. After his expulsion from the Communist International in 1929, and with his new transition to united front Luxemburgist politics following the debacle in China, Roy returned to Berlin and established the 'Group of Oppositional Indian Communists' as a affiliate organisation to the Communist Party of Germany — Opposition (KPD-O).[7] An official headquarter for the Indian Communist Party was set up in this same period in London, led by Rajani and Clemens Dutt.[8] Roy's Berlin group, by contrast, affiliated itself with the Indian National Congress, becoming one of the two 'German Branches' of the Congress in 1929.[9] With a number of Indian students working closely along with him, particularly Tayab Shaikh, Anadi Bhaduri, Sundar Kabadi and Brajesh Singh, Roy began setting up an organisation to protest the Comintern's stance of 'ultra-leftism' in India by advocating pro-Congress trade unionism. The leaders of the Communist Opposition in Germany, especially August Thalheimer, were similarly arguing the need to break out of the 'egg shell' of communist militancy, and to build strategic alliances with the Social Democrats, especially in the face of the rising Nazi threat.[10]

In May 1930, Roy's group in Berlin picketed the 1930 meeting of the executive committee of the Socialist Labour International, drawing attention to the Socialists' unwillingness to condemn British imperialism.[11] Roy wrote an 'Open Letter' of protest addressed to the Socialist International meeting. But sensing that Berlin was not the proper stage for political activity, Roy sent his young deputies, Tayab Shaikh and Anadi Bhaduri, ahead to Bombay in June 1930, to prepare the groundwork for a Communist Opposition party in India. Arriving in August, the two gathered a core group of supporters, especially C. Y. Chitnis, Maniben Kara, Charles Mascarenhas, A. N. Shetty, M. R. Shetty and V. B. Karnik. The group called itself the Committee of Action for Independence of India.[12]

Meanwhile the Nazis secured a major success in the German federal elections on 14 September 1930. And at the end of October, Roy embarked by ship for Bombay on a forged German passport, and arrived in December 1930.[13] In the coming months, he met a number of the leading political leaders of the time, including Bhulabhai Desai, B. R. Ambedkar, N. M. Joshi and Yusuf Meherally.[14] Meanwhile, the majority of his colleagues in the Communist Party of German Opposition, many of whom were Jewish, relocated to Paris by 1933.

Roy had discussions with the most eminent young leaders of the Congress left, Jawaharlal Nehru and Subhas Chandra Bose, at the Karachi Congress of March 1933 where he contributed to drafting the 'Fundamental Rights Resolution' on social justice passed at the Congress that year.[15] His main organiser, Tayab Shaikh, began editing a journal of the Roy group, *The Masses*, meanwhile Charles Mascarenhas started a second affiliated journal, *Independent India*. Pointing to the transnational public sphere that Roy inhabited, his articles in *The Masses* were also sent to Berlin for publication in *INKOPP (Internationale Nachrichten der Kommunistischen Opposition)*, a journal he had co-edited before his return to India. It was not long before a small political party developed, making swift progress in organising trade union activity in Bombay. By December 1930, M. R. Shetty, a member of the Roy Group, had become the leader of the Bombay Dockworkers Union. And at the conference of the All India Trade Union Congress that met in July 1931, members of Roy's party secured three executive positions in the organisation, ending the communist hold on that trade union.[16]

But Roy would not see these developments as a free man. On 21 July 1931, he was woken up from sleep at 5:00 a.m. by the Deputy Commissioner of Police and his raid party. Police had been tracking Roy's movements for some time, and Roy was not going out of his way to hide from them. Roy had written to his lover, Ellen Gottschalk, who was still in Berlin, 'I am taking risks these days, but it feels so exciting... We are turning out a large quantity of literature, mostly in Indian languages, in spite of very very strict censorship'.[17] Roy had also spent a few months in rural Uttar Pradesh, working with the non-payment of rent campaigns that arose there.[18] Hiding from the police would have entailed political inefficacy.

Roy's trial commenced the following month, August, and Jawaharlal Nehru was a member of Roy's Defence Committee. Roy was tried on charges first submitted during the Cawnpore trial of 1924 of 'conspiracy to deprive the King Emperor of the sovereignty of British India'.[19] He petitioned to have a trial by jury, but the Allahabad High Court dismissed the petition, claiming that the opinion of laymen should not handicap the expert view of judges. Taking place in a closed courtroom, an unusual measure, the trial resulted in the sentence of twelve years imprisonment in January 1932. In his own words, 'the blow was unexpectedly heavy'.[20]

Roy's imprisonment gave birth to an international campaign for his release. Coordinated from Paris by Ellen Gottschalk, a member of the Communist Party Opposition, letters of protest were sent to the British India Office by Roger Baldwin of the ACLU, as well as Fenner Brockway and James Maxton, members of the Independent Labour Party of Britain.[21] Even Albert Einstein, from Princeton, wrote to the American ambassador in Washington on Roy's behalf since he had known him from Berlin anti-colonial circles.[22] The *Workers' Age* of New York published an article about the conditions of his imprisonment in April 1932.[23] The *Arbeiterpolitik*, originally a Berlin labour journal, but recently located to Paris, published a report on his imprisonment around the same time.[24]

The Roy Group

During his six-year imprisonment, Roy continued to send letters to his Indian group outside of prison, relying on sympathetic wardens, jailers and other inmates to smuggle out his missives.[25] In Calcutta, Bombay, Ahmedabad and Ernakulam, inspired by M. N. Roy, activists made significant strides in trade unionism, and also in the creation of the Congress Socialist Party. The Congress Socialist Party, which traces its roots to meetings between prisoners at the Nasik jail in 1933, was officially inaugurated in 1934.[26] An early meeting of the Congress Socialist Party in Calcutta in 1934 centred around a critical discussion of M. N. Roy's letter from prison insisting that the group should only establish itself informally, as a working left consensus inside the Congress Party.[27] The decision of the CSP to form itself as a distinct political organisation would lead to a showdown with Roy after his release in 1937.

In the meantime, members of the Royist group comprised some of the most important members of the early Congress Socialist Party. Charles Mascarenhas of Goa, Rajani Mukherjee of Bengal and A. K. Pillai, a Kerala Congressman, were inaugural members particularly close to Roy.[28] Maniben Kara, one of the most influential members of the early Roy Group, became leader of Union of Bombay Municipal workers in September 1932.[29] In 1936, she became president of the All India Trade Union Congress (AITUC). Meanwhile Jayaprakash Narayan, perhaps the most important leader of the CSP, also relied heavily on M. N. Roy's theoretical and strategic writings. But the leaders among Roy's Group, especially V. B. Karnik, Tayab Shaikh and Maniben Kara, also sought out the perspectives of August Thalheimer, who wrote programmatic letters to them on techniques of united front politics from Paris in the early 1930s.[30] As opposed to the rise of a monolithic 'communist internationalism' in this period, it was precisely the fractures within communism, and especially the resistance of Opposition Communists against the Soviet hegemony from the late 1920s onwards, that fuelled left political movements.[31]

Prison Writings

Roy's prison notebooks, the nine volumes of writings that remained within his journals in jail, were composed of philosophical contemplations. Roy wrote about 3,750 pages while in prison — a testament to the importance of writing in defying the oppression of the prison cell. The original prison manuscripts of M. N. Roy are today preserved at the Nehru Memorial Museum and Library in New Delhi. These were written between 11 November 1931 (when the first notebook is dated) and 26 November 1936 (when Roy left jail) in four prisons: Cawnpore, Bareilly, Almora and Dehra Dun, all towns in Uttar Pradesh. Significant portions of Roy's prison writings are dedicated to theoretical meditations on historical materialism, as well as philosophical implications of new discoveries in theoretical physics, an interest Roy shared with August Thalheimer in Berlin.[32]

M. N. Roy's writing during six years of rather strenuous Class B imprisonment was broken up into notebooks granted at the warden's discretion, and his letters to his European colleagues, recently relocated to Paris after the rise of the Nazis, bore the blotches of prison censor's red ink.[33] Any information Roy provided about his physical health was cancelled out before mailing. The darkness of the prison cell, and the slow physical destruction brought about by long-term colonial imprisonment had a powerful effect on Roy's constitution. Over the course of his six years in prison, his medical report shows that he suffered from cardiac dilatation, digestive disturbances, rheumatic pain in the shoulder joint, pyorrhea (inflammation of the teeth/gums), pains in the pectoral region, pain in the waist, and that he had three teeth pulled (unnecessarily) because a dentist could not be requisitioned in time.[34] Roy was a body in pain.[35] He was provided with medical care, but only after long periods of waiting. His request to be transferred to a prison in a cooler climate was granted but only after years of petition.

Jawaharlal Nehru kept abreast of Roy's condition in prison, and was appalled at his treatment. He wrote, in 1936, to the Chief Minister of U.P., Govind Ballabh Pant, 'Even if his release cannot be hastened, he ought at least to be examined thoroughly by competent outside doctors. He is being kept, and he has been there a long time now, in the female ward of the Dehra Gaol. You know well what an awful hole this is. I could not survive this place for many weeks'.[36] Roy reached the nadir of his mental state in early 1935. On 20 January 1935 he wrote to Ellen: 'I presume you are expecting some report about my work. Lately, not much was done. I have been feeling rather out of sorts — mentally'. The following months were the darkest period of his prison life, and suicidal thoughts began creeping in. 'My patience is getting exhausted. Nothing can stand endless strain. I might not be able to keep my record of a well-behaved prisoner intact; though, if I did anything too angry to protest against his grossly unfair treatment, that would not be misbehaving either morally or legally'.[37] In June, he wrote ever more grimly: 'In another month, I shall complete five years of this life; and it is practically certain that the end will be still several months off. I am still of the opinion that death is no worse than more than five years of living death. But these are temptations which weaken one's resolve'.[38] In July, he continued with even more despair: 'On the whole, I feel miserable and depressed, worse than ever during the last four years. Therefore, I am more confirmed than ever in my opinion that death would be preferable to more than five years (at a stretch) of this life. I hope it would not be necessary to make the choice actually'.[39] And by October, only one month before his planned release, the oppression of the imperial jail — the subtle, quiet violence that punished through silencing and depriving — had almost defeated Roy's spirit: 'I am tired of this world. It appears to be doomed to destruction or a possible rebirth after protracted period of torture and torment'.[40]

Yet, there was a counterpoint at work during these same six years. In the prison space of privation, of all places, Roy said he became an 'Epicurean'.[41] 'To seek happiness is the object of life. Epicurus taught that every pleasure is good, every pain is evil. Every pleasure is good because it results from knowledge; pain is evil, because it is caused by ignorance'.[42] This avowal led Roy to shift his attention to the problems of sexual politics. In the prison context of minimal allocations for daily life, he began to think more maximally about the requirements of individual freedom.

Cultural Criticism

The writings of M. N. Roy that remained within the prison cell, locked away in his prison notebooks until his release, launched a cultural critique of mainstream Indian nationalism by drawing attention to the relationship between nationalist politics and sexual oppression. Roy made reference not only to Freud's notion of repression, but also to Clara Zetkin and Alexandra Kollontai's way of connecting Marxist revolution with the end of male domination and women's sexual liberation.[43] In Roy's prison writings on sexual politics, he advocated a radically different approach from that of the great Indian psychoanalyst of Calcutta, Girindrasekhar Bose (1853–1939), who argued that Indian subjectivities, unlike European ones, did not have a submerged 'id' charged with sexual desire as existed in European civilisation.[44] Girindrasekhar Bose, as a member of the Swadeshi avant-garde, maintained that Hindu dharma created a social order in which polymorphous perversity was not at the base of personality, but rather a transcendent spiritual self.[45] While such a claim for the civilisational distinction of Indian psyches from Western psyches was opposed to M. N. Roy's insistence on the global commonality of repressed sexual drives across cultures, we should not miss that both Bose and Roy assumed that there was some hidden or shrouded force at the depth of the self.[46] The notion of deep selfhoods, out of which transcendent energies could spring, was a shared idea stemming from the nineteenth-century Bengali context. That Roy's discussion of sexual politics aimed at criticising the very notions of culture and Hindu dharmic order that thinkers such as Girindrasekhar Bose championed, does not mean that Roy's views simply ventriloquised Western values. Once we resist the binary between western knowledge and authentic Indian (Hindu) knowledge, we begin to appreciate Roy's position as an intermediary, expressing views that connoted the polyphony of the worlds he travelled between.

In his essay, 'Why Men are Hanged', written in 1932 in Bareilly prison, Roy provided examples from newspaper articles he read of individuals whose sexualities were constrained or dominated by oppressive social mores. First, he spoke of a young man from a small town who because of the level of sexual repression at home, was apparently driven to have a relationship with a relative. He also recounted the case of a young woman driven to kill her sixty-year-old husband due to the extent of her sexual frustration. In each case, social oppression in the realm of sexuality caused violent eruptions of individual agency. Roy concludes that the 'criminals' were not at fault, but the social order they lived in.

In early 1935, Roy records his increasing preoccupation with Freud, Adler and Jung.[47] 'Sex instinct is one of the two sovereign factors of organic existence (the higher form). It cannot be suppressed'.[48] In prison, Roy envisioned a utopia of sexual liberation. 'Let the Indian masses taste the joy of life, and their natural love of life will no longer be camouflaged in all sorts of religious superstition ... it will flow openly into real spiritual values'. This focus on sexuality, certainly informed by his 1920s Berlin background, provided him with another 'horizontal' category, apart from class, to affirm the ways Indians belong to the world. Roy asserted that all humans share their 'animal instincts' and biological drives in common. 'In reality, he is an animal. His whole being, including the much-vaunted spiritual qualities, is driven by impulses that are common to all the higher forms of organisms. He is so proud of his intelligence, but he knows so little of the animal instincts that dominate the thin layer of his conscious mind... Thus the superiority of the human being is a fiction...'[49]

Roy's vision of freedom entailed individuals engaging in unhindered traffic with their material surroundings, and free experience of the pleasure of the senses without the limitation of social codes or taboos. The insistence on the flux and traffic of sense enjoyment, not on an unchanging construct of authenticity, was Roy's 'Epicurean' path to freedom. 'Epicurean pleasure is not to eat, drink and be merry, but knowledge. Knowledge of the causes of the constantly changing things frees man from fear and anxiety which arise from the feeling of helplessness, and that freedom makes man happy'.[50] Roy again emphasised: 'To seek happiness is the object of life. Epicurus taught that every pleasure is good, every pain is evil. Every pleasure is good because it results from knowledge; pain is evil, because it is caused by ignorance'.[51]

Roy's focus on the freeing of sexual drives conflicted with the writings of many feminist nationalist writers of the time, such as Rameshwari Nehru, Annie Besant, Sarojini Naidu, Kamaladevi Chattopadhyaya and Lakshmi Menon, who presented women most often as mothers and wives, and situated women's welfare within the framework of national culture.[52] It is difficult to evaluate Roy's contribution to debates on Indian feminism and sexual politics. Some of his essays, which he deemed too controversial, were only published posthumously in 1957. Roy made no sustained contribution to the theory or practice of the Indian feminist movement after his release, apart from the publication of some prison writings. Instead, his prison preoccupation with sexual politics seemed to have chiefly served as an avenue for criticising forms of social oppression beyond the framework of class analysis.

Culture as Conformity

The discussion of sexual politics served Roy's larger intent, articulated from his prison years into the 1940s, of breaking the frame of a bounded national culture. Roy insisted that what he derisively called 'Gandhism' was dangerous because it construed culture as a corporate ahistorical entity, defined by dogmatic notions of authenticity, social hygiene and bodily discipline. 'Profession of spiritualism commits Gandhian materialists to the vulgarist, most-brutal practice of materialism... Spiritualist dogmas hide anti-democratic counter-revolutionary, tendencies of orthodox nationalism'.[53] For Roy, the 'vulgar materialism' of 'Gandhism' lay precisely in its insistence on authenticity — on unchanging boundaries of group identity.

Another aspect of Roy's prison writings focused on the implications of revolutionary discoveries in the field of physics, especially relativity theory and the quantum view of matter. Roy's interest in theoretical physics first developed while in Berlin, the world centre for the development of quantum theory, with Albert Einstein, Max Planck and Erwin Schrödinger working in the city, and Werner Heisenberg and Max Born not far off in Göttingen. The philosophical implications of the remarkable new discoveries of a non-Newtonian universe formed one of the favourite subjects of discussion between Roy and August Thalheimer. Thalheimer wrote an essay in 1925 on the philosophical implications of the interwoven fabric of space and time seen from a Marxist point of view.[54] Roy, in his prison writings, discussed the resonance of the new quantum theory of matter with Spinoza's monistic notion of the universe, and with Marx's historical materialism, both of which took no recourse to a transcendent or metaphysical realm. In prison, Roy wrote a number of essays along these lines. In an entry on the 'Theory of Knowledge', for example, he explained, 'Individual "self" is an arbitrary concept. It has no foundation than the mistaken notion that my body is a stable unit having an existence distinct from the rest of physical existence... My physical being is a continuously changing bubble in the ocean of cosmic flux, a mere ripple in the endless flow of becoming'.[55] It was the eradication of fixed differences, and the vindication of history not as a linear progression, but as a field of interconnection and relativity, that captivated Roy.

Individual egos and intelligences were interwoven into the physical universe of perpetual flux.[56] 'As a matter of fact', Roy wrote, the 'external world' is a misleading term. As integral parts of the world of experience, our bodies and our cognitive faculties... are themselves all parts of the world'.[57]

Thus the erection of an ahistorical realm of Indian culture based on reconstructed notions of Asian civilisation generated social violence, Roy believed. 'The nationalist leaders are opposed not only to socialism; they are antagonistic to a democratic reconstruction of the Indian society. Consequently, every one of these pompous fighters for "Purna Swaraj" is sheep in a tiger's skin. They will compromise with imperialism. They are bound to do so'.[58] Roy pointed out the affinity of many Indian nationalists of his day for the notion of 'race purity'. He mockingly remarked, 'The northern Indians are the stoutest protagonists of the cult of Aryanism. It is such a misfortune that they are so brown — to the extent of blackness!...'[59] Roy noted that in some circles, 'Germany [has become] the ideal of Indian nationalism. In as much as Hitler's Germany possessed all the "spiritual" characteristics and more, it is sure to have sympathisers among Indian nationalists of the orthodox school'.[60] Leaders from the Hindu Right such as Hedgewar and Savarkar publicly praised Hitler's pursuit of race purity. With the rise of interest in eugenics in India in the 1930s, including projects to 'Hinduise' the untouchables and to perfect the racial stock of India, Roy was responding to a not uncommon fascination with Nazi Germany in some Indian nationalist circles.[61]

Roy knew first-hand of the violence and vulgarity of the Nazis and fathomed the extent of the danger they represented. 'This wild paroxysm of a moribund social system has for the time overwhelmed Germany, and its poisonous infection seems to be threatening other countries ... the ideology of this bloodiest, vulgarism of materialist phenomena of the capitalist culture is intensely spiritualist'.[62] The vulgar materialism of 'spiritualist' ideology resided in the establishment of ahistorical categories of authenticity that shrouded the continually changing historical quality of human existence.

At the crux of Roy's prison writings was the reimagining of explosive subjectivities, pregnant with energy to destroy societal forms of stagnancy and oppression. Whereas he thought in terms of explosive dharmic energy during the Swadeshi years of his youth and of the eruption of peasant consciousness in 1920s Berlin, in prison he focused on the explosiveness of the sexual drives, and the ways in which sexual politics could be employed to transgress and critique the boundaries of collective identity. But, here too, one senses the traces of Brahmo exegesis, devoted, as it was, to reading interconnection and unity beneath the apparent world of distinct forms.

Notes

1. A. K. Hindi. 1938. *The Man Who Looked Ahead,* Ahmedabad: Modern Publishing House, p. 242.
2. In February 1933, Nazi police imprisoned Indian anti-colonial activists. The Communist Party was banned in March 1933. See OIOC: L/PJ/12/73.
3. Roy to Ellen Gottschalk, 11 August 1931, in M. N. Roy. 1943c. *Letters from Jail, Fragments of a Prisoner's Diary.* Dehra Dun: Indian Renaissance Association, p. 1.
4. David Laushey. 1975. *Bengal Terrorism and the Marxism Left.* Calcutta: Firma Mukhopadhyay, p. 192.
5. Rajnarayan Chandavarkar. 1994. *The Origins of Industrial Capitalism in India, Business Strategies and the Working Classes in Bombay, 1900-1940.* Cambridge: Cambridge University Press, pp. 236, 399ff.
6. This began in 1934. See Dipesh Chakrabarty. 1989. *Rethinking Working Class History: Bengal, 1890-1940.* Princeton: Princeton University Press, p. 127.
7. John Patrick Haithcox. 1971. *Communism and Nationalism in India: M. N. Roy and Comintern Policy.* Princeton: Princeton University Press, p. 166.
8. Gene Overstreet and Marshall Windmiller. 1959. *Communism in India,* Berkeley: University of California Press, p. 148.
9. See 'Indian Information Bureau and Chattopadhyaya', 15 May 1930, OIOC: L/PJ/12/223: 79-81. Compare Haithcox, *Communism and Nationalism,* p. 166.
10. August Thalheimer, *Zurück in die Eierschale des Marxismus?,* IISG: KPD-O, p. 12.
11. A. K. Hindi. 1938. *The Man who Looked Ahead,* Ahmedabad: Modern Publishing House, p. 220.
12. John Haithcox. 1971. *Communism and Nationalism in India.* Princeton: Princeton University Press, p. 175.
13. Sibnarayan Ray. 2005. *In Freedom's Quest: A Study of the Life and Works of M. N. Roy.* Calcutta: Minerva, vol. 3: p. 192.
14. V. B. Karnik. 1978. *M. N. Roy: Political Biography.* Bombay: Nav Jagriti Samaj, p. 339.
15. Ibid., p. 345, for assertion of Roy's involvement. Gandhi took this resolution with him to the Second Round Table meeting in London in 1930. Also, Leonard Gordon. 1990. *Brothers Against the Raj: A Biography of Indian Nationalists Sarat and Subhas Chandra Bose.* New York: Columbia University Press, p. 244; Nehru emphatically denied this assertion. See Nehru, *Autobiography,* 2003: 267, 268.
16. Haithcox, *Nationalism and Communism in India,* p. 175. G. L. Kandalkar and J. N. Mitra were vice presidents, and Tayab Shaikh was one of the secretaries.
17. Roy's Letter to Ellen, 6 February 1931, Nehru Memorial Museum and Library, Delhi (NMML): Ellen Gottschalk File.
18. Sumit Sarkar. 1983. *Modern India, 1885-1947.* Delhi: Macmillan, p. 315; Horace Williamson. 1976. *Communism and India,* chapter 17.
19. 'Judgment', OIOC: L/PJ/12/421: 13.
20. Roy to Ellen Gottschalk, 18 January 1932, NMML: Ellen Gottschalk File.
21. Ray, *In Freedom's Quest,* vol. 3: p. 283.
22. Einstein to the Ambassador of England, Washington, 17 September 1934. NMML: M. N. Roy Papers, 'Relation to Imprisonment'.

23. OIOC: L/PJ/12/421, p. 62.
24. 28 January 1932, OIOC: L/PJ/12/421, pp. 9, 28.
25. Karnik, *M. N. Roy: A Political Biography*, p. 199; M. N. Roy. 1932. 'My Defence'. Reproduced in: Sibnaryan Ray (ed.). 1990. *Selected Works of M. N. Roy*, pp. 573–646. M. N. Roy. 1938b. 'On the Congress Constitution', Calcutta: Independent India; M. N. Roy. '*Letters to the Congress Socialist Party (1934, 1935, 1936) in Selected Works of M. N. Roy*, Sibnarayan Ray (ed.). Delhi: Oxford University Press, vol. 4.
26. Sarkar, *Modern India*, p. 332.
27. Roy, *Letters to the Congress Socialist Party (1934, 1935, 1936) in Selected Works of M. N. Roy*, p. 4.
28. Karnik, *M. N. Roy: A Political Biography*, p. 407.
29. V. B. Karnik. 1960. *Indian Trade Unions*, Bombay: Labour Education Service, p. 93ff.
30. See Thalheimer to Karnik, 24 May 1934, Paris. NMML: Roy Papers, Karnik Files. The wording of this long letter makes clear that it is part of a lengthy series of correspondence. Thalheimer insists that 'a regular correspondence is essential...'
31. This is the case with the Roy Group and the CSP in India. But the fate of the POUM in 1936–37 in Spain provides another, fateful, example. See E. H. Carr. 1984. *The Comintern and the Spanish Civil War*. New York: Pantheon Books.
32. Roy mentions in a letter from prison the work that August Thalheimer had begun in finding applications of discoveries in theoretical physics to the theory of historical materialism. See *Letters from Prison*, Roy to Ellen Gottschalk, 16 February 1932; See August Thalheimer. 1928. *Spinozas Stellung in der Vorgeschichte des dialektischen Materialismus*. Wien: Verlad Fur Literatur und Politik. In prison Roy was reading Stanely Eddington and James Jeans. See Roy to Sneevliet, IISH: File of A. Pannekoek, 18 July 1934.
33. See M. N. Roy, *Letters from Prison*, footnote to 11 July 1932: 27, 'as a matter of fact, all references to my health and conditions of life in jail were struck out from my letters...'
34. Superintendent to Gottschalk, NMML: Bareilly Prison Files, 1933, p. 33, Roy to Gottschalk, 13 September 1920, NMML, Roy to Gottschalk, 22 September 1933, Roy to Gottschalk, 19 June 1934, Roy to Gottschalk, 24 February 1936.
35. Elaine Scarry's insights into the objectification of the body in pain are useful here. See Elaine Scarry. 1985. *The Body in Pain: The Making and Unmaking of the World*. New York: Oxford University Press, p. 147ff.
36. Jawaharlal Nehru, *Selected Works of Jawaharlal Nehru*, 7: 657, 658.
37. Roy to Ellen Gottschalk, 24 May 1936, NMML.
38. Roy to Gottschalk, 20 June 1936.
39. Roy to Gottschalk, 21 July 1935.
40. Roy to Gottschalk, 21 October 1936.
41. Prison Notebook 2, 91b, NMML.
42. Prison Notebook 2, 90b, NMML.
43. Roy to Gottschalk, 20 January 1935, NMML. Alexandra Kollontai. 1972. *Sexual Relations and the Class Struggle: Love and the Morality*. Bristol: Falling Wall Press, pp. 6–8.

44. Girindrasekhar Bose. 1921. *Concept of Repression.* Calcutta: n.p.
45. Ashis Nandy. 2004. 'The Savage Freud: The First Non-Western Psychoanalyst and the Politics of Secret Selves in Colonial India', in *Bonfire of Creeds*, p. 345.
46. See Christiane Hartnack. 2001. *Psychoanalysis in Colonial India.* New York: Oxford University Press, pp. 127–33; Ashis Nandy in his essay, 'The Savage Freud' in *Bonfire of Creeds*, p. 369.
47. Roy to Gottschalk, 20 January 1935, NMML.
48. Prison Notebook 5, 338, NMML.
49. Prison Notebook 5, 336.
50. Prison Notebook 2, 91b.
51. Prison Notebook 2, 90b.
52. Kumari Jayawardena. 1986. *Feminism and Nationalism in the Third World.* London: Zed Books 1986. The complexity of women's 'self-configuration' within the discourse of nationalist politics is addressed by Mrinali Sinha. 2008. 'Gender in the Critiques of Colonialism and Nationalism', Sumit and Tanika Sarkar (eds), *Women and Social Reform in Modern India.* Bloomington: Indiana University Press, pp. 452–72. On critiques of gender relations in literature of the time, particularly within the Progressive Writers Movement of this period, see Priyamvada Gopal. 2005. *Literary Radicalism in India: Gender Nation, and the Transition to Independence.* London: Routledge, p. 65ff. On the role of men in feminist movements in India, see Gail Minault. 1998. *Secluded Scholars: Women's Education and Muslim Social Reform in Colonial India.* Delhi: Oxford University Press, p. 11.
53. Prison Notebook 5, 164a, NMML.
54. August Thalheimer. 1925. 'Über einige Grundbegriffe der physikalischen Theori der Relativität von Geschichtspunkte des dialektischen Materialismus' in *Unter dem Banner des Marxismus*, vol. 1. pp. 203–338.
55. Roy, Prison Notebook 7, 'Theory of Knowledge', p. 183. Several of Roy's essays on the theme of science were published later in the volume *Science and Philosophy.* Calcutta: Renaissance Publishers, 1947.
56. Prison Notebook 8, 98a.
57. Prison Notebook 2, 184.
58. Prison Notebook 8, 148b.
59. Roy to Gottschalk, 22 September 35, NMML.
60. Prison Notebook 8, 161a.
61. Themes of corporatisation, public works, eugenics and social regeneration received much shrift in Indian political science of the day. Keshav Baliram Hedgewar founded the Rashtriya Swayamsevak Sangh in 1925, and the group grew quickly in the 1930s. Leaders such as, M. S. Gowalkar, expressed early support for the Nazi Lebensraum offensives, and conceived of Hindus as an ethnos that had to likewise claim living space from the Muslim populations. See Walter Andersen and Shridhar Damle. 1987. *The Brotherhood in Saffron.* Boulder: Westview Press, p. 40ff.
62. Prison Notebook 3, 128b.

5

Interstitial Politics

Roy's travel through the deterritorial body of India created a mediated worldview that could not be assimilated into the mainstream political camps of the day. One consequence of the deterritorial nationalism of the early twentieth century was that it produced in-between figures such as M. N. Roy, on the margin of multiple worlds, but centred in none. In the period from 1936, after his release from prison, up until 1946 when he decided to exit political life, Roy positioned himself outside three regimens of anti-colonial form, Gandhian nationalist discourse at the All-India level, the neo-Swadeshi politics of Bengal led by Subhas Chandra Bose, as well as the orthodoxy of communist internationalism. As opposed to notions of cultural continence, Roy continually advanced his scandalous political project of cultural and conceptual promiscuity. His two major causes in the years of the Second World War — strident anti-fascism and the support of the war, and the campaign for Hindu–Muslim solidarity — show in practical ways how he insisted on the need to mediate identity divides. By trying to bridge and amalgamate domains seen as opposed, Roy made himself a *persona non grata* in Indian politics in the specific context of the Second World War.

Anti-colonial struggle in the twentieth century depended on a set of modernist styles for contemplating value, truth, social change and the form of the anticipated good society. It was partly marked by the pursuit of form, of boundaries of moral order, and what Axel Honneth has called the pursuit of 'self-esteem'.[1] But anti-colonialism also sought the transgression of boundaries and the mediation of identitarian boundaries, what we might call, following Honneth, the wish for 'solidarity'.[2] In his discussion of modern patterns of self-realisation, Honneth speaks of the development of 'internal freedom' by the cultivation of respect through 'group-pride and collective honor'.[3] The anti-colonial struggle can be understood as such a form-centred project. However, this pursuit of internal freedom is supplemented by the effort to create trans-group sympathies. 'Solidarity can be understood as an interactive relationship in which subjects mutually sympathize with their various different ways of life because, among themselves, they esteem each other symmetrically'.[4] According to Honneth, the internal freedom derived from group-pride and the 'symmetrical recognition' beyond the boundaries of group identity with other groups constitutes two aspects of the modernist pursuit of political freedom.[5] Roy's thought represents a heightened case in a broad family relation of anti-colonial discussions about solidarity and the building of trans-group sympathy.

On Stepping Out of Prison

Roy stepped out of prison in November 1936. The new constitution promulgated in 1935, the Government of India Act, threw down a new gauntlet to anti-colonial leaders. By 1937, the Indian National Congress formed provincial Ministries, an act spoken of as the 'rightward shift' of Congress politics in these years, both in terms of a growing de-emphasis on questions of social reform, but also a growing stress on constitutionalist as opposed to radical politics.[6] Nehru was at the peak of his 'infatuation with mass politics' in 1936, but by the time of the formation of ministries in 1937, the Congress was coming under the increasing control by a conservative high command.[7] In the first years after his emergence from prison, Roy concerned himself chiefly with orienting himself within this new field of politics. He not only emerged physically diminished, but appeared to some onlookers within the nationalist mainstream as a man deformed first by his deep immersion in international communism, and then again by his rancorous break with it. To many, Roy represented a disruption of the regimen of anti-colonial autonomy. 'I find myself in a rather peculiar position', Roy noted soon after his release. 'One section of the Congress looks upon me with suspicion, as a dangerous communist intriguer, trying to press through some invidious scheme, and another section, the Socialist Section, says that here is a man who is a traitor to communism... But I have walked into that position with open eyes and I stand to-day with clear conviction and these doubts and disbeliefs about me will be dispelled before long, and that will be done by my action'.[8]

As a communist, Roy proved himself a contrarian, a rebel against relays of institutionalising power within the Communist International. Now after six years in prison isolation, Indian anti-colonial nationalists of many walks were suspicious of him — suspicious of where he owed his allegiance and what he intended to do. The fear and distrust of M. N. Roy from within mainstream anti-colonial movements, the way in which he was pictured by some as a figure deserving scorn, suggests that he was more than contrarian — he was interstitial and taboo. His life course and his political philosophy epitomised a temporality of global circulation that seemed to contaminate and infect the regimens of anti-colonial morality and discipline. The global crisis of the Second World War, and the sense in these years that radical political change was imminent had the effect of strengthening party disciplines and group identities in the anticipatory competition for representation in the postcolonial state apparatus.

The Gandhian National Body

The suspicion accorded to Roy throughout the 1940s was largely due to his unyielding criticism of regimes of cultural continence and his resistance to retrenchment by the Indian National Congress and other groups as they articulated visions of strong autonomy.[9] On the All-India level, Mahatma Gandhi focused on building self-esteem for independence by training Indians in cultural continence, austerity, and the practices of a territorialised selfhood.[10] Gandhi wrote in his journal, *The Harijan,* of 1934 that 'culture is the fruit of compulsory continence... If there is no compulsory pre-nuptial continence, a society will display little energy'.[11]

Gandhi's practice of political liberation, from the early experiments at the Phoenix colony to the concluding period during the Second World War, concentrated on the organisation of a continent and autonomous Indian nation body, both in the physical and the political sense. This can be seen in his critical reinterpretation of the term 'Swadeshi' during the decline of the movement after the First World War. As we saw, Swadeshi, under Gandhi's revision, referred to the practices necessary for constituting Indian autonomy.[12] He pursued a reorganisation of individual physiques as part of the symbolic warfare orchestrated against British domination. His practices of renunciation and personal discipline aimed to attain 'non-violence and truth'. The *satyagrahi* 'must have a living faith in God ... he must be leading a chaste life and be ready and willing for the sake of his cause to give up his life and his possessions ... he must be a habitual khadi-wearer and spinner. This is essential for India. He must be a teetotaller and be free from the use of other intoxicants in order that his reason may be always unclouded and his mind constant'.[13] Gandhi also recommended purges and fasting, especially in his 1920s *Young India* journal. He favoured experiments with dietetics, including vegetarianism and eating 'unfired foods'. These would train both the physical body and the nation-body to be continent, to wean itself off spiritual subjection to the West, which '[had] germs in it, certainly, of the true type'.[14] On specific occasions, Gandhi undertook spectacular fasts, 'fasts until death', in order to provide an example of autonomy and continence.

To protest the divisive scheme for political representation of untouchables outlined in the 1932 Communal Award, Gandhi went on 'indefinite' hunger strike, eventually lasting three weeks, and culminating in the Poona Pact. Speaking of his decision to begin the fast, Gandhi commented, 'unfortunately for me, God or Truth has sent me this as it appears to me, much later than it should have come. But as I cannot be the judge of God Himself, I have submitted to His peremptory injunction'.[15] In 1939, shortly before the Tripuri Congress, Gandhi again began the spectacle of a grand fast, this time to protest the incarceration of political prisoners at Rajkot. As a commentator in the *Harijan* noted 'it is purer than any previous fast undertaken by Gandhiji — excepting the Three Weeks' Fast of 1933 (*sic*)... It has been described as a Christ-like "self-imposed death"... resolved upon in order that others may live'.[16] The timing of the fast, however, also suggests that it was also intended to 'purify' the Congress, which met at Tripuri at the same time and threatened to swerve towards the competing principle of Subhas Chandra Bose's neo-Swadeshi politics. 'In my opinion', wrote Gandhi in this context, 'the one and only task before the Congress is to make supreme efforts to clean the Congress house of proved corruption and impurities. The strongest resolutions that the Congress may pass will be of no value if there should be no incorruptible organisation to enforce them'.[17]

Control of the appetite and cleansing of the body also related to abstinence from sexual activity. 'From that day when I began brahmacharya, our freedom began', Gandhi commented in his *Autobiography*. 'My wife became a free woman, free from my authority as her lord and master, and I became free from my slavery to my own appetite which she had to satisfy'.[18] Gandhi insisted that abstinence was a necessity for ethical political action. 'Chastity is one of the greatest disciplines without which the mind cannot attain requisite firmness. A man who is unchaste loses stamina, becomes emasculated and cowardly. He whose mind is given over to animal passions is not capable of any great effort'.[19] His speaking tours throughout villages and towns in India often touched on the theme of abstinence, sometimes even receiving the weight of his attention as with his tours in the context of the Poona Pact of 1932 and his insistence on Hindu unity across caste boundaries.[20] This was far from a question of the regulation of intimate bodily functions alone. It was a politically efficacious practice of autonomy that Gandhi wanted, creating a culture among much larger swathes of the population beyond the elites. Bodily asceticism was a means of counteracting what elite anti-colonial politicians called 'Mobocracy', in the pursuit of a new populist form of political mobilisation that would successfully coordinate insurgency across classes.[21] 'Thirty-four years of continuous experience and experimenting in truth and non-violence have convinced me that non-violence cannot be sustained unless it is linked to conscious body-labour and finds expression in our daily contact with our neighbours', retorted Gandhi to his critics.[22] The practice of sexual continence had the effect of giving the nation–body dignity, of inspiring self-esteem, and of defining clear boundaries of separation and austerity from the lures of Anglicised colonial power and status. The special capacity of Indians, as a national group, to perform autonomy in the midst of colonial oppression characterised India's special message to the world, Gandhi maintained. 'India has, I think, a peculiar place today in the colonies of the world. It has both a moral prestige and organisational strength enjoyed by few colonies. The others look to it for a lead in many matters...'[23] Roy spoke of a different principle of anti-colonial struggle, which operated through bridging boundaries, deterritorial eruptive acts of creative amalgamation, and the striving for cultural unions.

Non-Indian Indian

Roy understood himself in his post-prison years as a non-Indian Indian. The notion of the non-Jewish Jew was used by Isaac Deutscher to describe a category of Jewish intellectuals situated on the borderlines of European Jewish communities, while also standing on the margins of European nation–state cultures.[24] It is a particularly apposite concept to use in connection with M. N. Roy, since Deutscher's interest in the cultural location of the doubled outsider stemmed from his own experience as a member of the Polish–Jewish communist community of 1920s and 1930s, a group Roy knew well, given his close association with the German Communist Party Opposition. Roy too felt himself to be a misfit to linear traditions and thus to 'comprehend more clearly the great movement and the great contradictoriness of nature and society'.[25]

Upon Roy's release from prison, he ostensibly had all the needed credentials for becoming a major player on the stage of national politics, and he wasted no time in arriving at his 'Waterloo', as one observer at the time commented.[26] After prison, he travelled directly to Bareilly to meet Jawaharlal, where the two held long talks. Roy recalled, 'we discussed a number of current political problems and found ourselves in agreement on most of them... I can say that I shall be able to work in close cooperation with him'.[27] Jawaharlal Nehru, in his presidential speech, welcomed the recently alighting Roy at the Faizpur Congress of 1936, saying 'Comrade M. N. Roy has just come to us after a long and most distressing period in prison... he comes with fresh mind and heart...'[28] He had 'a halo around his name', Subhas Chandra Bose remembered, and young intellectuals crowded to listen to his speeches.[29] Roy was viewed as a 'mystery man' in the press, with a formidable revolutionary pedigree but his cards still to be played. After listening to Roy's programme for social revolution, Gandhi offered Roy the biting advice that he should rest and stay out of active politics.[30] At the inception of Roy's new weekly magazine, *Independent India* in 1937, Gandhi asked him to 'render mute service to the cause of Indian freedom'.[31]

In 1938, Roy's name was mentioned in league with Rajendra Prasad, Subhas Chandra Bose and Jawaharlal Nehru as among the young leaders of national struggle. And yet, at this same time, he was already writing in letters to friends of his sense of unease with the Congress institution.[32] Adherence to Gandhian discipline would be the deal-breaker between Nehru and Roy. If Roy was a heretic within the context of the Comintern of the 1920s, a fringe communist who continually criticised the Eurocentrism and the regimentation of the organisation, he situated himself in a similarly contrarian position within the Indian National Congress of the late 1930s. By 1939, in the context of the incipient world war, Nehru began to appraise Roy as a threat to Congress unity.[33] While Nehru praised Roy's intellectual work as 'the only attempt to develop a definite [social] policy', he also commented that it was 'clearly at variance with anything we have done so far', and 'a complete break with the past'. For Nehru, Roy was making it all too clear that he was 'utterly out of touch with realities in India to-day'.[34]

Such critiques at first only heightened Roy's conviction to nevertheless still find a fringe for himself within the Congress organisation as a critic of the Gandhian leadership. Roy's main critique of the Congress after 1937 centred on the increasingly regimented political party, what he called an anti-colonial 'army' headed by Gandhi and his inner circle that 'imposed from above' their tactics on the 'rank and file'.[35] On the workings of the Congress, Roy said, 'there is more than enough of centralisation, but it is not democratic centralisation. It is rather authoritarian–dictatorial'.[36] The criticism recalled his stance towards the Comintern in the late 1920s before his return to India.

Foreshadowing his official break with the Congress in August 1940, he wrote to Gandhi, 'if, for no other fault than the courage of our conviction and our devotion to the cause of Indian freedom, we shall ever be driven out of the Congress, then the responsibility of weakening and destroying this organisation will belong to others'.[37] In 1940, when Roy ran for Congress president on an 'anti-fascist', pro-war stance, he received a mere 183 votes compared with Abul Kalam Azad's 1,864 votes.[38] The electoral insignificance of M. N. Roy by 1940 shows how much things had changed in just three years, since the initial Congress excitement over his release.[39]

Neo-Swadeshi Deterritorial Nationalism

If Gandhi's Swaraj politics envisioned territorialisation of the Indian nation–body, there was another powerful trajectory of Indian anti-colonialism that originated in Bengal, and asserted that autonomy could best be established through deterritorial practices of travel, coalition-building and modernist cultural promiscuity. It was most strongly represented by the neo-Swadeshi global nationalism of Subhas Chandra Bose in the 1930s and 1940s. Ever since the early 1920s, when Gandhi was establishing his major role in All-Indian politics, Bengali Left politics defined itself in contradistinction to him. Elements in the Bengal Congress remained a prodigal son to Gandhi's national paternalism. The birth of the communist politics in Bengal — a region in which it had one of its most important expressions in the 1930s onwards — was also often phrased in anti-Gandhian terms.[40] Many leaders in the Bengal Congress, typified in these years by the charismatic Subhas Chandra Bose, grew organically out of the Swadeshi underground of the early part of the century and favoured eruptive revolution and global travel through the deterritorial body of India. In his famous 1922 Congress presidential speech, the famed Bengali leader, Chittaranjan Das, the mentor of Subhas Chandra Bose, asserted the aims of anti-colonial nationalism as part of a larger global movement. He enunciated a new direction for the anti-colonial struggle that diverged from a politics of physical and political continence and spiritual purity.

In his critique of the Gandhi's Swaraj politics of abstinence and inwardness, C. R. Das proclaimed, 'I admit that our freedom must be won by ourselves but such a bond of friendship and love of sympathy and cooperation, between India and the rest of Asia, nay, between India and all the liberty loving people of the world is destined to bring about world peace. World peace to my mind means the freedom of every nationality, and I go further and say that no nation on the face of the earth can be really free when other nations are in bondage'.[41] This Swadeshi-era emphasis on deterritorial politics gave birth to the claim that Indians must participate in alliances of global reach.[42]

There was an interplay between autonomy and solidarity in Subhas Chandra Bose's politics and thought. He typified the workings of neo-Swadeshi politics in the 1930s and 1940s, and represented a style of politics different from Gandhi's more emphatic insistence on austere autonomy, and M. N. Roy's heightened argument for radical solidarity and amalgamation. The style of Bose's politics derived directly from the global temporal and spatial framework of avant-garde Swadeshi politics. He established his political base in Vienna in 1933, travelling to Czechoslovakia, Poland and Germany, France and Italy. In 1934, he travelled through Romania, Turkey, Bulgaria and Yugoslavia. On all of these journeys, he met political dignitaries, spoke of the future needs of independent India, but also placed himself in the position of an observer, remarking on social organisation, administration, scientific developments and cultural norms of the societies he encountered, with the intent of bringing the best of these influences back to India.[43]

After a period back in India, Subhas Chandra Bose again travelled abroad as a worldly envoy of Indian autonomy in 1937, making stops in Naples and London, again meeting dignitaries, academics and anti-colonial comrades such as Irish President de Valera. And finally, in 1941, Bose made his grandest gesture of deterritoriality by escaping British house arrest and travelling with the help of supporters to Kabul, then on by train to Moscow to finally reach Hitler's Berlin. Subhas Chandra Bose had been attempting to re-establish an interconnected infrastructure for deterritorial nationalism for a decade. He had sought assistance wherever it was offered, including from the Nazi regime. By invigorating the deterritorial body of India through various means: travel abroad by prominent Indians, the invitation of foreign scholars to India, the production of radio broadcasts and the distribution of interviews, the proliferation of images of India in global newspapers and film, and the encouragement of social mixing between Indians and foreigners, the englobement of India would lead to its ability to overwhelm the increasingly brittle axis of British rule, Bose insisted.[44] A host of other Indian travellers in the late 1920s and 1930s, many with roots leading back to the Swadeshi Movement, were likewise involved in projects of global cultural diplomacy, including Taraknath Das in New York, Kalidas Nag in Calcutta, Benoy Kumar Sarkar in Munich, Mohammad Shedai in Rome, Krishna Menon and Shapurji Saklatvala in London, Virendranath Chattopadhyaya, Maulana Obeidullah Sindhi and Shahid Suhrawardy in Moscow, Vithalbhai Patel and Rattan Singh in Geneva and A. C. N. Nambiar in Berlin.

But M. N. Roy, who himself was born of the Swadeshi deterritorial political context, began to voice strident criticism of neo-Swadeshi global nationalism, especially in the context of the Second World War. Travelling the world with a nationalist imagination, and attempting to utilise global circuitry for specifically nationalists ends would lead to destructive consequences, possibly even devastation, especially given the rising spectre of world fascism, Roy maintained. For him, national struggle was to be totally subordinated to the pursuit of international solidarity.

For some time after his release, Roy collaborated closely with mainstream forces of Bengali regional politics. M. N. Roy championed some of the concrete political causes of neo-Swadeshi activism: a decentralised Congress, the 'guidance and control of respective provincial Congress organisations', emphasis on social policy and insistence on the global itineraries of Indian anti-colonialism.[45] He also demanded the release of Bengali political detainees from the last major phase of insurgency in 1933–34 who were still being held in colonial jails.[46] In a tone much different from his humanist meditations in prison, Roy, upon his release could be heard calling for an eruption of anti-colonial insurgency and the immediate end of British imperialism. 'We must regard Congress men in office as the vanguard of the revolutionary army which is penetrating the citadel of the enemy and they must open up breaches in the ramparts of the enemies' citadel. Once that is done the task before us is to lead the entire army on the trail blazed by the vanguard'.[47] And from his release in 1937 until the beginning of the World War, British surveillance officials considered M. N. Roy to represent the threat of renewed radicalism in Bengal.[48]

At the 1939 Tripuri Congress, Roy, now a member of the Provincial Congress of the United Provinces, supported the re-election of Subhas Chandra Bose as Congress President. Subhas Chandra Bose and Sarat Bose represented a stable base of opposition to the Bengal Gandhians led by B. C. Roy in the 1930s.[49] Members of the Congress Right submitted a resolution that Subhas Chandra Bose should choose his Committee in strict conformity with Gandhi's wishes.[50] Roy and his followers voted with Subhas Bose in opposition to the Pant group. The Congress Socialists and the Communists, who each were trying to lead their own 'consolidation of the left' voted against Bose and allowed the resolution to pass. Bose finally stepped down, unable to choose his own Working Committee, and the Gandhian presidential replacement, Rajendra Prasad, ensured that the Congress Working Committee would be free of the radical left.[51] Gandhi's behind-the-scenes orchestration of these events, especially his Rajkot fast and his statement that 'the defeat of my candidate is my defeat', sealed M. N. Roy's conviction to break away from the National Congress organisation. After Tripuri, in an open letter to Gandhi in his journal *Independent India* of 1939, Roy lamented: 'since I returned to this country with no other object than to place my services at the disposal of the great organisation leading our struggle for freedom, I have been looked upon with suspicion, treated as an outcaste (*sic.*), although I have the poor satisfaction of seeing some of my modest contributions going home, often much too belatedly and indirectly'.[52]

Roy increasingly seemed a strange life-form in the ecosystem of 1930s Indian anti-colonialism — identifiable by genus but not by species. His break with the Congress after Tripuri spurred by his support for Subhas Chandra Bose and his critique of Gandhi did not lead to his integration into Bengali regional politics. Instead of joining Bose's Forward Bloc that was formed in the aftermath of Tripuri, Roy set up his own organisation, the League of Radical Congressmen on 1 May 1939.

In May 1939, Roy went further in his insubordination by deciding that his Radical Congressmen group would not even affiliate itself with Bose's Forward Bloc. When Bose established the Left Consolidation Committee to bring together groups of dissenting leftist parties to counter the Gandhian centre and proclaimed an All India Protest Day in June 1939, Roy called the move 'hasty and ill-advised', and withdrew the support of his group 'at the eleventh hour'.[53] In the very same month as the Forward Bloc's All-India protest day, he presided over the first All-India conference of the League of Radical Congressmen in Poona. The meeting attracted 250 delegates from eleven Congress provinces.[54] It passed a resolution of 'co-operation on concrete issues' with the Forward Bloc, but refused to merge with it. In 1940, Rajkumar Sinha, publicity secretary to the Forward Bloc, declared the Bloc's virulent opposition to Roy's candidacy for Congress President as due to the latter's sense of 'amplified self'.[55] Subhas Bose later appraised the misfit: '[M. N. Roy] is too individualist and cannot go in for teamwork. That is a great drawback for him'.[56]

Roy's old comrades from the Swadeshi revolutionary milieu, old revolutionaries who participated in the Jugantar and Anushilan samitis during the Swadeshi years, were among his most active supporters in the years after his release. These included especially Jibanlal Chatterjee, Bhupendra Kumar Datta, his cousin Hari Kumar Chakravarty, and Amarendranath Chatterjee.[57]

Political detainees in Bengal, suspected 'terrorists' held in camps for prolonged periods without trial according to the provisions of numerous Bengal Criminal Law Amendments passed between 1925 and 1934, were finally released from British prisons in 1937 and 1938 to mark the inauguration of the Government of India Act. These ex-detainees tended to join the leftist groups within the Indian National Congress, and distributed themselves among Subhas Chandra Bose leadership, the Congress Socialist Party, the Communist Party of India and the Royists, and other small groups of the left. A significant number of the Bengali ex-revolutionaries joined Roy's political group after their release, and thought of Roy as a Swadeshi revolutionary who had returned to Bengal.[58] Others among the old revolutionaries, however, were immediately skeptical of his erudite Marxism. Jadugopal Mukherjee, a famed Swadeshi revolutionary and now leader of a major faction of Bengali radicals, had recommended the young Narendranath in 1915 to the charge of his brother, Dhangopal Mukherji, at Stanford when Roy first went abroad. However, by 1938, Jadu Mukherjee chastised Narendranath, a.k.a. M. N. Roy, for the transformations he had undergone, 'I wish I could say — instruct you — for goodness sake, to desist from blurting out your philosophical Marxism either in the press or from the platform. You do not know by doing this, I think unnecessarily, you have antagonised many of [the] sincerest friends, admirers and well-wishers, supporters and sympathisers... From members of the public comes the criticism "Roy babbles in a subject for which he has no competence"'. Subhas Chandra Bose, who had much more patience for Roy's scholarly approach, nevertheless felt that Roy had arrived to fragment Bengali politics and aggrandise himself. Roy protested in response that he '[had] no missionary spirit, and shall leave Bengal to her fate'.[59]

But it was the pitch of Roy's critique of Subhas Chandra Bose that would really account for his estrangement from Bengal politics. While a number of Bengali groups remained skeptical of Subhas Chandra Bose's contact with the Nazi regime, and also criticised the Gandhian resistance to joining the war, Roy's attacks on Bose's involvement with the

Axis powers, and his bitter warnings that the evil of fascism knew no boundaries, led to his almost total loss of resonance on the Bengal political stage. Jibanlal Chatterjee, once a leader of Jugantar in the Swadeshi years, and a long-time close associate and associate of Roy, broke with Roy in 1943, and formed his own party.

Soon other old revolutionaries and colleagues began to separate themselves from Roy. Gracefully bowing out, Amanendranath Chatterjee wrote to Roy, 'I am feeling I am aging. You are younger than myself by at least a dozen of years'.[60] Students at Presidency College were cautioned by communist intellectuals not to attend Roy's lectures.[61] And the Pleiades of Bengali Marxism such as Hirendranath Mukhopadhyay and Sushobhan Sarkar viewed Roy as a vain and oppor-tunistic meddler, out of touch with Indian culture and society.[62]

If there were a group with which one would have expected Roy to form cordial ties, it would have been the Congress Socialists. But in March 1937, Roy instructed his group to leave the Congress Socialist Party (CSP). Almost all of Roy's followers during his years of imprisonment had joined the CSP upon its founding in 1934, and played, by all accounts, an important role in establishing the party platform.[63] Originally, the leaders shared many of Roy's views and admired him as an intellectual émigré to Weimar Germany.[64] Jayaprakash Narayan finished advanced studies in the United States; Rammanohar Lohia received his doctorate from Berlin; Minoo Masani completed a degree at the London School of Economics and took the occasion to travel to Moscow during one of his breaks to 'glimpse the workers' fatherland'.[65] Charles Mascarenhas, a Royist, was directly involved in the founding of the Congress Socialist Party in 1934, and both J. P. Narayan and Minoo Masani spoke explicitly of Roy's influence on them.[66]

But in three letters written from prison between 1934 and 1937, Roy made it clear that he would have trouble breaking bread with a distinct Congress Socialist Movement.[67] Instead of forming a named party within the Congress, the proper strategy for radicalising it from within was to be 'an organized left-wing of the Congress, acting, as such with no other party label...'[68] The CSP would tend to divide the Congress into camps, Roy wrote, and would hamper the ability to win over those radical anti-imperialist elements who did not identify themselves with socialism.[69]

Minoo Masani commented that the young CSP theoreticians were 'rather shaken and somewhat shattered when [they] met Roy. He no longer seemed the revolutionary [they] had once known'.[70] Jayaprakash Narayan reflected on Roy's sour disposition after exiting prison: 'the entire responsibility for disrupting the measure of unity that had been achieved must be laid at the door of the Royists, and above all of Shri Roy'.[71] Narayan continued, 'perhaps he had come to realise that the Congress Socialist Party could not be a plaything in his hands, nor a platform that he could use to boost his own ego...'[72]

Beginning in 1936, the Communist Party of India embarked on its People's Front policy, a 'minimal programme' articulated in the Dutt–Bradley Thesis, promoting the affiliation of communists and other leftist parties.[73] The Indian Communist Party, which had fallen into a lull by the mid-1930s due to its Moscow-derived policy restricting collaboration with other parties from 1928–35, subsequently grew by leaps and bounds as it began to build up its supporters within the Congress and the CSP. At the beginning of 1937, the so-called 'Lucknow Pact' between Communist and CSP leaders signalled their intent to form a common platform.[74] The Roy Group, which had been a part of the CSP since its inception in 1934, resigned from the organisation in March 1937.

Communists on the national stage attacked Roy as a 'unscrupulous liar' and a traitor — epithets which were historically rooted in his excommunication from the Comintern almost a decade earlier, but flared up again due to his seeming unwillingness to work for Left consolidation.[75] Communists libelled him as 'trying to disrupt the Left Wing radical movement in this country', and declared 'Royism... the greatest enemy which must be combated before Imperialism'.[76] P. C. Joshi, leader of the All-India Communist Party, asserted that Roy was 'a Rightist of the Rightists, more reactionary than the so-called Gandhian reactionaries and less progressive than the holy monks of the Wardha shrine'.[77] In another statement he continued, 'Roy shouts... about anti-Fascism, but only as a cover to his policy of disruption on the national and labour fronts. Like all renegades, Roy is an adept at using revolutionary phrases in order to confuse and divide the people'.[78] Continuing to invoke Roy as a 'renegade', the official Indian Communist Party presented him as a heretical exegete of the Marxist texts.[79]

Ironically, the Communist Party of India's (CPI) strategy was looking ever more like that ex-pounded by Roy, especially after the 1935 communist change of course to the collaborative 'people's front' approach. Eminent CPI intellectuals such as Gangadhar Adhikari articulated similar ideological emphases on internationalism, anti-fascism, and the critique of Hindu majoritarianism.[80] Shortly after 1935, Roy wrote an open letter to the Communist International: 'practically, all my views, condemned previously, have now been accepted. Why I am still treated as an *"outcaste"* and castigated as a culprit, is more than I can say'.[81] But the perennial problem for Roy, both the source of his ability for fresh thought and the cause of his status as an 'outcast' to multiple political regimes, was his way of continually breaking out of the regimens of group identification. This self-marginalisation was itself a feature of his politics, as a thinker who viewed the position of the outsider as a privileged standpoint for critique.

The dislike for M. N. Roy, even the derision of him, became a strong feature among Calcutta's left intelligentsia, with the charge led already in 1938 by eminent figures such as writer and political leader Hirendranath Mukhopadhyay, the historian Sushobhan Sarkar and the poet Manik Bandopadhyay. In Calcutta, during the 1930s, communism became the hegemonic intellectual culture, the source for symbols and institutional discipline for status competition among the urban Bengali intellectual elites.[82] Writing in the Bengali communist literary journal, *Parichay*, or participating in its *adda*, or Bengali-medium salon, bestowed on intellectuals a high social standing, and the ability to project his views broadly among the urban middle-class. In Calcutta, the dislike of left intellectuals for M. N. Roy resulted both from the threat to the established status hierarchy he represented, as well as from ideological disagreement on substantive points of politics.

One gets a sense for the degree of dislike of Roy by considering Syamal Krishna Ghosh's diary of the *Parichayer adda* meetings from 1936 to 1941, a book that reads like a hidden transcript of the week-to-week discussions within the group. *Parichay*, founded in 1931 as a modernist literary journal, was eventually transformed into the premier organ of the Calcutta communist intelligentsia. Along with the print organ, *Parichay* magazine also supported an *adda* that often took place in the home of its founding editor, Sudhindranath Datta. Datta eventually became one of Roy's closest friends in the 1940s, and distanced himself increasingly from the more orthodox communist line of *Parichay*. According to Ghosh's vivid account, there was indeed some discussion of M. N. Roy's thought during the *adda*, but it tended to take the form either of older members of the *adda* teaching younger members about Roy's shortcomings, or of sarcastic dismissal of his views.

In January 1938, Sajjad Zaheer, the Muslim writer originally from Lucknow who co-founded the Progressive Writers Association, commented in the group, 'Not a word of response has been given to Roy's invitation to Bengalis... He is trying to court the Muslims, but he will see that there are many political thinkers much more perceptive than himself here'.[83] On other occasions, Sushobhan Sarkar, a renowned professor of History at Presidency College and perhaps the most influential Bengali communist thinker of his day, counselled younger members of the *adda* to recognise Roy's failings and stay away from him. For example, on 4 February 1938, Sarkar delivered a lecture on the historical role of capitalists in supporting militarism and war. From the audience came a question regarding M. N. Roy's writings on a similar theme. The famed professor responded by asking the young inquirer: 'But do M. N. Roy's ideas have any following among any group (in India)?' Referring to Roy's decision to work within the Congress after his release from prison, Sarkar continued: '[Roy] wants to first win the medal of Independence, and then turn to the social questions. There is neither any truth, nor any success to be had in this line of thinking'.[84] The *adda* space was a place for intellectual debate, but also for the assertion of status hierarchy among camps, and for older members to train younger ones to maintain this hierarchy.

Status could be affirmed didactically, through a lecture or a pedagogical assertion, or more indirect, as with the multiple examples of 'M. N. Roy sarcasm' that laced the *adda* discussion. In April 1940, Hiren Mukherjee, graduate of Oxford and leader of the underground Communist Party of Bengal, was heard to say, 'Would someone care to straightforwardly ask him [Roy] why he decided to return from Moscow anyway?'.[85] On another occasion, a member of the *adda* group jokingly announced that 'it would be more amusing to read Hitler's writings or Gandhi's letters' than to go too deeply into M. N. Roy's counsel.[86] And another time, in 1941, amidst laughter, someone wondered out loud why M. N. Roy was still staying so close to 'Uncle Joe' (Stalin).[87]

If M. N. Roy had become something of a risible figure among the communist intelligentsia of Calcutta, his importance was also diminishing within the eyes of British observers. In 1938 and 1939, British surveillance followed Roy's activities doggedly, believing him to be a source of renewed unrest in Bengal. Yet, his early support of the British war effort against Nazi Germany led, ironically, to his dismissal as a viable political ally for colonial administrators.[88] By late 1940, British officials had a very low estimation of Roy as an intermediary, a non-Indian Indian, who did not belong squarely in any of the representative camps of Indian political identity. After having once feared him in 1930, as one of the most dangerous revolutionaries in India, an official in the Criminal Investigation Department now contentedly reported about his post-prison activities in 1940: 'in short Roy's political achievement has so far been nil. It is indeed difficult to see how a man with Roy's vanity and arrogant personality, listening to none and only stopping to pause when an old ally has to be discarded or a new one appears at the scene, can never be expected to make an effective leader of a coalition'.[89] Stafford Cripps said of Roy in a report during his war mission: 'I have always regarded Mr. Roy as an unreliable and self-seeking politician and I do not think he has any real influence in India'.[90] Roy did not fit into the cultural-symbolic regimens of wartime Indian politics, organised as it was increasingly according to the imperative of national autonomy.

In the late 1930s, Roy challenged the status hierarchies and discipline of established political camps, and this was the true source of his downfall, not any supposed anti-nationalism or lack of Indian authenticity, as many of his opponents often maintained. Roy's outsider status does not mean that he did not identify with the anti-colonial cause or with the Indian nation. Rather, by the time of the Second World War, he argued that the freedom of the deterritorial body of India could only be achieved in solidarity with a global struggle against fascism. Roy proposed a mediated form of autonomy, instead of an insurgent one.

Geopolitical Shifts

The 1930s saw a reordering of the world, especially in the context of the Great Depression and what Karl Polanyi called the interwar failure of 'capitalist internationalism'.[91] Although Indian deterritorial energies remained as strong, or even more pronounced, than they had been during the previous decade, they were now channelled not only through the undergrounds of global cities and harbours, but also through the foreign ministries of authoritarian states, especially among the future Axis powers. Many of the infrastructures of big states, whether American, German, Ottoman, Japanese or Soviet, that had supported the global Indian anti-colonial networks of the early twentieth century up to the mid-1920s, had been greatly altered, both because of the fall of the empires (such as Germany or the Ottomans), and the new type of strong state governmentality, economic protectionism and surveillance control, including passport laws and immigration laws, that prevented Indian activists from easily or clandestinely exploiting major technology and communication hubs outside of the British Empire.[92]

The post-First World War cracks in the world order were being plastered over by the mid-1920s, and the reconfiguration of muscular nation–states and domains of autarchy soon surpassed the levels of the pre-war context.[93] The interwar years saw an accentuation of the dialectic between territorialisation and deterritorialisation. In the name of Italian *Romanità*, Japanese Greater Nippon and Nazi *Mitteleuropa*, militarised states began to metastasise over larger and larger domains supposedly in the attempt to extend state boundaries to incorporate 'irredenta' communities, such as the '*Auslandsdeutsche*', to pursue the alignment of state boundaries with mythic civilisational zones.[94] Of course, these projects to expand the state apparatus to corresponded with purported zones of civilisational unity had their precedent in the movement in Great Britain in the late Victorian period leading to new Commonwealth institutions of the 1930s, or the coeval rise of the Greater France idea, and American interwar paternalism.[95] Powerful states of mid-century justified their projects of expansive territorialisation in the name of calibrating state boundaries to the 'real' deterritorial civilisational or cultural domain of its people. In Germany, Japan and Italy, to a special extent, but also in Britain, France, the Soviet Union and the United States of America, economic corporatism, biopolitics and aggressive reterritorialisation preoccupied state elites.[96]

Gandhi's form of nationalist politics sought to carve out Indian autonomy from a global map increasingly ordered into power blocs of big powers: a capitalist West, a Nazi Central Europe, a Communist Eastern Europe, a Fascist Southern Europe, a Japanese co-prosperity zone. Gandhi began his *Purna Swaraj* campaign with the Dandi March in early 1930. The march had a powerful impact on India's political imagination, recalibrating Indian politics to the dimensions of a people–body — to its natural resources and its localities, as opposed to its deterritorial energies. His great fasts of 1934, 1939 and 1941 can also be understood in this context, as projects to 'bring anti-colonialism back home' as it were, and focus it inwardly, especially given the increasingly treacherous international political scene.

Subhas Chandra Bose, on the other hand, maintained that in order for the anti-colonial pursuit to progress, it had to work in and through the growing tensions between the world's major power blocs. Mussolini's Italy granted Bose the passport that facilitated his travels in 1941, and Hitler invited him to Berlin to establish an anti-colonial base for radio addresses and publication, and to establish the Indian National Army. Tojo facilitated his organisation of the INA in South East Asia. Subhas Bose's circulation through Hitler's Germany and Tojo's Japan represents the application of a long-standing tradition of Swadeshi deterritorial nationalism to use the conflicts of international relations in its nationalist struggle.

Global Civil War

But Roy felt that the Second World War was not just about geo-political conflict between nation-states, but primarily about the future of the people of the world as a whole. Ever since the beginning of the war in September 1939, much before it took on its fully global dimensions in 1941, Roy felt it was not localisable to a specific region or to specific theatres of conflagration. In August 1941, the Germans seized control of the Balkans, sent armies marching across Russia, and stood poised within range of the Suez Canal. From the vantage point of 1941, a great moment of contingency had arrived. It was a war in the world's body. 'The world is in the midst of a civil war, the severest battles of which are yet to be fought...', Roy wrote.[97] His notion of an 'international civil war' highlights the degree to which Roy perceived the world as a monad, marked by systemic interconnectedness between the local expression and the global embodiments of political forms.[98]

War was declared in Europe on 1 September 1939. The Congress initially postponed taking an official stance then declared a policy of 'neutralism' and non-co-operation with the war effort. Finally, it declared its outright opposition to the British in 1942, in the absence of a grant of immediate self-government. But already on 6 September 1939, Roy controversially commented in a public speech, 'all freedom loving people will congratulate the British Government on the decision, even though much belated, to put an end to Hitlerism which it has been encouraging all the time...'[99] Less than two weeks later Roy made statements in the press congratulating Britain on the 'war against fascism.'[100] On 14 September he admonished the Congress President in a letter, 'the Congress cannot but sympathise with the victims of Fascist aggression and be willing to co-operate in freeing the world from that standing menace.'[101] By the middle of October 1939, the League of Radical Congressmen, Roy's group, issued its official statement warning that the defeat of Hitler was the immediate task. 'The present war is not an imperialist war... it is not permissible for the fighters for democracy and freedom, not only in Europe, but throughout the world, including India, to be indifferent about the outcome of the conflict and its possible developments...'[102]

By contrast, the declaration of war between the Western Powers and the Axis was widely interpreted in India as 'sharpening the anti-imperialist struggle', as Subhas Chandra Bose called it. The Congress Working Committee responded to the viceroy's unilateral declaration of India as a belligerent in the war by stating that 'India cannot associate herself in a war said to be for democratic freedom when that freedom is denied her'.[103] The call for Congress ministries to resign in protest came in the third week of October. The communists, given the Nazi–Soviet pact of August 1939, made the most forceful anti-British declaration: 'the most effective way in which the Indian people can serve the cause of world peace and democracy is by striking for their own freedom and weakening British imperialism...'[104] This stance eventually landed many CPI members in jail in March 1940.[105] Yet after their shift to a pro-British stance in late 1941 following Hitler's invasion of Russia, Indian communists soon won the trust of the government and were released from jail and legalised for the first time since 1934.

Already in May 1940, a month after Hitler's successful assault on Western European countries, Belgium, Holland, Denmark and Norway, Roy expressed to his group at a League of Radical Congressmen retreat, 'Every morning I open the newspaper with a shudder. I have no love for imperialist France and Britain. But I cannot think of the possibility of the Fascisation [*sic*] of European without horror...'[106] France was conquered by the Nazis the following month. Given the rising pitch of the war in Europe, and Roy's growing sense that cataclysm was imminent, the Radical Congressmen carried out anti-fascist demonstration on 1 September 1940, the one-year anniversary of the start of the war. As a result, Roy was expelled from the Congress for his insubordinate action.

His response was to form a new independent political party, the Radical Democratic People's Party, whose first conference was held beginning on 21 December 1940.[107] By the following year, the organisation remained small, but not insignificant, with a membership numbering almost 2200.[108] And in July 1941, M. N. Roy's group formed a more consequential organisation, the Indian Federation of Labour (IFL) by breaking away from the AITUC to promote worker collaboration with the war effort.[109] The IFL went on to become one of the largest and most important umbrella organisations for trade unions of the 1940s.[110] In the years after the war, the Indian labour movement was led by two major groups, the AITUC (communist) and the IFL (the Roy group).[111]

Global Fascism

Roy argued that imperialism had brought about a 'psychosis' among Indians, such that proper judgement of international politics as skewed. '[Nationalists] thought Imperialism was the greatest enemy of India.

Once upon a time it was. But now it is dying; and for the future of India, it is only a ghost'.[112] There were other, more substantial threats, Roy maintained. Chief among them was the global rise of fascism. Roy was not referring to a specific system of totalitarian rule, whether Nazi, Japanese or Italian, but rather to what he believed to be a more general style of politics of collective identity and cultural authenticity. 'In this new situation, we shall have to fight fascism on our home front'.[113] Roy saw fascism as a social phenomenon that could arise in any cultural setting of the modern world, on either side of the colonial divide. It was not a product of Western 'civilisation' as European thinkers assumed. Theodor Adorno, Max Horkheimer and Hannah Arendt and others insisted that the Nazis were only possible within Western civilisation alone.[114]

Roy challenged this geo-culturalist assumption. He insisted that fascism was 'a socio-political manifestation of our time, and its pattern is determined by the peculiarities of the country in which it grows. German fascism was different from Italian fascism, and the fascism in the East again was different from both. Therefore, we should not have an *a priori* notion about our enemy... To put the point straight: Indian Fascism will be cultural; it will be a cultural reaction. Therefore, violence may not be such a very outstanding feature of Indian Fascism... In India, Fascism may even be non-violent'.[115]

Roy saw the cultural features of an Indian fascism in Gandhi's politics of cultural continence and civilisationalism. In Gandhi's practice of anti-colonial politics in a culturalist key, Roy sensed an inkling of fascist discourse. 'In Germany, it was the old nationalist preoccupation and the readiness of the German people to accept regimentation and the militaristic tradition. The highest ambition of any German is to put on a uniform. When Hitler put all of them in uniforms, they believed they were all supermen, and followed him. Similarly, in our country also, the people are being put in a uniform: khaddar is a political uniform; and they also think that by donning the Mahatmic uniform, and a particular kind of headgear they become supermen'.[116]

A struggle for asserting cultural unity would be ultimately detrimental, argued Roy. The pursuit of mediation was equally important. 'The characteristic feature of Indian nationalism is to ignore the fact that India is a part of the world. If the aspirations of the nationalist and communalist politicians were not immediately fulfilled, the rest of the world might go to hell... the primary concern for those honestly fighting for the freedom and progress of the masses of the Indian people is to make the greatest possible contribution to the struggle for the destruction of Fascism'.[117] If Indians see themselves primarily as members of a world community, then the status of fascism as a universal threat, inherent in every society, would be clearly appreciated. Roy also criticised Subhas Chandra Bose's involvement with Nazi international politics. Roy attacked both the underlying logic of Bose's variety of neo-Swadeshi deterritorial nationalism, as well as the specific instance of engagement with European fascism.

> I had grave misgivings about the consequences of the experiment [of the Indian National Army]... My misgiving was based on experience. A quarter of a century ago, during the last world war, I tried to organise an I.N.A... Nevertheless, systematic efforts were made to invade India with an army raised in a neighbouring country, armed and equipped by an 'allied power', which happened to be Germany at the time... 'our ally' of that time sabotaged the plan...[118]

Roy saw Bose's politics as reminiscent of an older variety of Swadeshi internationalism, not yet able to grasp the monadic relationship between the microcosm of Indian context and the macrocosm of the world community. Elsewhere, he indirectly scorned Subhas Chandra Bose's inauguration of the Indian National Army in Nazi Germany, 'if you stand on the roadside and watch an I.N.A. demonstration, subconsciously your feet move as if marking time. So, you see how, dormant in every revolutionary, lies the counter-revolutionary'. In a letter to Humayun Kabir, Roy wondered whether representatives of Bengali radicalism, especially Subhas Chandra Bose, were going too far in their search for autonomy, to the point of developing admiration for the strong men of the fascist world. Roy believed that some in Bengal 'secretly wish Hitler to be victorious, not only because they like England to be humbled by someone else, but also they believe Hitler to be a superman entrusted with a divine mission'.[119] He thought neo-Swadeshi ways of relating the nation to the world could have treacherous results.

Through his critique of fascism, M. N. Roy was a figure of admiration for many leaders of the All-India Progressive Writers' Association. The group, which along with the Indian People's Theatre Association, grew into one of the most influential cultural forces in South Asia in the 1940s and 1950s, was first founded in London in 1935 and was galvanised by a series of international anti-fascism writers' conferences in London, Paris and Brussels over the coming two years. At this time, the main reference point was the civil war in Spain and the death toll caused by Franco's army, not the genocidal Nazi regime. Mulk Raj Anand and Sajjad Zaheer, the two early leaders of the movement's Indian branch, were present at the meetings in Paris in June 1935, in London in June 1936, and in Brussels in September 1936.[120] And the inaugural conferences of the Progressive Writers' Association took place in Calcutta in 1937, inaugurated by Rabindranath Tagore. Linked up to the international cultural programmes sponsored by the recently revived 'people's front' Communist International, progressive writers set out to 'to develop an attitude of literary criticism, which will discourage the general reactionary and revivalist tendencies on questions like family, religion, sex, war and society'.[121] Among those Indian members of this international writers' movement who admiringly spoke of M. N. Roy were Abu Syed Ayub, Humayun Kabir and Sudhindranath Datta in Calcutta, Khwaja Ahmad Abbas in Bombay, Mulk Raj Anand in London, Abburi Ramakrishna Rao in Hyderabad and Gopal Mittal in Lahore.[122] Mulk Raj Anand even incorporated M. N. Roy as a character in one of his novels.[123]

Policy Suggestions

Roy's social vision of Indian interconnectedness with the world was given shape in these years in two documents, the 'People's Plan for Economic Development of India' of 1943, and the 'Draft Constitution of India' of 1944. The 'People's Plan', penned by three of Roy's lieutenants, consisted in a summary of the programme articulated by Roy at the Indian Federation of Labour meeting of that year.[124] The publication of the economic plan slightly preceded the publication of the 'Bombay Plan' of 1944, which represented the Congress' blueprint for the post-Independence economy. The Bombay Committee led by P. C. Mahalanobis and M. Visveswaraya emphasised the nationalisation of heavy industry as the first priority, and the involvement of the state in organising a market for handicrafts.[125]

Roy, on the other hand, argued that the primary emphasis should lie on the rationalisation and modernisation of agriculture and the expansion of the domestic consumer market. The development of irrigation, communications (railways and roads) and basic rural industries (electrification, chemicals, engineering) should be first addressed. The starting point of Roy's proposal was that 'human freedom' had to be maximised, not 'economic benefits'.[126] This involved thinking in terms of how to best equate production with, what Roy called, 'human demand'.[127] The incomes of agriculturalists must rise so that they could consume above subsistence level, at a 'human level', and this would create a market for consumer goods that would drive economic development, the expansion of home industries and import markets, eventually the relocation of labour away from land towards industrial production. Roy insisted that India had to travel a non-aligned, third route, away from the model of the Soviet Union or the 'Fordist' democracy of the United States.[128]

Roy's second policy proposal, his 'Draft Constitution of India' of 1944 — we could call it a 'dream constitution' — consisted of thirteen chapters and 137 articles. The proportions of his alternative vision of post-independence India entailed the decentralisation of power to local people's committees in villages, towns and cities as the basis for the democratic States of the Indian Union. A similar idea was mentioned in C. R. Das' Draft Constitution of the Swaraj Party in 1923, and Gandhi too wrote extensively on the need for a decentralised *panchayati raj*.[129] In Roy's proposal, local committees would nominate candidates for the federal assembly and provincial council, and would be able to initiate legislation and demand referenda on any measure. The provincial governments would be formed by universal suffrage. All provinces would have the right to opt out of the federal union, but would be required to establish itself independently with a democratic constitution. Members to the federal assembly would be chosen by a college of electors, comprised of those from the 'learned professions'.[130] And a Council of State would be appointed by the provincial governments. Arguing for a postcolonial mediated autonomy, as opposed to a heroic, strongly autonomous one, Roy proposed that Indians form a 'British–Indian' cooperative Commonwealth, a federation of federations, as a full member in a post-imperial relationship.[131]

In debates about the constitution of an independent India in the mid-1940s, Roy argued for an Indian federation, 'composed of units based, as much as possible, on cultural, religious, linguistic and racial homogeneity. The idea of Federation implied autonomy on the part of the Constituent units of the Federation; and autonomy was an entirely meaningless term unless it carried with it the right of secession'.[132] The India that Roy envisioned, like many other anti-colonial leaders of the day, was an inclusive plurality. He insisted that a 'number of culturally heterogeneous communities can be artificially welded into a united nation without destroying culture'.[133] In terms of the idea of Pakistan, Roy wrote favourably in 1941, that it encouraged the birth of a non-centralised union of state. 'The Pakistan scheme as it stands today cannot be reasonably objected to. The objection comes from the fear that ultimately the Muslim units might also break away from India. I do not share that fear… Why should we establish a system of coercion in the name of national unity?'[134] Here, his writings anticipated the perspective of the Communist Party of India as articulated by Adhikari in 1943.[135]

⌈Thinking not in terms of a strong autonomous body but rather in terms of mediated autonomy within a transnational union put Roy in the company of a group of federative political thinkers of that time, from Muhammad Iqbal and Abul Hashim in India to H. N. Brailsford and H. G. Wells in Britain, to Ewald Ammende in Germany, to figures such as David Starr Jordan in the United States.⌋

By 1942, Gandhi was clear that the war offered Indians the moment to force the British from the country. 'I am convinced', he wrote in the *Harijan*, 'that time has come during the war for [non-cooperation], not after it, for the British and the Indians to be reconciled to complete separation from each other. That way and that way alone lies the safety of both and shall I say, the world'.[136] Chiang Kai-shek, long contending with Japanese occupation in China, travelled to India in February 1942 with hopes of convincing Congress leaders to support the war effort.[137] Gandhi, however, insisted on the granting of complete self-government before India would support the war. With the Quit India Movement of 1942, Gandhi took his 'do or die' stance and mass anti-British uprisings swelled up for the next three months. Whereas before imprisonment, Roy's critical practice aimed at critiquing the Soviet regime, calling it to a new Tsarist dictatorship, now, in the context of war, his target became the mainstream Congress. Coming to terms with the brinkmanship of Roy's rhetoric — his insistence on calling Gandhi's politics 'fascist' — requires us to correctly picture the countervailing brinkmanship of Congress politics in 1942.

The Divides of Nationalism: Hindu–Muslim Politics

Apart from the divide of India versus the West, there was another identity divide that Roy sought to mediate. The 1930s saw a ratcheting up of communitarian politics based on the Hindu–Muslim divide. To understand why Roy was such a misfit within Indian anti-colonialism of the 1930s and 1940s, we have to bring to light not only what he protested against, but also what he worked towards. In the context of economic crises in the countryside, social conflict and economic distress came to be increasingly 'politicised' in communal modes. The Hindu press in the 1930s built up a stereotype of the threatening, rioting Muslim peasants. Meanwhile the Muslim press deployed the trope of the unscrupulous and exploitative Hindu moneylender and landlord.[138] The ranks of the Hindu Mahasabha grew significantly in this period, as leaders of the party, such as L. B. Bhopatkar, suggested that the greatest threat to the Indian nation was that of 'Muslims [who] have been trying and directing their energy towards destroying the Hindu culture...'[139] And in 1938, V. D. Savarkar, the most celebrated figure of the *Mahasabha* and its president at the time said in a public lecture, '[Hindus] have borne the brunt of the fight, struggled single-handed down to this day while the other non-Hindu sections and especially the Mohammedans ... [are] nowhere to be found while the national struggle goes on and are always to be found in the forefront at the time of reaping the fruits of that struggle'.[140]

In this context, Roy's symbolic action revolved around crossing the Hindu–Muslim identity divide. To do this, he emphasised the mixed and mestizo nature of South Asian civilisation. In his years after prison, he sought to critique the notion of continent, linear civilisational divides that underlay much of regnant majoritarian and minoritarian Indian political discourse.

In July 1939, Roy organised a conference with radical and progressive Muslim politicians.[141] In Calcutta in 1939, he also spoke to the National Muslim Youth League at the invitation of Maulana Mohammed Akram Khan, and announced his new stance after the Tripuri Congress: '... our task is to destroy the Congress as well as the Moslem League and create in their place a great united political party of the Indian people, free from religious prejudices and communal narrowness. If that is your considered decision, come to me and I shall create a united party of India'.[142] In March 1940, in the context of the Lahore resolution on Pakistan, Roy made arrangements with Maulana Hazrat Mohani, a veteran of the Muslim League, who had played a major role in left ranks of the Congress in the 1920s, to combine the League of Radical Congressmen with the left wing of the Muslim League.[143]

Roy complemented this political pursuit with the publication of his new 'dream history', *The Historical Role of Islam*, which narrated Indian history in terms of the crossings and cultural fusion between Islam and other Indian traditions. Written in prison in 1932, M. N. Roy's treatise was particularly salient in 1939, the year of its publication. In the context of the rise of communitarian aggression in that year, Roy began on a note of irony, remarking that despite the population of Muslims outnumbering that of any Islamic land, Muslims were still considered an 'extraneous elements' to the mainstream Indian population.[144] 'This curious but extremely regrettable cleft in the loose national structure of India has its historical cause', Roy continued.[145] In the contemporary context of anti-colonial struggle, imaginary civilisational divides between Hindus and Muslims had been produced in nationalist discourses. 'A Hindu, who prides himself in the prosperity of the reign of an Akbar ... is even to-day separated most curiously by an unbridgeable gulf from his next door [Muslim] neighbour...'[146]

Roy's book undertook to revise the idea of Indian civilisation not as continent and pure, but as cosmopolitan. While in the West, the monotheism of Islam cleared away the 'dark superstition of the Magian mysticism, and the corrupt atmosphere of the Greek Church', the arrival of the Mughals also prepared the way for the cultural advancement of India, Roy argued. The spread of Islam produced the peace needed for the development of long-distance trade routes.[147] Islamic thought, and its rationalist fundaments, contributed to the development of scientific instruments and the acquisition of exact knowledge of the natural world.[148]

Roy insisted on the constructive consequences of the Mughal conquest of India, especially in terms of spurring social reform.[149] Roy's interest in using history to write across lines of genealogical purity resonated with a number of Muslim intellectuals. Humayun Kabir, a major Bengali Muslim intellectual and admirer of Roy, wrote in an article after Roy's death, 'it is not always realised that what we regard as ancient Indian civilisation was itself complex and composite. Till some forty years ago, we thought of ancient Indian history as a history of only the Aryans'.[150] Extending Roy's argument Kabir went on to note that all civilisations must thus be understood as 'complex'. 'Europe is as much a debtor to Asia as Asia is today a debtor to Europe. What we call western civilisation is the result of contribution from Hellenic, Hebraic, Egyptian, Iranian, Indian and Arab sources'.[151] M. N. Roy was admired by other Muslim intellectuals on the left, such as Ahsan Habib, Farrukh Ahmad, Syed Ali Ahsan, Abdul Gani Hazari and Syed Waliullah, while Roy became particularly close to Calcutta-based intellectuals, Humayun Kabir and Abu Syed Ayub.[152]

The Historical Role of Islam was widely read, generating both accolades and controversy. Some members of the Hindu Mahasabha went so far as to claim Roy had converted to Islam, mockingly calling him

'Maulana Roy'. And some Muslim leaders writing in the Urdu press criticised the book for 'harming [Muslim] religious sentiments'.[153] By evaluating Islam solely in terms of its social rationality and scientific genius, Roy failed to appreciate the specificity of the spiritual qualities of Islam, responses claimed. As was wont for Roy in his position as an intermediary, he defended himself before Hindu and Muslim critics alike. 'A scientific study of the history of all religions led me to the conclusions that Islam, being the most rigorous form of monotheism, is the purest type of religion... I fail to see how any Muslim can believe that I have disparaged his religion or been disrespectful to its Prophet'. By transgressing the Hindu–Muslim cultural divide, he perturbed the votaries of authenticity.[154]

Chosen Family

According to the round of opinions at the time, Roy was surly, contrarian, and to a point, egocentric. His in-betweeness made him an outcast, like Caliban, 'hag-born' to the world of 1940s Indian nationalism, not honoured with the shapeliness of national form. Roy, as a political and intellectual intermediary, tended to nonplus and perturb the regimens of Indian anti-colonialism nationalism. This was not only a choice. It was the historical effect of his lived experience of travel and social fusion. These 'defects of his character', as onlookers at the time were wont to describe, were the photo-negatives of his cosmopolitanism.

In 1938, Roy and his wife Ellen, decided to settle in Dehra Dun, the town where he spent the last phase of his imprisonment, from May 1935 to November 1936. It offered a cooler environment and a place on the peripheries where Roy could invent his own community and intellectual space. Even before Roy left prison, he thought about establishing a 'scientific institute' for the development of new thinking in India.[155] He took the first steps in that direction in 1943, when he set up his Renaissance Publishing House.[156] It would culminate in 1946 with the establishment of the Radical Humanist Movement. Roy wanted to create a space for his particular cosmopolitan worldview, as he sensed his growing estrangement from All-India and Bengal politics.

As well as his permanent exclusion from the ranks of international communist ranks, in 1940, he began forming a chosen family by holding 'study camps' in Dehra Dum. In April 1940, he held the first study camp of his associates.[157] The camp lasted for two weeks, with subsequent camps held intermittently — in 1942, 1946, 1948 and 1950. The aim was to carry out a critical exegesis of post-Soviet Marxism and to eventually develop a way of thinking beyond Marxist assumptions. 'Those doctrines of Marxism which cannot be reconciled with the (materialist) essence of Marxism, I reject as incompatible with Marxism. While Materialism is the essence of Marxism, Marx went far towards idealism in his economic and political doctrines'.[158]

Those who visited Roy's home in Dehra Dun remarked the presence of wine on the table, something most uncommon, and the way in which Roy would speak German with Ellen when they were in private conversation.[159] Roy's polyglot and transculturated home environment, mixing English, German and Bengali, was simply a different kind of play between cultural influences that was standard among colonial intellectuals, particularly of mid-century Calcutta. When Roy visited Calcutta and participated in Sudhindranath Datta's *adda*, discussion would flow freely in Bangla and English, with language often switching mid-sentence.[160] Colonial intellectuals exhibited a quotidian cosmopolitanism, shifting between languages and cultural symbols, not as habits derived from high philosophical reflection but rather from the sensibilities context of daily life.[161]

Roy's chosen family had global dimensions. After returning to India, he identified more closely with an invisible college of opposition. Jay Lovestone, leader of the American Communist Opposition Party and colleague of Roy in Moscow in the 1920s, helped organise the protest to have Roy released early from prison, and tried to convince Roy to move to Mexico after his release.[162] By the late 1930s, Lovestone became staunchly anti-communist by the 1940s. During the Cold War, he was sponsored by the CIA as a leader of the American Federation of Labour, and was also involved in the Congress for Cultural Freedom.[163] In the context of the Second World War, Lovestone began corresponding frequently with Roy, often encouraging him to take a more forthright and denunciatory stance towards the Soviet Union.[164] It is significant, however, that Roy chose not to attend the second Congress for Cultural Freedom conference in Bombay in 1951, sponsored by the U.S. government.[165] Minoo Masani and Jayaprakash Narayan were the lead figures in organising the event, which attracted over seventy Indian delegates.[166] Roy sent a letter of support, but was unwilling to repudiate the ideal of international communism fully. In fact, in his later years, he wrote openly of his admiration for Stalin's resolve to oppose the capitalist world order, while also deploring the Stalinist use of authoritarianism and terror.[167] A similar hedging was common among the global left, disheartened by the Soviet experiment but unwilling to participate in anti-communist demonisation campaigns.

Roy's closest companions from his Berlin days, August Thalheimer, Jan Pollack and Jakob Walcher, members of the German Communist Party Opposition, wrote to Roy from Paris in the late 1930s, where they had fled to escape the Nazis. [168] Connection was lost, however, as Jewish members of the KPD-O entered global diaspora in Palestine, the United States, Britain and Cuba as Hitler's armies expanded into France. [169] August Thalheimer emigrated to Cuba in 1940, where he began editing the *Internationale Monatlische Übersichten* in the hopes of providing new direction to the International Communist Opposition movement. Thalheimer wrote a number of essays on culture and philosophy, including on such diverse themes as phenomenology, revolutionary art, and Indian theatre. [170] But Roy and Thalheimer were never able to restart their correspondence, to Roy's disappointment. [171] Through this all, the closest connection Roy maintained to the critical communist milieu of the 1920s, the group he continued to call '*meine Familie*', was the company of his wife Ellen Gottschalk who had once worked as a secretary at the Comintern's Western Office in Berlin before travelling to India in 1936 to join Roy after his release. Gottschalk became a leader in the Radical Humanist movement in the 1940s. [172]

In the years after the war, Roy frequently wrote to American friends voicing his interest in coming to the United States for work and travel — a wish that would never be fulfilled. [173] Initially, he was not granted a visa by the United States government, but when the visa was finally obtained in 1952, he was too weak. [174] His articles, however, were published in foreign journals such as *The Pacific Affairs, The Manchester Guardian,* and *The Times Weekly Review*. [175]

In India, it was not a party or a particular ideological camp that defined Roy's intellectual community. Rather, it was a relatively small group of fellow intermediaries. There was the young Viennese convert to tantric Hinduism, Leopold Fischer (1923–92), who first came to India as a German infantrymen in Subhas Chandra Bose's Azad Hind Army. Fischer, of Czech Jewish descent, had actually converted to Hinduism much earlier, taking the name Ramachandra at the age sixteen while still in Vienna. [176] He adopted the name Swami Agehananda, meaning 'blissful homelessness' after release from a prison of war camp, and became a prolific writer and an advocate for the integration of sex into spiritual life. Fischer went on to take up a post at Syracuse University, New York, as an eminent scholar on

Hinduism beginning in the 1960s.[177] In 1948, Fischer, a newly-minted *sannyasi* at age twenty-five, contributed articles to Roy's *Marxian Way* press on spirituality. But it was not your typical spirituality. Leopold Fischer wrote, 'I constantly harp on and recur to sex, because I hold that the erotic part of it is the prototype and in a way the consummation of the rich life. I shall show you later that the monastic and mystical life are entirely based on a particularly set of experiences which are, in the last analysis, erotic'.[178] His interest in tantra, and the relationship between sexuality and spirituality attracted him to Roy's sensibilities. Roy also associated closely with Philip Spratt who had first come to India fresh out of Cambridge as an envoy of the Communist Party of Great Britain.[179] He was one of a handful of Britons imprisoned in the Meerut Communist Conspiracy Case of 1930. After his release, Spratt remained in India as a vocal critic of the Soviet allegiances of the Indian Communist Party. In the 1930s and 1940s, he began publishing his journal *MysIndia* from Madras, writing regularly with the aim of challenging the official Indian communist line. Spratt became a strong critic of both Russia and China by the late 1940s.[180]

Roy was attracted to the Bengali literary vanguard and found one of his closest friends in Sudhindranath Datta. A famed Bengali poet, leading figure among the Progressive Writers, and co-founder of the Comparative Literature Department at Jadavpur University in Calcutta, Sudhindranath proclaimed atheism, and evoked an aporetic and downcast existentialist perspective in his art. 'There is nothing in him that is happy or light or sparkling; all is dark, darkly and bitterly passionate', wrote Buddhadeb Basu about his friend and colleague.[181] All of these figures, although disparate, shared their interest in transgression and in challenging social orthodoxies. When he visited Calcutta, Roy had *adda* with Sudhindranath Datta, Abu Sayed Ayub, an intellectual force in the philosophy department at Presidency College, Humayun Kabir, a renowned social thinker, literary figure and politician — all leading members of the Progressive Writer's Association.[182] Roy also discussed issues frequently with Sushil Dey, a high-level member of Indian Civil Service who went on to become the Minister of State in the Government of India after independence. Dey had trained as an engineer in U.S.A. and wrote articles often critical of the British government under the pseudonym of Sikander Chaudhury.[183] Roy mentored a number of young intellectuals, many of them Bengali, especially the literary scholar Sibnarayan Ray, and the professor of economics, Amlan Datta. There was also Sitangshu Chatterji, a philosopher and expert on Spinoza, the historian Niranjan Dhar, and political scientist Gouripada Bhattacharya. A notable addition to the Bengali group was Surindar Suri of Lucknow, a young political philosopher who went on to write a book entitled '*Nazism and Social Change in Germany*' at the Frankfurt Institute for Social Research in 1957, before returning to India as a noted academic.[184] The film writer, director and producer, J. B. H. Wadia, provided Roy a *pied-à-terre* in Bombay, and financially supported the founding of the Indian Renaissance Institute.[185] And finally there were the members associated closely with the trade union organisation, the IFL. Many powerful labour organisers, known as the Old Royists, especially V. B. Karnik and Maniben Kara, were operating from Bombay. Meanwhile V. M. Tarkunde, G. D. Parikh and R. D. Nigam became forces behind the political organisation of Roy's Radical Democratic Party.

By challenging boundaries and transgressing the symbolic orders delimiting nation, culture and civilisation, Roy had long felt that underlying all human difference there was a unity. And yet, such an assertion was critical in intent. In the context of the rise of what Roy termed the 'collective ego' in different mid-century forms, from culturalism to civilisationalism, nationalism to corporatism, a countervailing critique of those categories was necessary. Roy wanted to create distance from identity categories such that they could be critiqued, revised and kept open. The symbolic action of M. N. Roy involved a critical in-betweenness that must not be mistaken for betrayal of the anti-colonial cause or an unresolved heteronomy to the West. Roy belonged to multiple social and intellectual emplotments, and in that sense, was defined by an excess of interconnection, not a condition of political loneliness.

Roy said at a Radical Congress Youth Conference at Madras, in 1937, 'Revolution does not mean only a change in the political administration of a country. It is a more far-reaching event. It replaces a decayed social order by a new one. Each social order has a philosophy of its own; its subversion, therefore, must be preceded by a critique of its philosophy'.[186] He insisted that it was not merely an economic system, but a 'historical and cultural background' that had to be upset.[187] Whereas Roy came to criticise the pursuit of strong, heroic, autonomy, he proposed not subservience to Western culture, but mediation across the borders of autonomy.

Notes

1. Axel Honneth. 1995. *The Struggle for Recognition: The Moral Grammar of Social Conflicts.* Cambridge: Blackwell, pp. xi–xii, 129.
2. Roy overtly said that he valued the 'culturally Dionysian', see M. N. Roy. 1953c. 'In Power by Proxy', *Radical Humanist*, 19 July, vol. 17: p. 343.
3. Honneth, *The Struggle for Recognition*, p. 128.
4. Honneth, *The Struggle for Recognition*, p. 128.
5. Ibid., p. 179.
6. David Washbrook. 1990. 'South Asia, the World System and World Capitalism', in S. Bose (ed.), *South Asia and World Capitalism*, p. 42. See Sumit Sarkar. 1983. *Modern India, 1885–1947.* Delhi: Macmillan, pp. 259, 351. But there was also a rising 'leftwardism' in 1936 and 1937, with the rise of trade union politics, and Nehru's two consecutive socialism-oriented speeches as Congress president. See Sanjay Seth. 1995. *Marxist Theory and Nationalist Politics: The Case of Colonial India.* New Delhi: Sage Publications, p. 161.
7. Vivek Chibber. 2003. *Locked in Place: State-Building and Late Industrialization in India.* Princeton: Princeton University Press, p. 115; Rajnarayan Chandavarkar. 1998. *Imperial Power and Popular Politics: Class Resistance and the State in India, c. 1850–1950.* Cambridge: Cambridge University Press, p. 299.
8. 'Communism or Socialism', *Madras Mail*, 27 July 1937.
9. A polemical account of the battle for political hegemony in India is offered by Shashi Joshi and Bhagwan Josh. 1992. *Struggle for Hegemony in India, 1920–47: the Colonial State, the Left and the National Movement.* New Delhi: Sage Publications, vol. 1: pp. 25–41.
10. Ranajit Guha. 1997. *Dominance without Hegemony*, Cambridge: Harvard University Press, p. 135.
11. V.G.D. (Valji Govindji Desai), 1934. 'Culture is the Fruit of Compulsory Continence', *The Harijan*, 21 September, vol. 2, p. 254.
12. Lisa Trivedi refers to 'making an "Indian" body' in Lisa Trivedi. 2007. *Clothing Gandhi's Nation.* Bloomington: Indiana University Press, pp. 113ff., 67–80. Trivedi's discussion of the 'geo-body' resonates with Sumathi Ramaswamy's discussion of the relationship between nationalism and national corporeality. Sumathi Ramaswamy. 2002. 'Visualizing India's Geo-body', in *Contributions to Indian Sociology*, 36(1–2): 151–89.
13. M. K. Gandhi, 1939d. 'Requisite Qualifications', *Harijan*, 25 March, vol. 7, p. 64.
14. M. K. Gandhi, 1938. 'Choice Before Congressmen', *Harijan*, 3 September, vol. 6, p. 24.
15. Quote of M. K. Gandhi in interview with Mahadev Desai, 'Sparks from the Sacred Fire', *Harijan*, 13 May 1933, vol. 1, p. 4.
16. Mahadev Desai, 1939. 'A God-Given Fast', *Harijan*, 11 March, vol. 7, p. 41
17. M. K. Gandhi. 1939c. 'The One and Only Task', *Harijan*, 5 November, p. 43.
18. M. K. Gandhi, 1939b 'My Life', *Harijan*, 4 November, vol. 7, p. 325.
19. Gandhi. 1997. *Hind Swaraj and Other Writings.* Anthony Parel (ed.). Cambridge: Cambridge University Press, p. 96.
20. For example, a note in the *Harijan* reads: 'Abstinence: Propaganda for abstinence has been made in all the districts of Orissa. Gandhiji stressed this point in all

his speeches. Much useful work has been done in the direction in the district of Ganjam'. Nandakisandas, 'Utkal Report for 8 Months Ending 31-3-34', *Harijan*, 19 October 1934, vol. 2, p. 282.

21. Guha, *Dominance without Hegemony*, pp. 135–51.
22. M. K. Gandhi, 1949. 'Ahimsa in Practice', *Harijan*, 27 January, vol. 8, pp. 428-29.
23. M. K. Gandhi, 1939a. 'India's Attitude', 14 October, *Harijan*, vol. 7, p. 1
24. Isaac Deutscher. 1968. *The Non-Jewish Jew and Other Essays*. London: Oxford University Press, p. 35. Fringe communism was one resolution of an insider-outsider identity. Also see Paul Mendes–Flohr. 1999. *German Jews: A Dual Identity*. New Haven: Yale, pp. 21–23, on the struggles of German Jewish intellectuals, especially Rosenzweig, in the 1920s to overcome assimilationist impulses, but also to preserve their sense of being at home in German mainstream culture. On a newer application of this claim, see Yuri Slezkine's discussion of European Jews as 'service nomads'. Yuri Slezkine. 2004. *The Jewish Century*. Princeton: Princeton University Press, pp. 39–40.
25. Deutscher, *Non-Jewish Jew and Other Essays*, p. 35.
26. Minocheher Masani. 1977. *Bliss Was It In That Dawn: A Political Memoir up to Independence*. New Delhi: Arnold-Heinemann Publishers, p. 98.
27. M. N. Roy, *On Stepping Out of Jail*, December 1936. Reproduced in Sibnarayan Ray (ed.). *Selected Works of M. N. Roy*, vol. 4: p. 635.
28. Quoted in V. B. Karnik. 1978. *M. N. Roy: A Political Biography*. Bombay: Nav Jagriti Samaj, p. 399.
29. Subhas Chandra Bose. 1964 rpt (1935). *Indian Struggle. 1920-1942*. Bombay: Asia Publishing House, p. 327.
30. S. M. Ganguly. 1984. *Leftism in India: M. N. Roy and Indian Politics, 1920-1948*. Calcutta: Minerva, p. 161.
31. Karnik, *M. N. Roy: A Political Biography*, p. 404.
32. See letter of Roy to Humayun Kabir, 15 September 1938, NMML: Roy Papers, Kabir File.
33. Jawaharlal Nehru, 'A. I. C. C. and After', 1939.
34. M. N. Roy. 1939b. 'Gandhian Policy Must Go', *Hindustan Standard*, 4 June.
35. M. N. Roy. 1938b. *On the Congress Constitution*, Calcutta: Independent India, p. 54.
36. Ibid., p. 4.
37. 'Letter from M. N. Roy to Gandhi', *Harijan*, 18 November 1939, pp. 341–43.
38. Sibnarayan Ray. 2005. *In Freedom's Quest: A Study of the Life and Works of M. N. Roy*. Calcutta: Minerva, 4(1): 40. Sitaramayya Pattabhi. 1946. *The History of the Indian National Congress*. Delhi: Chand Publishers, vol. 2: p. 166.
39. Sardar Patel had even organised an ostentatious and festive reception for Roy at Haripura the year after his release. *Ananda Bazar Patrika*, 29 December 1936.
40. Gitasree Bandyopadhyay. 1984. *Constraints in Bengal Politics 1921-41. Gandhian Leadership*. Calcutta: Sarat Book House, p. 279ff.; Leonard Gordon. 1974. *Bengal: The Nationalist Movement, 1876-1940*. New York: Columbia University Press, pp. 163–87; Dhananjay Das (ed.). 1972. *Marxbadi Sahitya-Vitarka*. Calcutta: Praima Publishing.
41. C. R. Das, Presidential Speech at the Thirty-seventh Session of the Indian National Congress, Gaya, 26–31 December 1922. Reproduced in A. Zaidi. 1985. *Congress Presidential Addresses*. New Delhi: Publication Department of the Indian Institute of Applied Research, vol. 4: p. 67.

42. Joya Chatterjee. 1994. *Bengal Divided: Hindu Communalism and Partition, 1932-1947*. Cambridge: Cambridge University Press, p. 51.

43. Leonard Gordon. 1990. *Brothers Against the Raj: A Biography of Indian Nationalists Sarat and Subhas Chandra Bose*. New York: Columbia University Press, pp. 271–75.

44. Leonard Gordon, *Brothers Against the Raj*, p. 280.

45. *Hindustan Standard*, 21 June 1938; 'Only Concern Must be Welfare of the Masses', *Indian Express*, 27 July 1937.

46. David Laushey. 1975. *Bengal Terrorism and the Marxist Left*. Calcutta: Firma Mukhopadhyay, p. 123; Many of these prisoners were released en masse in 1938.

47. 'Communism or Socialism Not the Immediate Issue', *Madras Mail*, 27 July 1937.

48. See the weekly gazetteers of the Criminal Intelligence Department, OIOC: L/PJ/12/401. A note from 9 February 1939, p. 54, reads: 'It seems therefore that the stage is gradually being set for M . N. Roy to take a prominent role in Bengal revolutionary affairs'.

49. Leonard Gordon, *Brothers Against the Raj*, p. 311ff.

50. For the Pant Resolution see Nripendra Nath Mitra (ed.). 1939. *The Indian Annual Register*. Calcutta: Annual Register Office, vol. 1: p. 332.

51. Ganguly, *Leftism in India: M. N. Roy and Indian Politics*, pp. 178–88.

52. *Independent India*, 26 November 1939.

53. M. N. Roy. 1939a. 'Fresh Blow to "Forward Bloc"', *Ananda Bazaar Patrika*, March; See Subhas Chandra Bose, *Indian Struggle 1920-1942*, p. 404.

54. Karnik, *M. N. Roy: Political Biography*, p. 426.

55. *The League of Radical Congressmen, Declaration of Objects and Constitution, 1940:* 29, quoted in Karnik, *M. N. Roy: Political Biography*, p. 427.

56. Subhas Chandra Bose. 1962. *Crossroads, 1938-1940*. New York: Asia Publishing House, p. 144. See Letter of Bose to A. N. Chattopadhyaya, 11 September 1939, NMML: Roy Papers, Amiya Nath Chattopadhyaya file.

57. See letter from Jibanlal Chatterjee to Roy, 24 July 1943 on the Jugantar group, NMML: Roy Papers, Jibanlal Chatterjee.

58. Jadugopal Mukerjee to Laushey, *Bengal Terrorism and the Marxist Left*, p. 126.

59. Jadugopal Mukerjee to Roy, 24 December 1939, NMML.

60. A. N. Chattopadhyaya to Roy, 9 September 1940, NMML.

61. Interview with Amlan Datta, who, as a young man, became an associate of M. N. Roy in the 1940s. 20 July 2008.

62. Perhaps the best testament to the disdain for Roy comes in Dhananjan Das' encyclopaedic chronicle of Bengali Marxist thinkers, *Marxbadi Sahitya-Vitarka*, pp. 7–12, in which M. N. Roy's name is not once mentioned. Roy's absence makes for an obvious omission, in an exhaustive catalogue of major Bengali Marxist thinkers of the day including Hirendranath Mukhopadhyay, Girijapati Bhattacharya, Nirendranath Ray, Hirenkumar Sanyal, Sushobhan Sarkar, Dhurjatiprasad Mukhopadhyay, Saheed Surawardy, Bishnu De, Muzaffar Ahmed, Bhupendranath Datta.

63. Gordon, *Brothers Against the Raj*, p. 315; Laushey, *Bengal Terrorism and the Marxist Left*, pp. 111-2; Karnik, *M. N. Roy: A Political Biography*, p. 383; Charles Mascarenhas, a member of the Roy Group, was one of the founders of the Congress Socialist Party.

64. Minocheher Masani and Jayaprakash Narayan both spoke of their great admiration for Roy's work. See Masani, *Bliss Was It In That Dawn*, p. 97.
65. Ibid., p. 29.
66. See discussion in Karnik. 1978. *M. N. Roy: A Political Biography*, p. 383.
67. Collected by A. K. Pillai and published after Roy's release as M. N. Roy. 1997. *Letters to the Congress Socialist Party*, (1934, 1935, 1936), in Sibnarayan Ray (ed.), *Selected Works of M. N. Roy*, Delhi: Oxford University Press, vol. 4.
68. M. N. Roy, 'To the Executive Committees of the Congress Socialist Party', 42, February 1936, *Letters of M. N. Roy*.
69. John Patrick Haithcox. 1971. *Communism and Nationalism: M. N. Roy and Comintern Policy*. Princeton: Princeton University Press, p. 250.
70. Masani, *Bliss Was It In That Dawn*, p. 97.
71. Jayaprakash Narayan, *Socialist Unity and the Congress Socialist Party*, 1971, pp. 6–8.
72. Lakshmi Narayan Lal. 1975. *Jayaprakash: Rebel Extraordinary*. Delhi: India Book Company, p. 92; Seth, *Marxist Theory and Nationalist Politics*, pp. 151–57.
73. Rajani Palme Dutt and Ben Bradley. 1936. 'The Anti-Imperialist People's Front', *International Press Correspondence*, 29 February, pp. 297–300.
74. Overstreet and Windmiller, *Communism in India*, p. 164.
75. *The Communist*, 5 May 1937.
76. *Madras Mail*, 25 July 1937.
77. 'The Presidential Election', *Hindustan Times*, 2 February 1940.
78. P. C. Joshi. 1942. 'Indian Communist Party, Its Policy and Work in the War of Liberation'.
79. See, for example, Ganga Narayan Chandra. 1939. *The Russian Revolution: How M. N. Roy Misinterprets it to the Young Intellectuals of India*. Chandernagore: Sambaya Publishing.
80. Gangadhar Adhikari, one of the leading Communist Party of India intellectuals, wrote on these various topics in the 1940s, including expressing excitement over the changes in China, arguing in favour of the Pakistan and pointing to fascism as the greatest danger. See Gangadhar Adhikari. 1943. *Pakistan and Indian National Unity: The Communist Solution*. Bombay: People's Publishing House.
81. M. N. Roy. 1938c. *Our Differences*. Calcutta: Saraswaty Library, pp. 20–21.
82. Even before Bourdieu's classic discussion of status and 'distinction', André Béteille's seminal work from the 1960s highlighted the importance of studying 'status groups', as opposed to class or caste entities, in Indian society, with special attention to the example of Calcutta. See Andre Béteille.1969. *Social Inequality Selected Readings*. Baltimore: Penguin Books. For a detailed discussion of the rise of this hegemonic communist intellectual culture in Western Bengal, see Rajarshi Dasgupta. 2003. *Marxism and the Middle Class Intelligentsia: Culture and Politics in Bengal 1920s-1950s*. PhD dissertation: Oxford University Press, p. 4.
83. Syamal Krishna Ghosh. 1990. *Parichayer Adda*. Calcutta: K. P. Bagchi, p. 27.
84. Ibid., 4 February 1938, p. 52.
85. Ibid., 11 April 1940, p. 201.
86. Ibid., 8 September 1939, *Adda*, p. 166.

87. Ibid., 24 January 1941, p. 238.
88. The Gazetteer focused on M. N. Roy's activities, as well as that of the Anushilan and Jugantar samitis, which were outright revolutionary organisations.
89. 'A Short Note on M. N. Roy', October 1940–January 1941, National Archives of India: Home/Poll/1941/F.128.
90. V. P. Menon, *The Transfer of Power in India*, 1957, 2: 340.
91. Dietmar Rothermund. 1996. *The Global Impact of the Great Depression, 1929–1939*. London: Routledge, 1996.
92. Gilles Deleuze and Felix Guattari. 1976. *Rhizome: Introduction*. Paris: Editions de Minute, p. 20. Christopher Torpey shows how a nineteenth century trend towards liberalisation of travel gave way to a phase of 'crustacean states' arising by the late nineteenth century. America ended its laissez faire policy on immigration in 1917 and remained relatively impermeable until the 1960s. See Christopher Torpey. 2000. *The Invention of the Passport: Surveillance, Citizenship, and the State*. Cambridge: Cambridge University Press, p. 93ff. Radhika Mongia considers the Canadian passport policies instituted during the first decade of the twentieth century in Radhika Mongia. 1999. 'Race, Nation, Mobility: A History of the Passport', *Public Culture* 11(3): 527–55. On the introduction of identity papers for Indians after the Mutiny/Rebellion see Radhika Singha, 'Colonial Law and Infrastructural Power: Reconstructing Community, Locating the Female Subject', *Studies in History* (2003) 19:1, pp. 87–126.
93. John Agnew and Stuart Corbridge. 1995. *Mastering Space: Hegemony, Territory and International Political Economy*. London: Routledge, pp. 34–35. Karl Polanyi. 1944. *The Great Transformation* New York: Rinehart, pp. 226–48.
94. See, for example, Max Günther. 1924. 'Das politische Ende des deutschen Volkes', *Deutsches Volkstum*, August, vol. 12, p. 458. On *Romanità* see the excellent paper by Fabrizio de Donno, 'Aryanism and 'Romanità' in Post-unification Italian Indology' presented 27 October 2006 at 'Exchange of Ideas and Culture between South Asia and Central Europe' conference, Heidelberg.
95. Duncan Bell. 2007. *The Ideas of Greater Britain: Empire and the Future of the World Order, 1860–1900*. Princeton: Princeton University Press; Gary Wilder. 2005. *The French Imperial Nation-State: Negritude and Colonial Humanism between the Two World Wars*. Chicago: University of Chicago Press.
96. Mark Mazower mentions these as characteristic of the governmentality of the interwar years. In the hankering after empires instead of only nation-states, in the desire to conquer healthy bodies and do away with sick ones, and in the response to the global crisis of capitalism through not only protectionist, but autarchic policies, the political DNA was in place for the rise of totalitarian regimes on a global scale. See Mark Mazower. 1996. *Dark Continent: Europe's Twentieth Century*. New York: A. A. Knopf. See Chapters 1–3. Roger Griffin. 2000. 'The Primacy of Culture: The Current Growth (or Manufacture) of Consensus within Fascist Studies', *Journal of Contemporary History*, 32(1): 21–43.
97. M. N. Roy. 1949. *The Russian Revolution*. Calcutta: Renaissance Publishers, p. 356. Originally published in 1937 and incorporated into 1949 edition.
98. M. N. Roy, 'International Civil War', *War and Revolution*, 1942c.: 47.
99. M. N. Roy. 1942b. 'Introduction'. *India and World*. Lucknow: Radical Democratic Party, p. 1.

100. See Roy to Bhupen Kumar Datta, September 1939, NMML: Roy Papers, Datta File.
101. Roy, *India and War*, Introduction, pp. 1–2.
102. Roy, 'Thesis adopted by the Radicals in the middle of October 1939', *India and War*, p. 52.
103. Roy, 'Resolution of 14 September 1939. Reprinted in *Congress and War*, 1939. Quoted in Sanjay Seth. 1995. *Marxist Theory*, p. 181.
104. A. K. Ghosh. 1939. 'What True Internationalism Demands', *National Front*, 22 October, p. 501.
105. Overstreet and Windmiller, *Communism in India*, p. 183.
106. M. N. Roy. 1940a. *The Alternative*. Bombay: Independent India, pp. 75–76. Quoted in Karnik, *M. N. Roy: Political Biography*, p. 453.
107. Roy, 'Participation in War Efforts', *India and War*, Part 3: xxii.
108. Karnik, *M. N. Roy: Political Biography*, p. 526.
109. V. B. Karnik. 1966. *Indian Trade Unions*. Bombay: Labor Education Service, pp. 129–31.
110. Rajnarayan Chandavarkar. 1994. *The Origins of Industrial Capitalism in India: Business Strategies and the Working Class in Bombay 1900-1940*. Cambridge University Press, p. 420ff.
111. Dipti Kumar Roy. 1990. *Trade Union Movement in India: Role of M. N. Roy*. Calcutta: Minerva Associates.
112. M. N. Roy. 1946b. *New Orientation. Lectures Delivered at the Political Study Camp held at Dehra Dun from May 8-18, 1946*. Calcutta: Renaissance Publishers, p. 173.
113. Ibid., p. 10.
114. Horkheimer and Adorno situated the roots of totalitarianism within the 'Enlightenment', and further suggested that the Enlightenment tradition stretched as far back as the ancient Greeks. Max Horkheimer and Theodor Adorno. 1987 (1944). *Dialectic of Enlightenment*, trans. John Cumming. New York: Herder & Herder, p. 36ff.
115. Roy, *New Orientation*, p. 180. 'We are living in an atmosphere pervaded with the spirit of Fascism. Our fight, therefore must be fought on the home front'. M. N . Roy. 1941c. 'Our Task', *Independent India*, 24 August.
116. Roy, *New Orientation*, p. 180.
117. Roy, 'War and Revolution', December 1942, in *People's Plan for Economic Development*, 1944: 35.
118. M. N. Roy. 1946a. 'I. N. A. and the August Revolution', Calcutta: Renaissance Publishers, p. 4.
119. Roy to Kabir, 17 August 1940, NMML: Roy Papers, Kabir Files.
120. These meetings were sponsored by the Soviet Union, although officially did not take place under its banner. This renewed a form of Soviet internationalism, that is the use of so-called 'front organisations', common before the 6th Congress of 1928. See Pradhan. 1979. *Marxist Cultural Movements in India*, pp. iii–xii.
121. The Seventh Congress of the Comintern met in Moscow in July 1935. Just preceding the Congress, an International Peace Conference of Writers was held in Paris in June, establishing a broad tent among left intellectuals. Also see the Manifesto of the All India Progressive Writers' Conference, Calcutta 24–25 December 1938. Quoted in Pradhan, *Marxist Cultural Movements in India*, p. 19.

122. On M. N. Roy and Abburi Ramakrishna Rao, the Telegu poet, see *Abburi and M. N. Roy, 1996:* pp. 25–63. On Mulk Raj Anand and Roy see 'A Decadent Society Needs Renewal', *The Hindu,* 11 December 1983. On Roy's influence on K. A. Ahmad see Walter Ruben. 1959. *Über die Aufklärung in Indien.* Berlin: Akademie Verlag, p. 16.

123. M. N. Roy appears as a somewhat over-academic though perspicacious revolutionary, under the alias of 'Professor Verma', in Mulk Raj Anand's 1941 novel, *The Sword and the Sickle.*

124. B. N. Banerjee, G. D. Parikh and V. M. Tarkunde. 1994. *People's Plan for Economic Development of India,* Calcutta.

125. For an excellent discussion of the plan see Benjamin Zachariah. 2005. *Developing India.* New Delhi: Oxford University Press, p. 224. See also Vivek Chibber. 2003. *Locked in Place: State Building and Late Industrialization in India.* Princeton: Princeton University Press.

126. M. N. Roy. 1942e. 'The Philosophy of the Twentieth Century', *Scientific Politics,* 197–98.

127. Banerjee et al., *People's Plan: For Economic Development in India,* 1944: 4.

128. Roy, *New Orientation,* p. 165. 'The practice of "Western Democracy" is equally disappointing'. On not following either the American or the Russian model, but developing a new approach to development, see M. N. Roy. 1948b. 'Our Future', *Independent India,* 28 November: 572–3.

129. Sugata Bose. 1997. 'Instruments and Idioms', in Frederick Cooper (ed.), *International Development and the Social Sciences,* p. 52.

130. M. N. Roy. 1945a. 'Constitution of Free India: A Draft' in B. S. Sharma (ed.), *Radical Humanism of M. N. Roy,* p. 20. The Council of State was to be selected by a group of engineers, economists, scientists, medical men, jurists and historians.

131. Ibid., p. 21.

132. M. N. Roy. 1941b. 'New Federal Scheme for India', *Independent India,* 9 March.

133. M. N. Roy. 1952. 'Nationalism and Freedom', editorial, *Radical Humanist,* 25 May.

134. Speech delivered speech in Madras, 22 February 1941. Quoted in Karnik, *M. N. Roy: A Political Biography,* p. 506.

135. M. K. Gandhi, 1942. 'One Thing Needful', *Harijan,* 10 May, vol. 9, p. 148.

136. M. K. Gandhi. 1942. 'One Thing Needful', *Harijan,* 10 May.

137. *Independent India,* 22 February 1942.

138. Tanika Sarkar. 1985. 'Communal Riots in Bengal', in Mushirul Hasan (ed.), *Communal and Pan-Islamic Trends in Colonial India.* Delhi: Manohar Publications, p. 296; Sugata Bose. 1986. *Agrarian Bengal Economy, Social Structure, and Politics.* Cambridge: Cambridge University Press.

139. Speech given at Poona on 2 September 1939, quoted in Joshi and Josh, *Struggle for Hegemony India,* vol. 2: p. 222.

140. V. D. Savarkar at the 19th session of All India Hindu Mahasabha held at Ahmedabad, Lahore. Central Hindu Yuvak Sabha, 1938.

141. See M. N. Roy to Habibur Rahman, 30 July 1939, NMML: Roy Papers, Rahman File.

142. M. N. Roy. 1939. 'Mr. M. N. Roy's Call to Muslim Youths', *Amrita Bazaar Patrika*, 5 April.
143. 'Mohani to Join Radicals', *Amrita Bazar Patrika*, August 1939; Hirendranath Mukhopadhyay. 1983. *Under Communism's Crimson Colors: Reflections on Marxism, India and World Scene*. New Delhi: People's Publishing House, p. 112.
144. Joya Chatterji, *Bengal Divided: Hindu Communalism and Partition, 1932-1947*, p. 15.
145. M. N. Roy. 1974. *Historical Role of Islam: An Essay on Islamic Culture*. Lahore: Sind Sagar Academy, p. 1.
146. Ibid., pp. 2-3.
147. Ibid., p. 18.
148. Ibid., p. 67.
149. Ibid., p. 90.
150. Humayun Kabir. 1958. 'Rationalism, Democracy, Humanism', *Radical Humanist*, 21 February, p. 597.
151. Humayun Kabir. 1958. 'Radicalism, Democracy and Humanism: Islam in Indian History', *Radical Humanist*, 21 December, p. 597.
152. See Ray, *In Freedom's Quest*, vol. 4: p. 99; See correspondence between Roy and Abu Syed Ayub beginning in April 1949, NMML: Roy Papers. They largely dealt on evaluation of the Soviet Union. They discuss Ayub's formulations of a humanistic perspective 'beyond Marxism'.
153. 'Mr M. N. Roy's Reply to Critics', *Statesman*, August 1938.
154. Ibid.
155. Letter from Ellen Gottschalk to Jawaharlal Nehru, 10 September 1938, NMML: Roy Papers, Ellen Gottschalk correspondence.
156. Ray, *In Freedom's Quest*, 4(1): 162.
157. *Independent India*, 7 April 1940.
158. Roy to Sushil Dey, 5 July 1947. NMML: Roy Papers.
159. Oral history interview with R. M. Pal, 19 January 2005, Delhi.
160. Syamal Krishna Ghosh reproduces some of Roy's half-Bengali, half-English sentences in Sudhindranath Datta's *adda* of 1941. See Ghosh, *Parichayer Adda*, p. 235.
161. The lived versus the self-reflective forms of cosmopolitanism can be distinguished. Within the massive literature on this distinction, Kwame Anthony Appiah. 2000. *Cosmopolitanism: Ethics in a World of Strangers*. New York: Yorton, offers a particularly precise discussion.
162. Lovestone to Roy, 5 October 1934, NMML: Roy Papers.
163. Ted Morgan. 1999. *A Covert Life: Jay Lovestone, Communist, Anti-Communist, and Spymaster*, Robert Alexander. 1981. *The Right Opposition: The Lovestoneites and the International Communist Opposition of the 1930s*, Westport: Greenwood Press.
164. Their debates were particularly intense in 1937, during the Spanish War. See Roy to Jay Lovestone, NMML, 19 October 1937. Roy's stance moved in Loveston's direction by the end of the Second World War. Alexander, *The Right Opposition: The Lovestoneites and the International Communist Opposition of the 1930s*.

165. Karnik, M. N. Roy: Political Biography, p. 591.
166. Peter Coleman. 1989. The Liberal Conspiracy: The Congress for Cultural Freedom and the Struggle for the Mind of Postwar Europe. New York: Free Press, pp. 149–53.
167. M. N. Roy. 1953e. 'Stalin's Obituary', Radical Humanist, 15, 17 March; Roy was critical of the U.S. involvement in the Korean War. Radical Humanist, 8 April 1952.
168. See Roy correspondence with J. Walcher and Jan Pollack in 1939, NMML, Roy Files. Walcher immigrated to the United States in 1941, but returned to the GDR in 1946 to take up activity in the trade union movement.
169. August Thalheimer and Heinrich Brandler ended up in Cuba. Meanwhile many of the KPD-O members in Paris travelled on to the United States. Others such as Theodor Bergmann fled to Palestine.
170. Many of Thalheimer's manuscripts were destroyed during a hurricane. One completed essay, 'Über die Kunst der Revolution und die Revolution der Kunst', is available in the FZH (Hamburg) Archive. See Theodor Bergmann. 2004. Die Thalheimers: die Geschichte einer Familie undogmatischer Marxisten. Hamburg: VSA-Verlag, p. 194ff.
171. Thalheimer passed away in 1948. A number of Roy's letters to Jay Lovestone in the 1940s contain inquiries about the whereabouts and activities of August Thalheimer.
172. He regularly spoke of 'his family'. See, for example, 'I am glad to know that our family (the international organisation of Opposition Communists) remains so firm and optimistic', Roy to Ellen Gottschalk, 7 December 1932, Letters from Jail, 1943: 39.
173. Roy to Lovestone, 3 May 1937, NMML: Roy Papers.
174. Oral history interview with R. M. Pal, Delhi, 19 January 2005.
175. See Ray, In Freedom's Quest, 4: 2, 2007: 358.
176. Swami Bharati Agehananda. 1961. The Ochre Robe. London: George Allen & Unwin. See also an excellent discussion of Agehananda's life and work in Jeffrey Kripal. 1995. Roads of Excess, Palaces of Wisdom: Eroticism & Reflexivity in the Study of Mysticism. Chicago: University of Chicago Press, pp. 207–49.
177. Kripal, Roads of Excess, Palaces of Wisdom, p. 221.
178. Swami Bharati Agehananda, Dear Lalita, 1962: 50, quoted in Kripal, Roads of Excess, Palaces of Wisdom, p. 251.
179. On Spratt's arrival in India in May 1926, see OIOC: L/PJ/12/308, p. 5. He was closely associated with Muzaffar Ahmad from 1928 till the Meerut Conspiracy Trial of 1933.
180. Phillip Spratt. 1955. Blowing Up India: Reminiscences and Reflections of a Former Comintern Emissary. Calcutta: Prachi Prakashan, pp. 91–100.
181. Buddhadeb Basu. 1948. An Acre of Green Grass. Calcutta: Papyrus, p. 65
182. Kabir was co-founder of the important Calcutta literary magazine, Chaturanga, along with Buddhadeb Basu in 1938.
183. Vivid and detailed descriptions given in Ray, In Freedom's Quest, 4(2): 257–58. On S. K. Dey in the United States see Ramachandra Guha, How Much Should A Person Consume?: Environmentalism in India and the United States, 2006: 50.

184. Max Horkheimer to Ellen Roy, 6 June 1956, Frankfurt University, Horkheimer Nachlass: III-11-298-301. See Surindar Suri. 1959. *Nazism and Social Change*. Calcutta: K. L. Mukhopadhyay. Suri also published a number of studies in German, including *Der Kommunismus in Südostasien*, in *Schriftreihe der Nierdersäschischen Landeszentralefür Politische Bildung*, Heft 3, 1965.

185. See extensive correspondence between Roy and Wadia in the NMML Roy Papers, spanning 1939 to 1953. Wadia was a founding trustee of the Indian Renaissance Institute. See *Independent India*, 3 November 1946, p. 631.

186. Anonymous. 1937. 'Pure Philosophy of Materialism', *Madras Mail*, 25 July. Article reproduces excerpts from M. N. Roy's presidential speech at the Madras Presidency Radical Youth Conference on July 25 1937.

187. Ibid.

6

Radical Humanism

As the South Asian nation–states were established in 1947 and the sense of the givenness of their arrival set in, the principle of hope and anticipation of new time, always present in Roy's intellectual project, was set in increasingly stark relief. If Roy once waged a revolutionary war on colonial universalism using the tool of futuristic imaginings and 'dream histories', now, in the context of the creation of India and Pakistan, his project consisted in preserving or protecting hope from the occurrences of the present. Roy's final utopian writings bridged intellectual debates occurring within regional, national and international spheres of intellectual debate, about Indian anti-colonial cosmopolitanism, the Bengali avant-garde's views of selfhood and creativity, and post-Marxist humanism.

Utopia could no longer be achieved by overt political action under current conditions, Roy believed. His Radical Humanist Movement, inaugurated in 1946, was a project to preserve notions of freedom obscured by the political tectonics of the partition years and the geo-political tensions of the Second World War era. Freedom, in its truest form, he concluded, was the ability for individuals to find their own secret meanings within the accepted canons of knowledge, as well as the capacity for individuals to deploy their bodily and mental energies to the fullest extent. Both exegesis and ascesis played an important role in Roy's late theory of postcolonial freedom. Yet, there was also something of the consolatory and therapeutic at work, as opposed to the revolutionary and agentive.

Roy made the position of interstitiality a place from which to define selfhood. If Gandhi imagined a continent self, Roy imagined a 'shiftless, but also truly adventurous' one.[1] He declared himself a 'man from nowhere' and a 'heretic', disappointed by communism, proudly estranged from anti-colonial nationalism, critical of Swadeshi internationalism and sensitive to the complexities of a fractal earth.[2]

Social displays of estrangement and loneliness became important elements of Roy's self-fashioning. One must not forget that the figure of the renouncer had a cultural resonance for him. The ascetic, or *sannyasin*, who leaves society and retreats for spiritual contemplation enjoyed a special status in the cultural field of Roy's Bengali Hindu background.[3] Roy said in a statement to the members of his own party in 1946, 'You simply disregarded my ideas, took up a tolerant attitude: the man seems to have gone a little out of his mind, and is talking all manner of strange things; nevertheless, occasionally he does have good ideas; that may be enough for the time being, eventually, we shall drift back to our spiritual home and this interregnum will pass over as a nightmare'.[4] At his August 1946 Radical Humanist study camp, Roy spoke about his 'lonely road'.[5] In a 1949 letter to Bertram Wolfe at Stanford, a friend from his days in Mexico City, he mused that 'it is less humiliating to plow one's lone furrow', than to have compromised one's convictions.[6] He often employed another religious image, the 'heretic', as a favourite term of self-description. In 1946, Roy described himself as 'a tormented soul...' whose 'political practice, be it liberal, democratic

Illustration 6.1   Roy in 1953.

Source: Sibnarayan Ray, *In Freedom's Quest: Life of M. N. Roy*, vol. 4, Part 2. Used with permission.

or proletarian' had failed to produce the 'promised result'.[7] In India he fashioned himself increasingly as a persecuted outcast from the power centres of anti-colonial struggle. On another occasion he said, 'I have had enough of politics. If the chance for democracy came again, I hope others would make a better job'.[8]

Anti-Colonial Cosmopolitanism

But Roy was not so distant from mainstream modes of anti-colonial thought as his own claims suggested. His project can be understood as belonging to the same conversation as thinkers such as M. K. Gandhi, Rabindranath Tagore and Muhammad Iqbal, all of whom contemplated the requirements and possibilities of anti-colonial cosmopolitanism in India. As Indian thinkers articulated visions of difference and cultural autonomy, they also simultaneously imagined new circuits for travelling beyond the limits of group identity toward larger solidarities. Imagining the self beyond local or familiar bounds was deeply rooted in anti-colonial thought. We cannot understand Gandhi's discussion about the continent nation-body without also relating it to his vision of a new internationalism born of mutual recognition and esteem among cultures worldwide.[9] The end of Swaraj was to help create a peaceful human community, Gandhi stressed. Gandhi wrote in 1939, 'India has therefore to tell a very distraught and maddened world that there is another path that humanity must tread if it would save itself from these periodical disasters...'[10] Ashis Nandy has analysed at least six avenues through which Gandhi's thought aimed at reworking the assumptions of global human exchange.[11] Discourses on universalism and humanity were important implements in the toolbox of anti-colonial thinkers, providing the ethical context in which the nation could be imagined.

The point is not to argue that Roy prescribed mediation and the bridging of borders, meanwhile other, more mainstream, anti-colonial intellectuals solely pursued autonomy and the strengthening of bounded selfhoods. Such a juxtaposition would be facile and incorrect. The task is to understand what was distinctive about M. N. Roy's variety of anti-colonial cosmopolitanism, and how that difference relates to the other conversation games he participated in.

Indian cosmopolitan discourse was traditionally phrased in terms of civilisational continuity and exchange between high traditions.[12] In the writings of diverse thinkers of the early twentieth century, and perhaps most explicitly in the work of M. K. Gandhi, Rabindranath Tagore and Muhammad Iqbal, an insistence on some notion of civilisational continuity played an important role. Civilisation, as a supranational domain of cultural holism, provided an important ethical basis for grounding possible forms of Indian national autonomy. These notions of civilisation, such as Tagore's notion of Greater India, or Iqbal's Islamic Universalism, or Gandhi's view of shared Sanskritic civilisation, all established the contours of a collective identity that ran deep into the past, but that also facilitated ethical exchange and interaction across cultural bounds.[13]

Communist internationalism, as it was rigorously interpreted by M. N. Roy, once had inspired him to deny notions of inheritance and tradition altogether, and to assert that only the cross-cutting sociological category of class properly defined social collectives. Yet, by his late writings, disillusioned with communist internationalism, Roy felt that it was not philosophically satisfactory to speak of a free-floating self adrift in a boundless human universe, solely relating to others in terms of production relations. Inheritance, traditions and belonging played an important role in defining not only the social experience, but the moral sensibilities of individuals, Roy came to believe. 'What is necessary to-day is to draw inspiration from the store of the civilised man's spiritual heritage. That alone can guide the steps of mankind out of the present impasse and towards a still unexplored future believed to be full of promise'.[14]

If we read his texts *Materialism* (1940) and *Reason, Romanticism and Revolution* (1952–55) together, we see that the term 'civilisation' begins to play an increasingly important role in Roy's late thought, although he uses it in an uncommon and avant-garde way. In his late phase, Roy maintained that it was up to the individual to imagine his own 'dream' civilisation, with like-minded thinkers stretching into the past. Roy spoke of his 'brotherhood of men attracted by the adventure of ideas, keenly conscious of the urge for freedom'.[15] While Roy criticised notions of cultural holism, he introduced his own chosen regime of authenticity by creating a chosen lineage.[16]

Roy's late works were utopian genealogies of this hidden cosmopolitan humanist tradition in which he fit. He focused on uncovering a lineage of humanists and heretics, and on grafting himself onto that line as a modern interpreter and renovator. He traced a submerged tradition that ran through the writings of Anaxogoras, Heraclitus, Pythagoras, Democritus, Diogenes. It also ran through Kanada, Kapila, Gautam, through Vaisheshik and Sankhya philosophy, through the

Gita and the writings of Sankaracharya, through the Carvaka system of philosophy and Buddhist thought. The tradition connected him to the German *Aufklärung*, as well as the *Sturm und Drang*, and to thinkers such as Spinoza, Hegel and Marx. Roy maintained that all these figures together formed an inheritance through space and time, and at the crux of their disparate systems and thought was a 'materialist monism', that all life was matter and all matter was one. Finally, contemporary experimental sciences were carrying this tradition forward. 'The space–time conception of the Theory of Relativity is yet another step in advance towards a materialist monism... Even the electron has been traced down to a state where particles disappear. Today the substratum of the world has been revealed to be an all-pervasive substance'.[17]

Radical Humanism

The Radical Democratic Party failed to win a single seat in the Constituent Assembly elections of early 1946. Roy was forced to recognise the limitations of his abilities as a mobiliser in the field of party politics. There was not much place for interstitial politics in the context of postcolonial arrival. 'After much thought, I finally came to the conclusion that our party had no root. We are neither Marxist nor Communists nor anything else...', he said to his group at their annual meeting in 1946.[18] This played a major role in his decision to disband his political party after its fourth All-India meeting in December 1948. Reflecting on the fits and starts of his organisational attempts since 1937, Roy said, 'the Party never claimed a strong mechanical apparatus with huge mass membership which could be no more than a blind following... but it did surpass any other group in the country in respect of its intellectual integrity and spiritual strength'.[19]

Roy proposed to deterritorialise his movement, to make it a borderless community of like-minded individuals. 'Whoever agreed with us, we do not ask them to become members of any organisation; but we shall expect them to act according to their conviction. We are giving up a rigidly organised existence because we do not want to create a barrier around us, excluding anybody as outsiders. We do not want to monopolise the result of our efforts'.[20] The name of his magazine *Independent India* was changed to *The Radical Humanist* in April 1949, the *Marxian Way Quarterly* was renamed the *Humanist Way*. Roy finally set himself to work on establishing his Frankfurt School in India, the Indian Renaissance Institute at Dehra Dun.[21]

Roy's 'radical humanism' declared modernist faith in the 'laws of science', and in evolutionary biology as setting forth undeniable common principles for all life. The 'biological urge to life' was that which 'developed into the conscious need of a human being to evolve his personality, his individuality'.[22] At the heart of this 'urge to life' was the '...harmony and law-governedness inherent in man. They are the foundation of the special human qualities'. Thus, following Roy's utopian logic, selfhood arises out of the biological urges, and the desires of the self accord with the inherent order of the universe.[23]

Fundamentally, what the human animal desired in Roy's interpretation, was 'spiritual freedom', something even more satisfying than economic or political liberation. 'The urge for spiritual freedom ... has been the lever of entire human development, ever since the birth of the species. It is the striving to feel that man is a free agent, that he can act according to his judgment and is capable of discriminating good from evil and right from wrong without being haunted by the preoccupation that he is helplessly at the mercy of some capricious superhuman power'.[24] In his monistic view, the mind and the body, the judgements and the instincts, were identical. 'If the Universe is a cosmos, it is arbitrary to break it up into matter and mind. A monistic naturalism does not allow evolutionary ethics to distinguish a world of values from a world of facts'.[25] Roy's notion of 'monistic naturalism' obviously resonated with the religious discourses that galvanised the Swadeshi avant-garde in their destruction of colonial universalism's gradient of consciousness.[26]

But Roy's interest in biology, science and spirituality was also informed by debates on the civic role of scientific discovery that had reached a peak in the interwar years. While in prison, Roy read books by Albert Einstein, Bertrand Russell, Arthur Stanley Eddington, James Jeans and Erwin Schrödinger, all written in the 1920s and 1930s, with the aim of proposing applications for the new discoveries in theoretical physics, as well as insights from logic and mathematics, to questions of epistemology, as well as to problems of ethics.[27]

Roy's Radical Humanist Movement proposed to combine 'scientific rationalism' with the 'romantic faith' that 'man is the maker of his world'. Revolution, in Roy's late writings, no longer had a direct referent in the material or social world, but referred specifically to an alteration of consciousness. It entailed mental process and a shift in viewpoint.[28] 'I am of the opinion that the solution to our problems, which in varying manifestations are confronting the whole world, will be to make individuals conscious of their almost unlimited potentialities, and of the rights and responsibilities which flow from these'.[29] The revolution that would change society and recreate the world would entail a mental act, namely the realisation that it was in the biological nature of the individual to continually reinvent itself. Human existence consists in 'endless processes of unfoldment of the potentialities which are of biological heritage'.[30] The advent of revolution would come, wrote Roy, when individuals realised that the claims of science and those of romanticism were at one. It was not that Roy was escaping into a utopian conception, or that he was receding into the solipsistic interiority of the bourgeois self, but rather he was struggling to distil out the essence of his Swadeshi–Marxist hope. If the contents of anti-colonial hope could be distilled and articulated in their purest form, then they could also be preserved for use at a more opportune time in the future. And this distillation produced, in Roy's view, a postcolonial sublime: 'That philosophy is sublime which opens up before mankind the vista of infinity without deluding it into the wilderness of metaphysical abstractions'.[31]

Post-Swadeshi Modernism

Roy's late thought resonated with that of many contemporary Swadeshi modernists. Rabindranath Tagore at his Viswa Bharati University at Shantiniketan founded institution in order to cultivate imagination (*kalpana*), creativity (*srsti*), and essence (*rasa*) in his students as ambassadors of Indian and Asian culture to the world.[32] '*Rasa* is not static', Tagore wrote. 'It is not rigid, but soft, and mobile everywhere. It can be widely dispersed, and because of this it can shake the world with its ability to create variations. There is no end to its novelty'.[33] Aurobindo Ghosh offered another expression. He exited politics after emerging from imprisonment in 1909 on charges of Swadeshi insurgency. Moving to Pondicherry in 1910 he established a renowned yoga ashram that drew a large international following.[34] Aurobindo expounded the notion of 'integral yoga' that 'hastens the soul's development'.[35] 'Each man who enters the realms of yogic experience is free to follow his own way...', he wrote. In his *Future Evolution of Man* (1962) and *The Future Poetry* (1953) he argued that an unprecedented evolution of mankind was still to be expected, in which spiritually enlightened humans would glimpse the transcendent universal principle at the centre of all being.[36]

Roy's Indian Renaissance Institute, founded in the hill station of Dehra Dun in Uttar Pradesh in 1949, stood in family relation to a number of post-Swadeshi modernist institutes, such as Rabindranath Tagore's Viswa Bharati University (founded 1921), Aurobindo Ghosh's Pondicherry Ashram (founded 1926), Girishchandra Bose's Indian Psychoanalytic Society (founded 1921), and Kalidas Nag's Greater India Society (founded 1923). Another member of this cohort, Meghnad Saha, a world-renowned physicist who collaborated with Einstein, established the National Academy of Science (founded 1930).[37] Meanwhile, Prasanta Mahalanobis, a member like Kalidas Nag of Tagore's inner circle of young modernists, set up the Indian Statistical Institute in 1931. Indeed, what could be more modernist than to ground a school or academy or to invent a movement? Benoy Kumar Sarkar, the great Swadeshi avant-garde thinker, saw this trend of founding schools as an affirmation of the abiding modernism of India. '*Parisats* or academies, whether stationary or peripatetic, have indeed existed in India since time immemorial', Sarkar wrote.[38] In the period from 1925 to 1938, Sarkar himself went on to found no less than eight institutes (all at the same address at 9 Panchanan Ghose Lane!), including the Bengali Society of Economics, the Bengali German Knowledge Society and the Bengali Dante Society.[39] Sarkar was hailed by his admirers, such as Radhakamal Mukerjee, as 'the idol of the young [Swadeshi] intellectuals, the focus of national idealism and the spear-head of the national education movement in later times'.[40] Unfortunately, space does not permit a detailed treatment of the web of the Swadeshi avant-garde thinkers in the interwar years; the topic certainly deserves a book of its own. The point to emphasise is that Roy's activities belonged to this same family relation of post-Swadeshi intellectual activism in the interwar years.

Global Humanism

Mid-century humanism sought to find meaning in the face of unprecedented human destruction. In 1952, Roy became the vice president of the inaugural session of the International Humanist and Ethical Union in Amsterdam, although he could not attend due to ill health. The Union was established among British, American, Dutch, Austrian, Belgian organisations, as well as the Indian Radical Humanists.[41] Critics at the time said that 'Royists of tomorrow aspire, through political action, to create a new heaven on earth before long'. It represented a 'dogmatism of "scientific materialism", which was just as bad as a "dogmatism of religion"'.[42]

The 1940s and 1950s were decades in which a worldwide group of thinkers were discussing 'Man' before the backdrop of unprecedented human destruction. Following the end of the Second World War, a flurry of international summits arose to ensure the birth of a new internationalism.[43] Radhakamal Mukherjee's assertion that an earth 'radiant with calamity' provided the background needed to see an inclusive family of humankind, recalled Kant's statement during the European world war of 1793 that contemplating a possible 'vast grave' of humankind was the only truly effective spur to resolving a cosmopolitan peace.[44] Erik Erikson remarked after the war that the possibility of 'species-wide destruction' was making possible, for the first time, a 'species-wide identity'.[45] The particular quality of mid-century humanism, with its concern for the cross-cultural category of 'man', arose from experiences of devastation and vulnerability, not from the bravado of 'grand theory narratives'.[46]

Hannah Arendt reflected on the new era of the 1950s, observing 'man [is] being thrown back upon himself'.[47] And Ernst Cassirer put it slightly differently in his 1944 *Essay on Man*, 'Man is declared to be that creature who is constantly in search of himself — a creature who in every moment of his existence must examine and scrutinize the conditions of his existence. In this scrutiny, in this critical attitude toward human life, consists the real value of human life'.[48] French existentialism explored the possibility of humanism in the midst of devastation and absurdity. Jean-Paul Sartre became a symbol of the existentialist resolution with his 1946 manifesto, 'Existentialisme c'est un humanisme'.[49] Meanwhile Christian thinkers such as Reinhold Niebuhr and Jacques Maritain proposed that only a rebirth of Christian faith could ground humanism in the wake of Marxism's secular failure. The New Left in Europe and America, with major exponents such as Herbert Marcuse and his championing of the pleasure principle and polymorphous perversity, spoke of transforming the whole notion of class revolution to one of sexual revolution, to give occasion to a less destructive and more creative social order.[50]

Roy regularly and critically reviewed European monographs in the *Marxian Way*, including books by Ernst Cassirer, Reinhold Niebuhr, Sidney Hook, Jacques Barzun, P. A. Sorokin and Jacques Maritain.[51] Roy's philosophical journal, *The Radical Humanist*, published both commissioned and reprinted articles by Arthur Koestler, Erich Fromm, Raymond Aron, C. S. Lewis, H. R. Trevor-Roper, Isaac Deutscher, Heinrich Brandler, and others, showing how attuned it was to European and American philosophical and social scientific discussions.[52] There were discussions of French existentialism, the Frankfurt School and the intellectual Left in Britain.[53] Occasionally, the Indian Renaissance Institute would receive visitors from abroad. The young Gloria Steinem wrote an article for *The Radical Humanist* in 1957 after her visit to the institute.

M. N. Roy's thought was a Swadeshi–Luxemburgist contribution to this humanist conversation, clearly working from some shared assumptions, but also drawing on resources outside European discourse. The influence of Brahmo exegesis, dharmic asceticism and the Swadeshi avant-garde left traces in Roy's work, just as much as did 1920s German Marxist thought. M. N. Roy situated the self athwart the constructs of the 'West' and the 'East', in a sublime realm of 'the human' characterised by underlying unity. He would retort to some European humanists that a peaceful universal community of man was possible not because Western universalism had spread to the ends of the earth, and not because the West and the East were finally able to meet on equal footing after postcolonial independence, and certainly not because the East had come bearing spiritual peace, but because human bodies had urges, regardless of their cultural location, and these urges were universally shared among all humans, and also reflected in the very order of the natural world.[54] Once all peoples came to recognise this deep monism at the heart of existence, then all configurations of culture, civilisation and nation would be seen in the light of a higher sublime truth. My point here is that this idea cannot be traced solely to deep traditions of Indian thought, nor to Western Marxist conceptions — it arose from the amalgamation and admixture of diverse thought traditions under the global horizon of nineteenth and twentieth-century modernism, as well as Roy's own efforts to make sense of his social experience as an intermediary and traveller between very different social worlds. The hermeneutic 'middle world' in which varied influences meet and fuse is a more appropriate field for situating M. N. Roy's ideas, as opposed to attempting to assimilate him to problematically reified categories of either 'indigenous' or 'Western' thought.

Return of Hope

The old often return to the questions first posed in youth, surprised they had in fact not travelled so far. In the years before his passing, Roy took stock of his life of crossings. After a major fall down a steep craggy hill in Mussoorie in 1952, his health, already fragile, began to quickly deteriorate. In August he suffered a cerebral thrombosis resulting in partial paralysis. And two years alter, after some periods of improvement, he passed away on 24 January 1954. His friends and associates recalled the following excerpt from his 1946 writings:

> When, as school body of fourteen, I began my political life, which may end in nothing, I wanted to be free. Independence, complete and absolute, is a newfangled idea. The old-fashioned revolutionaries thought in terms of freedom. In those days, we had not read Marx. We did not know about the existence of the proletariat. Still, many spent their lives in jail and went to the gallows. There was no proletariat to propel them. They were not conscious of class struggle. They did not have the dream of Communism. But they had the human urge to revolt against the intolerable conditions of life... I began my political life with that spirit, and I still draw my inspiration farther from that spirit than from the three volumes of *Capital* or three-hundred volumes by the Marxists.[55]

Roy had spent his lifetime fusing conversations and ideologies that circulated in regional, national and international zones of thought and debate. His distinction lay not only in his particular political objective, and his anticipatory vision of the Indian future, but also in his unusually open disposition towards the many new conversation games and social worlds he joined over the course of his life.

In his last years, he tempered his views on Gandhi, and even started adopting Gandhian language to describe his own political ideals.[56] In 1946, he proclaimed that his own organisation required a period of 'spiritual purging and self-examination'.[57] Reflecting on his relationship to Gandhi since the 1920s, the role of the Mahatma as his anti-muse, Roy said, 'as a student of philosophy, I have tried to appreciate the positive aspects of Gandhism. But at the same time, I could not overlook its obvious defects and fallacies... The most laudable aspect of Gandhism was the desire to purify public life and raise the moral standards of politics... But Gandhism also stands for human freedom. It has even been called a sort of humanism... But in distinction to Marxism, Gandhi brought back religion into politics, in social science and even in economics'.[58] In a critical obituary, Roy criticised Gandhi for inadvertently fanning the flames of Hindu nationalism in India, despite his efforts to bring communal harmony.[59] But later, a full year after Gandhi's death, Roy commented, 'the practice of the precepts of purifying politics with truth and non-violence alone will immortalise the memory of the Mahatma. Monuments of mortar and marble will perish, but the light of the sublime message of truth and non-violence will shine forever'.[60]

Talk of anti-culturalism and revolutionary politics during the war years gave way in Roy's work to a more meditative language that sounded old and wise, 'Humanist politics must be a moral force; it must get out of the struggle for power of the political parties'.[61] Roy was conscious of this increasing resonance with Gandhian ethics, even as he came to this appreciation in retrospect.

The poet Sudhindranath Datta soliloquised, in his obituary tribute, that M. N. Roy had 'retired into the wilderness... Inevitably, therefore, he was widely misunderstood in India where virtue has been either cloistered or compartmentalised, and as he refused to compromise, or to subordinate reason to emotion, or break up the unity of the world by arbitrary hostility to some parts, militant nationalism, whether of the old or the new school, went so far as to consider him an enemy of the State'.[62] At the very end, Roy's was a sublime conception, characterised by the location of human meaning beyond the immediate world and in an enduring unity of human and natural life.

With the arrival of nation–states in South Asia, Roy felt that preserving his hope in its sublime form was the best way to protect it from the degradation of the present.[63] This was a period of unexampled bloodshed and violence. The Calcutta killings of August 1946 left more than 4,000 dead. Riots in Bombay, Noakhali, Tippera, Garhmukteswar and in areas of Bihar added to the year's number of casualties. Riots followed in a number of other regions throughout the following year. And this led to the holocaust that began in August 1947, to more than an estimated three million missing people by 1951.[64] On the coming of Independence, Roy wrote: 'On August 15th, the vocal section of the Indian people, drugged and duped into a delirium, will ceremoniously enthrone the Leviathan. The exacting deity will demand more and more sacrifice. Eventually, he will thirst for blood. The Leviathan is the God of War'.[65]

In a surrealist essay, Roy imagined an angel flying to India in 1942 and returning in 1946 to 'have a closer look at things'. The situation he met did not evince jubilation, but '[he] returned to [his] oblivion with a heavy heart, and for these four years kept on sorrowfully watching things go from bad to worse. [His] gloomy view about the future of Asia was born out by the march of events'.[66]

Whereas in the 1920s, it was clear that utopianism was used as a tool or weapon in the charged effort to blast apart the 'is' with the 'ought', it seemed now that hope had to be preserved and protected. In the study of M. N. Roy's thought, we seem to encounter something of a life-cycle of utopianism. As the structures of the world changed, so too did Roy's interpretative responses. Perhaps Roy's notion of utopia was not dissimilar from that of Walter Benjamin as he wrote of the 'Angelus Novus' while fleeing from the Nazis in 1940. The 'angel of history' is caught in a storm blowing from paradise, Benjamin imagined. 'This storm irresistibly propels him into the future to which his back is turned'. Benjamin's angel has 'eyes staring, mouth open, and wings spread' as 'he sees one single catastrophe which keeps piling wreckage upon wreckage and hurls it in front of his feet'. In the case of M. N. Roy's angel, whom he imagines flying to earth in 1946, the creature concludes its autumnal comments, 'let me finish on a note of cautious optimism. Even a confirmed pessimist like myself can see a dim ray of hope in the midst of a suffocating gloom. When the war comes Indian fighters of freedom will have a chance to turn the tide of history'. In the case of both angels, in the case of both men, keeping hope had become a matter of seeing a secret promise hidden amidst debris.

Notes

1. Erik Erikson. 1964. 'Identity and Uprootedness in Our Time', in *Insight and Responsibility: Lectures on the Ethical Implications of Psychoanalytic Insight*. New York: W. W. Norton, p. 99.
2. Bert Gasenbeek and Babu Gogineni (eds.). 2002. *International Humanist and Ethical Union, 1952–2002: Past, Present and Future*. Utrecht: De Tijdstroom, p. 14.
3. Romila Thapar. 2001. 'Dissent and Protest in the Early Indian Tradition', in *Cultural Pasts: Essays in Early Indian History*. New Delhi: Oxford University Press, p. 215.
4. M. N. Roy. 1946b. *New Orientation: Lectures Delivered at the Political Study Camp held at Dehra Dun from May 8–18, 1946*. Calcutta: Renaissance Publishers, p. 62.
5. Ibid., p. 7.
6. Roy to Bertram Wolfe, 21 September 1949, NMML: Roy Papers.
7. *Independent India*, 11 December 1946, p. 746.
8. Roy to Louis Coney, 20 August 1952, NMML: Roy Papers.
9. A powerful expression of Gandhi's cosmopolitanism is provided in his letter exchange with Rabindranath Tagore, collected and edited by Sabyasachi Bhattacharya. 1997. *The Mahatma and the Poet: Letters and Debates Between Gandhi and Tagore, 1915–1941*. Delhi: National Book Trust India. 1997.
10. M. K. Gandhi. 1939a. 'India's Attitude', *Harijan*, 14 October, vol. 1.
11. Nandy brilliantly discusses the critiques of scientism, technicism, professionalism, hyper-adulthood, hyper-masculinity, among other dimensions, in Gandhi's thought. See Ashis Nandy. 1987. 'From Outside the Imperium: Gandhi's Cultural Critique of the West', in *Traditions, Tyranny and Utopias*, Delhi: Oxford University Press, pp. 127–62; See Leela Gandhi. 2006. *Affective Communities: Anticolonial Thought, Fin-de-Siècle Radicalism, and the Politics of Friendship*, on Gandhi's alternative of a 'politics of friendship', pp. 85, 86.

12. See Cemil Aydin. 2007. *The Politics of Anti-Westernism in Asia: Visions of World Order in Pan-Islamic and Pan-Asian Thought.* New York: Columbia University Press, pp. 59–68.
13. Shashi Joshi and Bhagwan Josh. 1992–94. *Struggle for Hegemony in India, 1920–47: the Colonial Stale, the Left and the National Movement.* New Delhi: Sage Publications, vol. 3: pp. 200–03. Also see Javed Majeed. 2007. *Autobiography, Travel and Post-national Identity: Gandhi, Nehru and Iqbal.* New York: Palgrave Macmillan, pp. 19–40, 52–69.
14. Roy, *New Orientation,* p. 158.
15. M. N. Roy. 1953f. 'Our Creed', *Radical Humanist,* 1 February.
16. Pheng Cheah. 1997. 'Given Culture: Rethinking Cosmopolitical Freedom in Transnationalism', *Boundary 2* , 24 (2): 157–97.
17. M. N. Roy. 1982. *Materialism: An Outline in the History of Scientific Thought.* Delhi: Ajanta Publications, p. 51
18. Roy, *New Orientation,* p. 164.
19. M. N. Roy. 1960. *Politics, Power and Parties,* Calcutta: Renaissance Publishers, pp. 98–99.
20. Roy, *Politics, Power and Parties,* p. 107.
21. V. B. Karnik. 1978. *M. N. Roy: Political Biography.* Bombay: New Jagriti Samaj, p. 553.
22. Roy, *Politics, Power and Parties,* p. 36.
23. Ibid., p. 136.
24. Reproduced in M. N. Roy. 2004. *M. N. Roy Radical Humanist Selected Writings.* Innaiah Narisetti (ed.). Amherst: Prometheus Books, p. 173.
25. Roy, *Politics, Power and Parties,* p. 10.
26. J. C. Bose, an eminent Bengali scientist (1858–1937), famously wrote on the monistic principle uncovered through scientific research, and how this accorded with the 'Hindu' worldview. See Ashis Nandy. 1995. 'Defiance and Conformity in Science: The World of Jagadish Chandra Bose' in *Alternative Sciences: Creativity and authenticity in two Indian scientists,* Delhi: Oxford University Press, pp. 17–87.
27. He read Eddington's *New Pathways in Science* and *The Nature of the Physical World*; James Jeans, *The Universe around Us*; Émile Meyerson's *Réel et déterminisme dans la physique quantique* (1933); Erwin Schrödinger, individual titles not listed in file; Bertrand Russell, individual titles not listed in file. See Prison Notebooks, vol. 2, pp. 187–91 and vol. 5, p. 481ff.
28. M. N. Roy. 1952–55. *Reason, Romanticism and Revolution,* Calcutta: Renaissance Publishers, vol. 1: p. 16.
29. M. N. Roy. 1957. 'Humanism — The Answer to our Basic Problems', *Radical Humanist,* 7 July, p. 333.
30. Roy, *Reason, Romanticism, Revolution,* vol. 2: p. 264.
31. Roy, *Reason, Romanticism, Revolution,* vol. 1: p. 16.
32. Prathama Banerjee. 2005. 'The Work of Imagination: Temporality and Nationhood in Colonial Bengal', *Subaltern Studies,* vol. 12: pp. 280–322; Tapati Guha-Thakurta.1992. *The Making of a New 'Indian' Art: Artists, Aesthetics, and Nationalism in Bengal, C. 1850–1920.* Cambridge: Cambridge University Press, pp. 146–84.

33. Rabindranath Tagore. 1973. *Racanabali*, Calcutta: Viswa Bharati, vol. 8: p. 546.
34. Sugata Bose. 2007. 'The Spirit and Form of an Ethical Policy: A Meditation on Aurobindo's Thought', in *Modern Intellectual History*, vol. 4: pp. 129–44.
35. Wilhelm Halbfass. 1988. *India and Europe: An Essay in Understanding*, 249.
36. Aurobindo Ghosh. 1949. *The Life Divine*, pp. 856, 857.
37. Meghnad Saha's journal *Science and Culture*, which begun in 1934, advanced themes that were very resonant with M. N. Roy's own views on intellectual agenda in India. Saha contributed occasionally to Roy's press, for example in 'New Philosophy of Life', which appeared in Roy's *Independent India* magazine on 27 January 1928, and 'Philosophy of Industrialisation' on 4 September 1938.
38. Benoy Kumar Sarkar. 1937. *Creative India, From Mohenjo Daro to the Age of Ramakrsna-Vivekananda*. Lahore: Motilal Banarsi Dass, p. 143.
39. Report on the Bangiya Jarman Vidya Samsad in 1933, National Library of India, Kolkata: File 149.B.311.
40. Radhakamal Mukerjee. 1997. *India: The Dawn of a New Era: An Autobiography*. New Delhi: Radha Publications, p. 53.
41. Gasenbeek and Babu Gogineni. 2002. *International Humanist and Ethical Union*, p. 14.
42. Review of *In Man's Own Image* in *The Times of India*, 30 August 1949.
43. Especially the Inter-Asia Conference held in Delhi in 1947; The Progressive Writers' Conference held in Lahore in 1949, the Bandung Afro-Asia Conference of 1955, the 1958 Afro-Asia Writers Bureau Conference in Tokyo, the Cairo Afro-Asian Women's Conference of 1961, the Non-Aligned Movement Conference in Belgrade of 1961, the 1966 Tricontinental Conference. See Vijay Prashad. 2007. *The Darker Nations: A People's History of the Third World.* New York: New Press.
44. Radhakamal Mukerjee begins his *The Way of Humanism*, 'Mankind has never before so endangered its very existence as in this epoch, dividing itself into two vast, hostile blocs struggling for world domination'. Mukerjee, *The Way of Humanism. East and West.* Bombay: Academic Books, p. v. The book, written in 1968, redresses many of Roy's arguments from the 1940s without mentioning him by name; Immanuel Kant. 2006. *Toward Perpetual Peace and Other Writings*, trans. David Colclasure. Yale: Yale University Press, p. 81.
45. Erik Erikson, *Insight and Responsibility*, p. 242.
46. A later postmodernist critique of 'grand narratives' would obscure the historical context of war devastation that informed 1940s and 1950s thought. See, for example, Jean-François Lyotard. 1988. *The Differend: Phrases in Disputes.* Minneapolis: University of Minnesota Press.
47. Hannah Arendt. 1958 rpt (1951). *Origins of Totalitarianism*, New York: Meridian Books, p. 320.
48. Ernst Cassirer. 1944. *An Essay on Man: An Introduction to a Philosophy of Human Culture.* Garden City: Doubleday, p. 5.
49. Originally published in German in 1947, and translated into French in 1952.
50. Herbert Marcuse. 1972. *Counterrevolution and Revolt.* Boston: Beacon Press, Alain Schnapp et al. (eds). 1969. *Journal de la Commune Etudiante.* Paris: Editions du Seuil.

51. He reviewed the following in *The Marxian Way*, later *The Humanist Way* after 1949: Cassirer's *Die Philosophie der Aufklärung*, 2 April 1946; Reinhold Niebuhr's, *The Children of Light and the Children of Darkness*, 1 March 1946; Sidney Hook's *The Hero in History*, 1943; Jacques Barzun's *Romanticism and the Modern Ego*, 1 April 1949; P. A. Sorokin's *The Crisis of Our Age*, 2 January 1946.
52. Following articles were published in the *Radical Humanist*: Raymond Aron. 1960. 'Europe's Resurgence', 1 March. Erich Fromm. 1960. 'The Present Human Condition', 23 January p. 39; Isaac Deutscher. 1958. 'Act Two of Hungary's Tragedy', 18 October, p. 517.
53. Sachin Roy. 1958. 'Existentialist "New Humanism" in France', *Radical Humanist*, 12 May, p. 234. Also see M. K. Halder. 1958. 'Man in the Modern World', *Radical Humanist*, 24 August, p. 401. Sachin Roy. 1957. 'Beyond Communist towards Humanism', *Radical Humanist*, 19 May, p. 251.
54. Roy mocked this view repeatedly, particularly sarcastically in, M. N. Roy. 1946a. 'Four Years Later'. Here he styles himself as a mythic messenger of Asia who is a 'confirmed pessimist' and '[preaches] revolutionary defeatism...' in *I.N.A. and the August Revolution*, p. 105.
55. Roy, *New Orientation* , p. 183.
56. *Independent India.* 1947. 28 September.
57. Roy, *New Orientation*, p. 164.
58. M. N. Roy. 1955. 'Gandhism, Marxism, Humanism', *Radical Humanist*, 19 June, pp. 294–95.
59. M. N. Roy. 1948a. 'The Message of the Martyr', *Independent India*, 8 February
60. *Independent India.* 1948. 22 February, p. 47.
61. Roy, *Politics, Power and Parties*, p. 121.
62. Sudhindranath Datta. 1995. 'Homage to M. N. Roy', in *M. N. Roy: Philosopher-revolutionary*. Sibnarayan Ray (ed.). pp. 194–96.
63. Saranindranath Tagore, 'Benjamin in Bengal: Cosmopolitanism and Historical Primacy' in Sugata Bose and Kris Manjapra (eds), *Cosmopolitan Thought Zones of South Asia* [forthcoming].
64. Asim Khwaja. 2008. 'The Big March: Migratory Flows After the Partition of India', *Economic and Political Weekly*, vol. 43: p. 35.
65. *Independent India*, August 1947, quoted in Karnik, *M. N. Roy: A Political Biography*, p. 563.
66. Roy, 'Four Years', in *I.N.A. and the August Revolution*, p. 94.

Epilogue

In 1950, Roy was mostly bed-ridden and otherwise barely able to walk. Nevertheless, he implored those taking care of him to drive him to the Hindu holy town of Haridwar for the Kumbhamela festival. This seems a strange demand from an ex-communist revolutionary and proponent of secular humanism. Roy's protestations were so strong that only the firm intervention of a doctor, insisting that the trip would do harm, could put plans in abeyance.[1] The fact that Roy fervently wanted to see the Kumbhamela in his final years suggest the way in which religious sensibilities continued to animate him. Roy read Marxism canonically, as an exegete, and he continuously envisioned deep subjecthoods, pregnant with world-changing creative energies, cultivating and socially distributing these energies through ascesis. This book has suggested that the palimpsest of discourses in Roy's thought blurs distinctions, least of which is that between the 'spiritual' and the 'secular' in philosophical discussions about meaning, value and 'new times' in the anti-colonial era.

M. N. Roy, despite all of his travels and transformations, persisted in contemplating three recurring themes: the eruption of energy out of form, the reading of underling unity out of apparent difference, and the articulation of mediated autonomy and solidarity. These can be taken as topoi of his life work, but also, perhaps, as central recurring themes in different forms of modernist thought and aesthetics of the twentieth century. The struggle to break the frame of linear temporal succession, and to define self within new universal communities, was at the heart of Bengali thought from the nineteenth century to the mid-twentieth century, just as much as it preoccupied German, Russian or other groups in the same period. Different local expressions of moder-nist avant-gardism arose like reflecting mirrors in the modern period.

Studying M. N. Roy's thought leads to more than an inquiry into an unusual life-arc, for he represented a nexus between some of the most powerful and historically significant discourses of the early to mid-twentieth century. We have come across Swadeshi global travellers, philosophers of anti-colonial cosmopolitanism, avant-garde expositors of temporal rupture and 'new time', and intermediaries working on the margins of identity divides. The history of the deterritorial body of India continually exceeds the bounds of the territory-bounded historical narrative. And the heightened case of M. N. Roy's anti-colonial cosmopolitanism opens up those middle worlds of circulation, travel and in-betweenness for further study, not as an alternative to the study of anti-colonial nationalism, but indeed, as central to it.

Roy's championing of solidarity and of mediated autonomy led to his own forgetting in a time when postcolonial nation–states were being born. But, one of the claims of this study has been that deterritorialisation, including the social and cultural effects that follow from it, was not the product of individual intentionalities or worldviews, but was an inherent force working itself out in the modern era. For this reason, global perspectives and cosmopolitanism continually resurfaced, with different aims, different eventualities, different ethical implications throughout the period. This, above all, is why Roy did not die lonely in 1954. For the birth of nation–states did not 'win out' over deterritorial forms of identification, thought and social existence. Roy's thought was not the occasion for a deterritorialised imagining. Rather, his ideas were the *consequence* of historical forces long at work.

Note

1. Oral history interview with R. M. Pal, 17 January 2005.

References and Select Bibliography

Primary Sources

REPORTS AND PROCEEDINGS

Communist International. 1919. *Bibliothek der Kommunistischen Internationale I. Manifest, Richtlinien, Beschlüsse des ersten Kongresses.* Hamburg: Hoym.

Communist International. 1920. *Theses and Statutes of the Third International: Adopted by the Second Congress 1920.* Moscow: Publishing Office of the Communist International.

Communist International. 1921. *Protokol des III. Kongresses der Kommunistischen Internationale.* Hamburg: Verlag der kommunistischen Internationale.

Communist International. 1922. *Protokol des IV. Kongresses der Kommunistischen Internationale.* Hamburg: Verlag der kommunistischen Internationale.

Communist International. 1920–29. *Protokoll. Weltkongresse der Kommunistischen Internationale. Vom 2 bis 6 Kongresse.* 1920–1929. Hamburg: Hoym.

India Office. April 1914–March 1915. *Proceedings of the Council of the Governor-General of India, assembled for the purpose of making laws and regulations.* vol. 53. Calcutta: Government Printing.

———. 1918. Report of Committee Appointed to Investigate Revolutionary Conspiracies in India.

———. 1919–20. Reichstag, Deutschland. *Untersuchungsausschuss über die Weltkriegsverantwortlichkeit.* Berlin: Deutsche Verlagsgesellschaft für Politik und Geschichte.

Report of the first League Against Imperialist Conference. 1927. *Das Flammenzeichen vom Palais Egmont: Offizielles Protokoll des Kongresses gegen Koloniale Unterdrückung.* Berlin: Neuer Deutscher Verlag.

ARCHIVES

Frankfurt University, Horkheimer Archive
III-11-298-301 Horkheimer Nachlass

Forschungsstelle für Zeitgeschichte in Hamburg, Hamburt Universität (FZH)
KPD-O Archive

German Foreign Office Archive, Berlin (AA)
21078-4
21079-2

Hoover Museum and Library, Stanford
Jay Lovestone Correspondence
M. N. Roy Correspondence

Humboldt Universität Archiv
Phil. Fak. 637 Gangadhar Adhikar File

International Institute of Social History, Amsterdam (IISG)
Fond 362 Sneevliet papers
Fond 62 Korsch papers
Fond 581 Borodin papers
KPD-O files

National Archives of India, Delhi
Home/Poll/1941/F.128 'A Short Note on M. N. Roy'

National Library of India, Kolkata
File 149.B.311 Report on the Bangiya Jarman Vidya Samsad,
Electronic collection of Bengali Journals: *Kallol*

Nehru Museum and Memorial Library, Delhi (NMML)

List 70: The Papers of M. N. Roy
'Relation to Imprisonment'
'Bareilly Prison Files'
'Prison Notebooks'

M. N. Roy correspondence with:
Abu Syed Ayub
Jibanlal Chatterjee
A. N. Chattopadhyaya
Amlan Datta
Bhupen Kumar Datta
Jibanlal Chattopadhyaya
Louis Coney
Sushil Dey
Ellen Gottschalk
Humayun Kabir
Maniben Kara
V. B. Karnik
Jay Lovestone
Jadugopal Mukherjee
R. L. Nigam
Jan Pollack
Habibur Rahman
Sibnarayan Ray
V. M. Tarkunde
J. B. H. Wadia
Bertram Wolfe

Ellen Gottschalk correspondence with:
Jawaharlal Nehru
Sibnarayan Ray

Oriental and India Office Collection (OIOC), British Library (now 'Asian and African Collections') Surveillance Files, 1919–54:
L/PJ/12/12
L/PJ/12/47
L/PJ/12/62
L/PJ/12/69
L/PJ/12/73
L/PJ/12/99
L/PJ/12/117
L/PJ/12/178
L/PJ/12/189
L/PJ/12/221
L/PJ/12/223
L/PJ/12/280
L/PJ/12/308
L/PJ/12/401
L/PJ/12/421

P. C. Joshi Archives, Jawaharlal Nehru University, Delhi
Pamphlets of the Communist Party of India, 1928–35

Préfecture de Police de Paris
BA 2184 148.800-C Reports on Activities of Indians

Russian States Archive of Social and Political History, Moscow (RGASPI)
Fond 495, Opus 68, File 4
Fond 495, Opus 68, File 20
Fond 495, Opus 68, File 36
Fond 532, Opus 1, File 375

Zentrum Moderner Orient, Berlin
Krüger Nachlass
Krüger Nachlass Annex

West Bengal State Archives
File No/100/23

AUDIOVISUAL SOURCE

Leon, Vladimir. 2006. *Le Brahmane du Komintern*. DVD. Paris: L'Institut National de L'Audiovisuel.

JOURNALS

Calcutta Review, Calcutta
Deutsches Volkstum, Hamburg

Dhumketu, Comilla
Gegen den Strom, Germany
Harijan, Ahmedabad
Independent India, Bombay
International Press Correspondence, Moscow
Internationale Presse Korrespondenz
Kallol, Calcutta
Langol, Calcutta
Marxian Way, Bombay and Calcutta
Masses of India, Berlin
Modern Review, Calcutta
Prabasi, Calcutta
Radical Humanist, Bombay and Calcutta
Revue du monde Musulman, Paris
Rote Fahne, Berlin
The Crisis, New York
Vanguard, Berlin
World Affairs Quarterly, Los Angeles
Young India, Ahmedabad

NEWSPAPERS

Amrita Bazar Patrika, Calcutta
Ananda Bazar Patrika, Calcutta
Bande Mataram, Calcutta
The Communist, Bombay
The Hindu, Madras
Hindusthan Standard, Calcutta
Indian Express, Delhi
London Times, London
Madras Mail, Madras
Manchester Guardian, Manchester
National Front, Bombay
Times of India, Bombay

ORAL HISTORIES

Oral History with Theodor Bergman, 30 October 2004 and November 1 2004
Oral History with Amlan Datta, 20 July 2008
Oral History with R. M. Pal, 19 January 2005
Oral History with Sibnarayan Ray, 12 December 2007
Oral History with Samaren Roy, 12 January 2005

Secondary Sources

Abelshauser, Werner, Anselm Faust et al. (eds.). 1985. *Deutsche Sozialgeschichte 1914–1945: ein historisches Lesebuch.* Munich: C. H. Beck.
Abendroth, Wolfgang. 1976. *Ein Leben in der Arbeiterbewegung.* Frankfurt: Suhrkamp.

Abendroth, Wolfgang. 1978. *Sozialgeschichte der europäischen Arbeiterbewegung.* Frankfurt: Suhrkamp.

Abu-Lughod, Janet. 1989. *Before European Hegemony.* New York: Oxford University Press.

Adhikari, Gangadhar. 1940. *Marxist Miscellany.* Bombay: People's Publishing House.

———. 1943. *Pakistan and Indian National Unity: The Communist Solution.* Bombay: People's Publishing House.

———. 1971. *Documents of the History of the Communist Party of India.* Delhi: People's Publishing House.

Agehananda, Bharati. 1961. *The Ochre Robe.* London: George Allen & Unwin.

Agnew, John and Stuart Corbridge. 1995. *Mastering Space: Hegemony, Territory and International Political Economy.* London: Routledge.

Ahmad, Muzaffar. 1962. *The Communist Party of India and its Formation Abroad.* Calcutta: National Book Agency.

———. 1970. *Myself and the Communist Party of India, 1920–1929.* Calcutta: National Book Agency.

Alavi, Seema. 2008. *Islam and Healing.* New York: Palgrave Macmillan.

Alexander, Robert. 1981. *The Right Opposition: The Lovestoneites and the International Communist Opposition of the 1930s.* Westport: Greenwood Press.

Almond, Gabriel A. and Sidney Verba. 1963. *The Civic Culture: Political Attitudes and Democracy in Five Nations.* Princeton: Princeton University Press.

Althusser, Louis. 1969. *For Marx.* New York: Pantheon.

Amin, Shahid. 1995. *Event, Metaphor, Memory: Chauri Chaura, 1922–1992.* Berkeley: University of California Press.

Anand, Mulk Raj. 1942. *The Sword and the Sickle.* London: J. Cape.

Andersen, Walter and Shridhar Damle. 1987. *The Brotherhood in Saffron.* Boulder: Westview Press.

Anderson, Benedict. 1983. *Imagined Communities: Reflections on the Origin and Spread of Nationalism.* London: Verso.

Anderson, Perry. 1979. *Lineages of the Absolutist State.* London: Verso.

Anonymous. 1937. 'Pure Philosophy of Materialism', *Madras Mail*, 25 July.

Apel, Karl-Otto. 1979. *Hermeneutik und Ideologiekritik, Theorie-Diskussion.* Frankfurt am Main: Suhrkamp.

Appadurai, Arjun. 1996. *Modernity at Large.* Minneapolis: University of Minnesota Press.

Appiah, Kwame Anthony. 2000. *Cosmopolitanism: Ethics in a World of Strangers.* New York: Norton.

Aron, Raymond. 1960. 'Europe's Resurgence', *Radical Humanist*, 1 March.

Arendt, Hannah. 1951. *The Origins of Totalitarianism.* New York: Meridian Books.

Armitage, David. 2007. *The Declaration of Independence: A Global History.* Cambridge: Harvard University Press.

Augé, Marc. 1995. *Non-Places*, trans. John Howe. London: Verso.

Aydin, Cemil. 2007. *The Politics of Anti-Westernism in Asia: Visions of World Order in Pan-Islamic and Pan-Asian Thought.* New York: Columbia University Press.

Bailey, F. M. 1946. *Mission to Tashkent.* London: Travel Book Club.

Baker, Ray Stannard. 1927. *Woodrow Wilson: Life and Letters.* Garden City: Doubleday.

Bandyopadhyay, Gitasree. 1984. *Constraints in Bengal Politics 1921–41: Gandhian Leadership.* Calcutta: Sarat Book House.

Banerjea, Benoyendranath, V. M. Tarkunde, et al. 1944. *People's Plan for Economic Development of India*. Delhi: Mukerjee.

Banerjee, B. N., G. D. Parikh and V. M. Tarkunde. 1944. *People's Plan for Economic Development of India*. Delhi: Indian Federation of Labour.

Banerjee, Prathama. 2005. 'The Work of Imagination: Temporality and Nationhood in Colonial Bengal', *Subaltern Studies*, vol. 12: pp. 280–322.

Banerjee, Sumanta. 1989. *The Parlour and the Streets*. Calcutta: Seagull Books.

Barakatullah, Mohammed. 1925. 'Une communication de M. Barkatullah', *Revue du monde Musulman*, vol. 62: pp. 157–58.

Barooah, Nirode Kumar. 2004. *Chatto, the Life and Times of an Indian Anti-Imperialist in Europe*. New Delhi: Oxford University Press.

Barzun, Jacques. 1945. *Romanticism and the Modern Ego*. Boston: Little Brown and Company.

Bartolovich, Crystal and Neil Lazarus. 2002. *Marxism, Modernity and Postcolonial Studies, Cultural Margins*. Cambridge: Cambridge University Press.

Basu, Buddhadeb. 1948. *An Acre of Green Grass*. Calcutta: Papyrus.

Bayly, C. A. 1986. 'The Origins of Swadeshi (home industry): Cloth and Indian Society', in Arjun Appadurai (ed.), *The Social Life of Things: Commodities in Cultural Perspective*. Cambridge: Cambridge University Press.

———. 1989. *Imperial Meridian: The British Empire and the World*. London: Longman, pp. 100–32.

———. 2004. *The Birth of the Modern World, 1780–1914: Global Connections and Comparisons*. Malden: Blackwell.

———. 2006. *Empire and Information: Intelligence Gathering and Social Communication in India, 1780–1870*. New York: Cambridge University Press.

Beals, Carleton. 1938. *Glass Houses: Ten Years of Free-lancing*. Philadelphia: Lippincott Company.

Bearce, George. 1965. 'Intellectual and Cultural Characteristics of India in a Changing Era, 1740–1800', *Journal of Asian Studies*, 25(1): 3–17.

Becker, Jens. 2001. *Heinrich Brandler: eine politische Biographie*. Hamburg: VSA-Verlag.

Benjamin, Walter. 1968. 'Theses on the Philosophy of History', in Hannah Arendt (ed.), *Illuminations*. New York: Harcourt, Brace & World.

———. 2003 reprint (1940). 'On the Concept of History' in Marcus Bullock, Howard Eiland and Gary Smith (eds), *Walter Benjamin Selected Writings*. Cambridge: Belknap Press.

Bell, Duncan. 2007. *The Idea of Greater Britain: Empire and the Future of the World Order, 1860–1900*. Princeton: Princeton University Press.

Berghaus, Günther. 1996. *Futurism and Politics: Between Anarchist Rebellion and Fascist Reaction, 1909–1944*. Providence: Berghahn Books.

Bergmann, Theodor. 1987. *Gegen den Strom: die Geschichte der Kommunistischen-Partei-Opposition*. Hamburg: VSA-Verlag.

———. 2004. *Die Thalheimers: die Geschichte einer Familie undogmatischer Marxisten*. Hamburg: VSA-Verlag.

Bergmann, Theodor and Mario Kessler. 2000. *Ketzer im Kommunismus: 23 biographische Essays*. Hamburg: VSA-Verlag.

Béteille, André. 1969. *Social Inequality: Selected Readings*. Baltimore: Penguin Books.

———. 1982. *Marxism, Pluralism, and Orthodoxy: M. N. Roy Memorial Lecture*. Dehra Dun: Indian Renaissance Institute.

Bhabha, Homi. 1994. *Location of Culture.* London: Routledge.

———. 1996. 'Unsatisfied', in Laura Garcia-Moreno et al. (eds), *Text and Nation*, pp. 191–207.

Bhattacharjee, G. P. 1971. *Evolution of Political Philosophy of M. N. Roy.* Calcutta: Minerva Associates.

Bhattacharya, Abinash. 1979 rpt (1962). *Iyorope Bharatiya Biplaber Sadhana.* Calcutta: Popular Library.

Bhattacharya, Sabyasachi (ed.). 1997. *The Mahatma and the Poet: Letters and Debates between Gandhi and Tagore, 1915-1941.* Delhi: National Book Trust India.

Bhattacharya, Tithi. 2005. *The Sentinels of Culture: Class, Education, and the Colonial Intellectual in Bengal (1848-85).* Oxford: Oxford University Press.

Bloch, Ernst. 1918. *Geist der Utopie.* Munich: Dunker & Humblot.

———. 1959. *Das Prinzip Hoffnung.* Frankfurt: Suhrkamp Verlag.

———. 1986. *Principle of Hope*, trans. - Neville Plaice et al. Oxford: Oxford University Press.

Bose, A. C. 2002. *Indian Revolutionaries Abroad.* Delhi: Northern Book Centre.

Bose, Girindrasekhar. 1921. *Concept of Repression.* Calcutta: n. p.

Bose, Subhas Chandra. 1962. *Crossroads, Being the Works of Subhas Chandra Bose, 1938-1940.* New York: Asia Publishing House.

———. 1964. *The Indian Struggle. 1920-1942.* Bombay: Asia Publishing House.

Bose, Sugata. 1986. *Agrarian Bengal: Economy, Social Structure, and Politics.* Cambridge: Cambridge University Press.

———. 1997. 'Instruments and Idioms', in Frederick Cooper (ed.), *International Development and the Social Sciences*, p. 52.

———. 2006. *A Hundred Horizons: The Indian Ocean in the Age of Global Empire.* Cambridge: Harvard University Press.

———. 2007. 'The Spirit and Form of an Ethical Policy: A Meditation on Aurobindo's Thought', in *Modern Intellectual History,* 4(1): 129–44.

Bose, Sugata (ed.). 1990. *South Asia and World Capitalism.* Delhi: Oxford University Press.

Brenner, Neil. 1997. 'Global, Fragmented Hierarchical', *Public Culture,* 10(1): 135–67.

Burns, Edward McNall. 1953. *David Starr Jordan: Prophet of Freedom.* Stanford: Stanford University Press.

Bynum, Carolyn. 1992. *Fragmentation and Redemption: Essays on Gender and the Human Body in Medieval Religion.* New York: Zone Books.

Cannadine, David. 2001. *Ornamentalism: How the British Saw their Empire.* Oxford: Oxford University Press.

Carr, E. H. 1954. *The Interregnum.* London: St. Martin's Press.

———. 1958. *Socialism in One Country.* New York: Macmillan Carr.

———. 1984. *The Comintern and the Spanish Civil War.* New York: Pantheon Books.

Cassirer, Ernst. 1932. *Die Philosophie der Aufklärung.* Tübingen: Mohr.

———. 1944. *An Essay on Man: An Introduction to a Philosophy of Human Culture.* Garden City: Doubleday.

———. 1951. *The Philosophy of the Enlightenment.* Princeton: Princeton University Press.

Césaire, Aimé. 2000. *Discourse on Colonialism*, trans. Joan Pinkham. New York: Monthly Review Press.

Chakrabarty, Dipesh. 1989. *Rethinking Working-Class History: Bengal, 1890 -1940.* Princeton: Princeton University Press, p. 127.

———. 1992. 'Postcoloniality and the Artifice of History: Who speaks for " Indian" Pasts?', *Representations.* California: University of California Press, vol. 32: pp. 1–26.

———. 2000. *Provincializing Europe: Postcolonial Thought and Historical Difference.* Princeton: Princeton University Press.

Chandra, Ganga Narayan. 1939. *The Russian Revolution: How M. N. Roy Misinterprets it to the Young Intellectuals of India.* Chandernagore: Sambaya Publishing.

Chandavarkar, Rajnarayan. 1994. *The Origins of Industrial Capitalism in India: Business Strategies and the Working Class in Bombay 1900-1940.* Cambridge: Cambridge University Press.

———. 1998. *Imperial Power and Popular Politics: Class, Resistance and the State in India, c. 1850-1950.* Cambridge: Cambridge University Press, p. 299.

Chatterjee, Partha. 1993. *The Nation and its Fragments.* Princeton: Princeton University Press.

Chatterji, Joya. 1994. *Bengal Divided: Hindu Communalism and Partition, 1932-1947.* Cambridge: Cambridge University Press.

Chattopadhyay, Bankimchandra. 2004. *Sahitya Samagra.* Calcutta: Tuli-Kalam.

Chattopadhyay, Nripendrakrishna. 1924. 'Russahitya o Tarun Bangali', *Kallol,* vol. 3: p. 59 ff.

Cheah, Pheng. 1997. 'Given Culture: Rethinking Cosmopolitical Freedom in Transnationalism', *Boundary 2,* 24(2): 157–97.

Chibber, Vivek. 2003. *Locked in Place: State-building and Late Industrialization in India.* Princeton: Princeton University Press.

Christian, William A. 1972. *Person and God in a Spanish Valley.* New York: Seminar Press.

Clayton, Anthony. 1986. *The British Empire as a Superpower, 1919-39.* Hampshire: Macmillan.

Clifford, James. 1997. *Routes: Travel and Translation in the Late Twentieth Century,* Cambridge: Harvard University Press.

Coleman, Peter. 1989. *The Liberal Conspiracy: The Congress for Cultural Freedom and the Struggle for the Mind of Postwar Europe.* New York: Free Press.

Collingwood, R. G. 1955. *The Idea of History.* New York: Oxford University Press.

Communist International. 1922. *Protokol des IV. Kongresses der Kommunistischen Internationale.* Hamburg: Verlag der kommunistischen Internationale.

Cutts, Elmer. 1953. 'The Background of Macaulay's Minutes', *American Historical Review,* 58 (4): 824–53.

Dange, S. A. 1921. *Lenin and Gandhi.* Bombay: Literature Library.

———. 1974. *Selected Writings of Lenin and Gandhi.* Bani Deshpande (ed.). Bombay: Vangmaya Griha.

Datta, Bhupendranath. 1958. *Biplaber Padacinha.* Calcutta.

———. 1983. *Bharater Dvitiya Swadhinatar Samgram: Aprakasita Rajnitik Itihas.* Calcutta: Nababharat Publishing.

Das, Dhananjay. 1975. *Marxbadi Sahitya-Vitarka.* Calcutta: Praima Publishing.

Das, Dineshranjan. 1925. 'Rolland o Tarun Bangla', *Kallol,* vol. 4: p. 791ff.

Das, Swadesh Ranjan. 1965. *Manabendranath, Jiban o Darsan*. Calcutta: Radical Humanist.

Dasgupta, Rajarshi. 2003. *Marxism and the Middle Class Intelligentsia: Culture and Politics in Bengal 1920s-1950s*. PhD Dissertation: Oxford University Press.

Dasgupta, Shashi Bhushan. 1946. *Obscure Religious Cults as Background of Bengali Literature*. Calcutta: University of Calcutta Press.

Datta Gupta, Sobhanlal. 1980. *Comintern India and the Colonial Question*. Calcutta: Centre for Studies in Social Sciences.

Datta Gupta, Sobhanlal, Hari Vasudevan, et al. 1997. *Indo-Russian Relations: Checklist of Documents*. Calcutta: Asiatic Society.

Datta, Sudhindranath. 1995. ' Homage to M. N. Roy', in Sibnarayan Ray (ed.), *M. N. Roy: Philosopher-Revolutionary*. Delhi: Ajanta Publications, pp. 194ff.

Davies, Cecil. 2000. *The Volksbühne Movement: A History*. Amsterdam: Harwood Academic.

Dayal, Har. 1911. 'India in America', *Modern Review*, July. 10(1): 1–11.

———. 1913. 'India and the World Movement', *Modern Review*, February, 13(2): 185–87.

Degras, Jane. 1956. *The Communist International: Documents, 1919-1943*. London: Oxford University Press.

Deleuze, Gilles and Félix Guattari. 1976. *Rhizome: Introduction*. Paris: Éditions de Minuit.

———. 1977. *Anti-Oedipus: Capitalism and Schizophrenia*. Translated by Robert Hurley, Mark Seem, and Helen Lane. New York: Viking Press.

———. 1987. *A Thousand Plateaus*. Translated by Brian Massumi. Minneapolis: University of Minnesota Press.

Derrida, Jacques. 2001. *Cosmopolitanism and Forgiveness*. London: New York.

Desai, Mahadev. 1933. 'Sparks from the Sacred Fire', *Harijan*, 13 May, vol. 1, p. 4.

———. 1939. 'A God-Given Fast', *Harijan*, 11 March, vol. 7, p. 41.

Desai, Valji Govindji. 1934. 'Culture is the Fruit of Compulsory Continence', *The Harijan*, September, 2 (21): 254ff.

Deutscher, Isaac. 1958. 'Act Two of Hungary's Tragedy', *Radical Humanist*, 18 October, p. 517.

———. 1959. *The Prophet Unarmed: Trotsky, 1921-1929*. New York: Oxford University Press.

———. 1963. *The Prophet Outcast: Trotsky, 1929-1940*. New York: Oxford University Press.

———. 1968. *The Non-Jewish Jew and Other Essays*. New York: Oxford University Press.

———. 2003 rpt (1954). *The Prophet Armed: Trotsky, 1879-1921*. New York: Oxford University Press.

Diouf, Mahmud. 2000. 'Senegalese Murid Trade Diaspora and the Making of Vernacular Cosmopolitanism', *Public Culture*, 12(3): 679–702.

Draper, Theodore. 1957. *The Roots of American Communism, Communism in American Life*. New York: Viking Press.

Du Bois, W. E. B. 1956. *The World and Africa*. New York: The Viking Press.

———. 1989 rpt (1903). *Souls of Black Folk*. New York: Bantam Books.

Dutt, Rajani Palme and Ben Bradley. 1939. 'The Anti-Imperialist People's Front', *International Press Correspondence*, 29 February, pp. 297–300.

Eaton, Richard Maxwell. 1978. *Sufis of Bijapur, 1300-1700: Social Roles of Sufis in Medieval India*. Princeton: Princeton University Press.

———. 1993. *The Rise of Islam and the Bengal Frontier, 1204-1760*. Berkeley: University of California.

Editorial. 1818. *Friend of India*, 1(1): 1.

Editorial. 1943. 'University College of Science, Calcutta', *Science and Culture*, 9(1): 43.

Edney, Matthew. 1997. *Mapping and Empire: The Geographical Construction of British India, 1765-1843*. Chicago: University of Chicago Press.

Edwards, Brent Hayes. 2003. *The Practice of Diaspora: Literature, Translation, and the Rise of Black Internationalism*. Cambridge: Harvard University Press.

Emmet, Dorothy. 1994. *The Role of the Unrealisable: A Study in Regulative Ideas*. New York: Macmillan Press.

Erikson, Erik. 1964. *Insight and Responsibility: Lectures on the Ethical Implications of Psychoanalytic Insight*. New York: W. W. Norton.

Fischer, Fritz. 1962. *Griff nach der Weltmacht: die Kriegszielpolitik des kaiserlichen Deutschland 1914-18*. Düsseldorf: Droste.

Fischer-Tiné, Harald. 2006. 'Indian Nationalism and the "World Forces"', *Journal of Global History*, 1(2): 325-44.

Forbes, Geraldine. 1975. *Positivism in Bengal*. Calcutta: Minerva.

Frölich, Paul. 1972. *Rosa Luxemburg: Her Life and Work*. New York: Monthly Review Press.

Fromm, Erich. 1960. 'The Present Human Condition', *Radical Humanist*, 23 January, p. 39.

Gadamer, Hans-Georg. 1993. *Truth and Method*. New York: Continuum.

Galison, Peter Louis. 2003. *Einstein's Clocks, Poincaré's Maps*. New York: W. W. Norton.

Gandhi, Leela. 2006. *Affective Communities: Anticolonial Thought, Fin-de-Siècle Radicalism, and the Politics of Friendship*. Durham: Duke University Press.

Gandhi, M.K. 1938. 'Choice Before Congressmen', *Harijan*, 3 September 1938, vol. 6, p. 24

———. 1939a. 'India's Attitude', *Harijan*, 14 October, vol. 7, p. 1.

———. 1939b. 'My Life', *Harijan*, 4 November, vol. 7, p. 325.

———. 1939c. 'The One and Only Task', *Harijan*, 5 November, p. 43.

———. 1939d. 'Requisite Qualifications', *Harijan*, 25 March, vol. 7. p. 64.

———. 1942. 'One Thing Needful', *Harijan*, 10 May, vol. 9, p. 148.

———. 1949. 'Ahimsa in Practice', *Harijan*, 27 January, vol. 8, pp. 428-29.

———. 1995. *Hind Swaraj and Other Writings*. Anthony Parel (ed.). Cambridge: Cambridge University Press.

Ganguly, Keya. 1984. *Leftism in India: M. N. Roy and Indian Politics, 1920-1948*. Calcutta: Minerva.

———. 2002. 'Adorno, Authenticity, Critique', in Crystal Bartolovich and Neil Lazarus (eds.), *Marxism, Modernity, and Postcolonial Studies*. Cambridge: Cambridge University Press.

Ganguly, S. M. 1993. *Manabendra Nath Roy: An Annotated Bibliography*. Calcutta: K. P. Bagchi & Co.

Garber, Marjorie. 1992. *Vested Interests*. New York: Routledge.

Gasenbeek, Bert and Babu Gogineni. 2002. *International Humanist and Ethical Union, 1952-2002: Past, Present and Future.* Utrecht: De Tijdstroom.

Gellner, Ernest. 1985. *Relativism and the Social Sciences.* New York: Cambridge University Press.

Ghose, Jogendra Chunder. 1906. *The English Works of Raja Rammohun Roy with an English Translation of "Tuhfatul Muwahhiddin".* Allahabad: The Panini Office.

Ghosh, A. K. 1939. 'What True Internationalism Demands', *National Front,* 22 October, p. 501.

Ghosh, Aurobindo. n. d. 'Nationalism is the Work of God', in Stephen Hay (ed.), *Sources of Indian Tradition.* New York: Columbia University Press.

———. 1949. *The Life Divine.* New York: Greystone Press.

———. 1959. *A Practical Guide to Integral Yoga.* Pondicherry: Sri Aurobindo Ashram.

———. 1974 rpt (1893). *New Lamps for Old.* Pondicherry: Sri Aurobindo Ashram.

———. 1990. *The Future Evolution of Man: The Divine Life upon Earth.* Pondicherry: Sri Aurobindo Ashram.

Ghosh, Barindrakumar. 1922. *The Tale of My Exile.* Pondicherry: Arya Office.

Ghosh, Durba and Dane Kennedy (eds.). 2006. *Decentering Empire: Britain, India, and the Transcolonial World.* Hyderabad: Orient Longman.

Ghosh, Suresh Chandra. 2005. 'The Genesis of Curzon's University Reform: 1899-1905', *Minerva,* 26(4): 463-92.

Ghosh, Syamal Krishna. 1990. *Parichayer Adda.* Calcutta: K. P. Bagchi.

Glissant, Edouard. 1997. *Poetics of Relation,* trans. Betsy Wing. Ann Arbor: University of Michigan Press.

Gopal, Primyamvada. 2005. *Literary Radicalism in India: Gender Nation, and the Transition to Independence.* London: Routledge.

Gordon, Leonard A. 1974. *Bengal: The Nationalist Movement, 1876-1940.* New York: Columbia University Press, pp. 163-87.

———. 1990. *Brothers against the Raj: A Biography of Indian Nationalists Sarat and Subhas Chandra Bose.* New York: Columbia University Press.

Gordon, Peter. 2003. *Rosenzweig and Heidegger: Between Judaism and German Philosophy.* Berkeley: University of California Press.

Goswami, Manu. 2004. *Producing India: From Colonial Economy to National Space.* Chicago: University of Chicago Press.

Gould, Harold. 2006. *Sikhs, Swamis, Students and Spies.* New Delhi: Sage Publications.

Graf, Rüdiger. 2008. *Die Zukunft der Weimarer Republik.* Munich: Oldenbourg.

Greenblatt, Stephen. 1980. *Renaissance Self-fashioning.* Chicago: University of Chicago Press.

Greene, Thomas. 1968. 'The Flexibility of the Self in Renaissance Literature', in Peter Demetz (ed.), *The Disciplines of Criticism.* New Haven: Yale University Press, pp. 241-64.

Griffin, Roger. 2000. 'The Primacy of Culture: The Current Growth (or Manufacture) of Consensus within Fascist Studies', *Journal of Contemporary History,* 32(1): 21-43.

Gross, Jonathan David. 2001. *Byron: The Erotic Liberal.* Lanham: Rowman & Littlefield.

Guha, Ramachandra. 2006. *How Much Should a Person Consume?: Environmentalism in India and the United States.* Berkeley: University of California Press.

Guha, Ranajit. 1997. *Dominance without Hegemony*. Cambridge: Harvard University Press.

Guha, Ranajit (ed.). 1988. *Selected Subaltern*. New York: Oxford University Press.

Guha-Thakurta, Tapati. 1992. *The Making of a New 'Indian' Art: Artists, Aesthetics, and Nationalism in Bengal, c.1850-1920*. Cambridge: Cambridge University Press.

Günther, Max. 1924. 'Das politische Ende des deutschen Volkes', *Deutsches Volkstum*, August, vol. 12, p. 458.

Gwynn, Charles William. 1934. *Imperial Policing*. London: Macmillan.

Haithcox, John Patrick. 1971. *Communism and Nationalism in India: M. N. Roy and Comintern Policy, 1920-1939*. Princeton: Princeton University Press.

Halbfass, Wilhelm. 1988. *India and Europe: An Essay in Understanding*. Albany: State University of New York Press.

Halder, M. K. 1958. 'Man in the Modern World', *Radical Humanist*, 24 August, p. 401.

Harrison, Peter. 1990. *'Religion' and the Religions in the English Enlightenment*. Cambridge: Cambridge University Press.

Harvey, David. 2000. *Spaces of Hope*. Berkeley: University of California Press.

Hartnack, Christiane. 2001. *Psychoanalysis in Colonial India*. New York: Oxford Univeristy Press, pp. 127-33.

Hasan, Mushirul. 1981. *Communal and Pan-Islamic Trends in Colonial India*. New Delhi: Manohar.

Hay, Stephen. 1970. *Asian Ideas of East and West: Tagore and his Critics in Japan, China, and India*. Cambridge: Harvard University Press.

Hay, Stephen et al. (eds). 1988. *Sources of Indian Tradition*. New York: Cambridge University Press.

Hegel, G. W. F. 1961. 'The Positivity of the Christian Religion (1795-96)', in T. M. Knox (trans. and ed.), *On Christianity: Early Theological Writings*. New York: Harper.

———. 1952 rpt (1822). *Philosophy of Right*, trans. T. M. Knox. London: Oxford University Press.

———. 1977 rpt (1807). *Phenomenology of Spirit*, trans. A. V. Miller. Oxford: Oxford University Press.

Heidegger, Martin. 1962. *Being and Time*. New Haven: Philosophy Education Society.

Hindi, A. K. 1938. *M. N. Roy: The Man who Looked Ahead*. Ahmedabad: Modern Publishing House.

Ho, Engseng. 2006. *Graves of Tarim: Genealogy and Mobility Across the Indian Ocean*. Berkeley: University of California Press.

Honneth, Axel. 1995. *The Struggle for Recognition: The Moral Grammar of Social Conflicts*. Cambridge: Blackwell.

Hook, Sidney. 1943. *The Hero in History: A Study in Limitation and Possibility*. New York: The John Day Company.

Hoover, Karl Douglas. 1989. *The German-Hindu Conspiracy in California, 1913-1918*. PhD Dissertation. University of California: Santa Barbara.

Horkheimer, Max and Theodor Adorno. 1987 rpt (1944), trans. John Cumming. *Dialectic of Enlightenment*. New York: Herder & Herder.

Huntington, Samuel. 1969. *Political Order in Changing Societies*. New Haven: Yale University Press.

Innaiah, Narisetti. 1995. *Evelyn Trent alias Shanti Devi: Founder Member of the Exile Indian Communist Party*. Hyderabad: Booklinks Corp.

Iqbal, Muhammad. 1930. *The Reconstruction of Religious Thought in Islam*. Lahore: n.p.

Jacobs, Dan. 1981. *Borodin: Stalin's Man in China*. Cambridge: Harvard University Press.

Jalal, Ayesha. 1995. *Democracy and Authoritarianism in South Asia: A Comparative Perspective*. Cambridge: Cambridge University Press.

Jalal, Ayesha. 2000. *Self and Sovereignty: Individual and Community in South Asian Islam since 1850*. New York: Routledge.

Jangfeldt, Bengt. 1976. *Majakovskij and Futurism 1917-1921*. Stockholm: Almqvist & Wiksell International.

Jayawardena, Kumari. 1986. *Feminism and Nationalism in the Third World*. London: Zed Books.

Jones, Gareth Stedman. 2007. 'Radicalism and the Extra-European World', in Duncan Bell (ed.), *Victorian Visions of Global Order*, pp. 186–214.

Jones, Jean. 1996. *The League against Imperialism*. London: Socialist History Society.

Jones, Richard. 1859. *Literary Remains, Consisting of Lectures and Tracts on Political Economy*. William Whewell (ed.). London: J. Murray.

Jordan, David Starr. 1922. *The Days of a Man*. Yonkers-on-Hudson: World Book Company.

Josh, Sohan Singh. 1978. *Hindustan Gadar Party: A Short History*. New Delhi: People's Publishing House.

Joshi, P. C. 1942. *Indian Communist Party, Its Policy and Work in the War of Liberation*. London: Communist Party of Great Britain.

Joshi, Shashi and Bhagwan Josh. 1992. *Struggle for Hegemony in India, 1920-47: The Colonial State, the Left and the National Movement*. New Delhi: Sage Publications.

Kabir, Humayun. 1958a. 'Rationalism, Democracy, Humanism', *Radical Humanist*, 21 February, p. 597.

———. 1958b. 'Rationalism, Democracy and Humanism: Islam in Indian History', *Radical Humanist*, 21 December, p. 597.

Kaes, Anton et al. (eds.). 1994. *Weimar Republic Sourcebook*. Berkeley: University of California Press.

Kaestner, Jürgen. 1982. *Die Politische Theorie August Thalheimers*. Frankfurt: Campus-Verlag.

Kale, Madhavi. 1998. *Fragments of Empire: Capital, Slavery, and Indian Indentured Labor Migration in the British Caribbean*. Philadelphia: University of Pennsylvania Press.

Kant, Immanuel. 1960. *Religion within the Limits of Reason Alone*, trans. Theodore Green and Hoyt Hudson. La Salle: Open Court.

———. 2006. *Toward Perpetual Peace and Other Writings*, trans. David Colclasure. Yale: Yale University Press.

Kanungo, Hemchandra. 1928. *Banglay Biplab Pracesta*. Calcutta: Kamala Book Depot.

Karl, Rebecca. 2002. *Staging the World: Chinese Nationalism at the Turn of the Twentieth Century*. Durham: Duke University Press.

Karnik, V. B. 1966 rpt (1960). *Indian Trade Unions*. Bombay: Labour Education Service.

———. 1978. *M. N. Roy: A Political Biography*. Bombay: Nav Jagriti Samaj.

Katz, Friedrich. 1981. *The Secret War in Mexico: Europe, the United States, and the Mexican Revolution*. Chicago: University of Chicago Press.

Kaviraj, Sudipta. 1986. 'The Heteronomous Radicalism of M.N. Roy', in Thomas Pantham and Kenneth L. Deutsch (eds), *Political Thought in Modern India*. New Delhi: Sage Publications.

———. 1995. *The Unhappy Consciousness: Bankimchandra Chattopadhyay and the Formation of Nationalist Discourse in India*. Delhi: Oxford University Press.

Kaye, Cecil. 1971 rpt (1924). *Communism in India*. Calcutta: Editions Indian.

Ker, James Campbell. 1973 rpt (1917). *Political Trouble in India, 1907–1917*. Calcutta: Superintendent Government Printing.

Kelley, Robin. 2000. 'Introduction', in Aimé Cesaire, *Discourse on Colonialism*, trans. Joan Pinkham. New York: Monthly Review Press.

Khan, Yusuf Hussein. 1956. 'The Educational System of Medieval India', *Islamic Culture*, 30: 119–22.

Khwaja, Asim. 2008. 'The Big March: Migratory Flows After the Partition of India', *Economic and Political Weekly*, vol. 43: p. 35.

Kohn, Hans. 1960. *The Mind of Germany*. New York: Scribner.

Köhnke, Klaus Christian. 1991. *The Rise of Neo-Kantianism*. Cambridge: Cambridge University Press.

Kojève, Alexandre. 1969. *Introduction to the Reading of Hegel*. New York: Basic Books.

Kolakowski, Leszek. 1978. *Main Currents of Marxism: Its Rise, Growth, and Dissolution*. Oxford: Clarendon Press.

Kollontai, Alexandra. 1972 rpt (1919). *Sexual Relations and the Class Struggle: Love and the New Morality*. Bristol: Falling Wall Press, pp. 6–8.

Kopf, David. 1969. *British Orientalism and the Bengal Renaissance: The Dynamics of Indian Modernization, 1773–1835*. Berkeley: University of California Press.

Korsch, Karl. 1970. *Marxism and Philosophy*. London: NLB.

Koselleck, Reinhart. 1979. *Historische Semantik und Begriffsgeschichte, Sprache und Geschichte*. Stuttgart: Klett-Cotta.

———. 1985. *Futures Past*, trans. Keith Tribe. Cambridge: MIT Press.

———. 2002. *The Practice of Conceptual History: Timing History, Spacing Concepts*, trans. Todd Presner. Stanford: Stanford University Press.

Kripal, Jeffrey. 1995. *Kali's Child: The Mystical and the Erotic in the Life and Teachings of Ramakrishna*. Chicago: University of Chicago Press.

———. 2001. *Roads of Excess, Palaces of Wisdom: Eroticism & Reflexivity in the Study of Mysticism*. Chicago: University of Chicago Press.

Lajpat, Rai. 2003. *The Collected Works of Lala Lajpat Rai*. B. R. Nanda (ed.). New Delhi: Manohar.

Lakoff, George. 1987. *Women, Fire, and Dangerous Things: What Categories Reveal about the Mind*. Chicago: University of Chicago Press.

———. 1996. *Moral Politics*. Chicago: University of Chicago Press.

Lal, Lakshmi Narayan. 1975. *Jayaprakash: Rebel Extraordinary*. Delhi: India Book Company.

Langels, Otto. 1984. *Die ultralinke Opposition der KPD in der Weimarer Republik*. Frankfurt am Main: Lang.

Laushey, David. 1975. *Bengal Terrorism and the Marxist Left*. Calcutta: Firma Mukhopadhyay.

Lazarus, Neil. 1990. *Resistance in Postcolonial African Fiction*. New Haven: Yale.

Lenin. 1920. Minutes from meeting on 3 June 1919. 'Manifest der Kommunistischen Internationale an das Proletariat der ganzen Welt' in *Bibliothek der Komintern*, vol. 1, Hamburg: Verlag der Kommunistischen Internationale, p. 13ff.

——. 1960. *Collected Works*. Moscow: Progress Publishers.

Leonhard, Wolfgang. 1970. *Die Dreispaltung des Marxismus. Ursprung und Entwicklung des Sowjetmarxismus, Maoismus und Reformkommunismus*. Düsseldorf: Econ-Verlag.

Lindqvist, Sven. 2000. *A History of Bombing*. New York: New Press.

Low, Michael. 2008. 'British Empire and the Hajj: Pilgrims, Plagues, and Pan-Islam under British Surveillance, 1865–1908' in *International Journal of Middle East Studies*, 40 (2): 269–90.

Lukács, Georg. 1971 rpt (1922). *History and Class Consciousness*, trans. Rodney Livingstone. Cambridge: MIT Press.

——. 1983. 'Tagore's Gandhi Novel', in *Reviews and Articles from Die Rote Fahne*, trans. Peter Palmer. London: Merlin Press.

Luxemburg, Rosa. 1906. *Massenstreik, Partei und Gewerkschaften*. Hamburg: E. Dubber.

——. 1922. *Die Russische Revolution, eine kritische Würdigung: Verlag Gesellschaft und Erziehung*.

——. 1972 rpt (1906). *Gesammelte Werke*. Berlin: Dietz.

Lyotard, Jean-François. 1988. *The Differend: Phrases in Disputes*. Minneapolis: University of Minnesota Press.

Maier, Charles. 2000. 'Consigning the Twentieth Century to History', *American Historical Review*, 105(3): 808.

Maine, Henry Sumner. 1966 rpt (1875). *Lectures on the Early History of Institutions*, 7th ed. New York: Kennikat Press.

Majeed, Javed. 1992. *Ungoverned Imaginings: James Mill's the History of British India and Orientalism*. Oxford: Oxford University Press.

——. 2007. *Autobiography, Travel and Postnational Identity: Gandhi, Nehru and Iqbal*. New York: Palgrave Macmillan.

Majumdar, Bimalendu. 1900. *Professor Max Müller on Ramkrishna and the World on Keshub Chunder Sen*. Calcutta: Lawrence Printing Works.

Manela, Erez. 2007. *The Wilsonian Moment: Self-Determination and the International Origins of Anticolonial Nationalism*. Oxford: Oxford University Press.

Manjapra, Kris. 2006. 'The Illusions of Encounter: Muslim "Minds" and Hindu revolutionaries', *Journal of Global History* 1(3): 363–82.

Marchand, Suzanne. (Forthcoming). 'On Orientalism and Iconoclasm', in Sugata Bose and Kris Manjapra (eds.), *Cosmopolitan Thought Zones of South Asia*. London: Palgrave Macmillan Press.

Marcuse, Herbert. 1955. *Eros and Civilization: A Philosophical Inquiry into Freud*. Boston: Beacon Press.

——. 1972. *Counterrevolution and Revolt*. Boston: Beacon Press.

——. 1978. *The Aesthetic Dimension: Toward a Critique of Marxist Aesthetics*. Boston: Beacon Press.

Markovits, Claude. 2004. *The Un-Gandhian Gandhi.* London: Anthem Press.

Marx, Karl. 1939. *Grundrisse der Kritik der politischen Ökonomie 1857–1858.* Moscow: Verlag für Fremdsprachige Literatur.

———. 2004 rpt (1867). *Das Kapital.* Cologne: Parkland Verlag.

Marx, Karl, Friedrich Engels, and Robert C. Tucker. 1968. *Karl Marx on Colonialism and Modernization.* Shlomo Avineri (ed.). Garden City: Doubleday.

———. 1972. *The Marx-Engels Reader.* New York: Norton.

Institute of Marxism-Leninism (Central Committee of the Communist Party of the Soviet Union). 1972. *Marx-Engels Gesamtausgabe.* Berlin: Dietz.

Masani, Minocheher. 1977. *Bliss Was It in That Dawn: A Political Memoir upto Independence.* New Delhi: Arnold-Heinemann Publishers.

Maslow, Abraham. 1954. *Motivation and Personality.* New York: Harper.

Mathur, P. N. 1977. *The Civil Service of India.* Jodhpur: Prabhat Prakashan.

Maugham, Somerset. 1936. *Ashenden.* London: Heinemann.

Mazower, Mark. 1996. *Dark Continent: Europe's Twentieth Century.* New York: A. A. Knopf.

McKay, Claude. 1922. 'Report on the Negro Question' in: *International Press Correspondence,* vol. 2, 3 January 1925, pp. 16–17.

McLane, Charles. 1966. *Soviet Strategies in Southeast Asia.* Princeton: Princeton University Press.

Mehta, Uday Singh. 1999. *Liberalism and Empire: A Study in Nineteenth-Century British Liberal Thought.* Chicago: University of Chicago Press.

Mendes-Flohr, Paul. 1999. *German Jews: A Dual Identity.* New Haven: Yale University Press.

Menon, Dilip. 1994. *Caste, Nationalism and Communism in South Asia.* Cambridge: Cambridge University Press.

———. [Forthcoming]. 'A Local Cosmopolitan: "Kesari" Balakrishna Pillai and the Invention of Europe for a Modern Kerala', in Sugata Bose and Kris Manjapra (eds.), *Cosmopolitan Thought Zones of South Asia.* London: Palgrave Macmillan.

Menon, V. P. 1957. *The Transfer of Power in India.* Bombay: Orient Longmans.

Mignolo, Walter. 1995. *The Darker Side of the Renaissance: Literacy, Territoriality, and Colonization.* Ann Arbor: University of Michigan Press.

———. 2000. *Local Histories/Global Designs: Coloniality, Subaltern Knowledges, and Border Thinking.* Princeton: Princeton University Press.

Mill, James. 1820. *History of British India.* London: Baldwin, Cradock, and Joy.

Minault, Gail. 1982. *The Khilafat Movement: Religious Symbolism and Political Mobilization in India.* New York: Columbia University Press.

———. 1998. *Secluded Scholars: Women's Education and Muslim Social Reform in Colonial India.* Delhi: Oxford University Press.

Mitra, Nripendra Nath. 1939. *The Indian Annual Register.* Calcutta: Annual Register Office.

Mitter, Partha. 2007. *Triumph of Modernism: India's Artists and the Avant-Garde, 1922–1947.* London: Reaktion Books.

Mongia, Radhika. 1999. 'Race, Nation, Mobility: A History of the Passport', *Public Culture,* 11(3): 527–55.

Morgan, Ted. 1999. *A Covert Life: Jay Lovestone, Communist, Anti-Communist, and Spymaster.* New York: Random House.

Mukerji, Dhan Gopal. 1923. *Caste and Outcaste.* New York: E. P. Dutton & Company.

Mukerjee, Radhakamal. 1940. *Man and his Habitation: A Study in Social Ecology.* London: Longmans Green.

———. 1961. *Ways of Dwelling in the Communities of India.* Evanston: Row, Peterson and Company.

———. 1968. *The Way of Humanism, East and West.* Bombay: Academic Books.

———. 1997. *India, the Dawn of a New Era: An Autobiography.* New Delhi: Radha Publications.

Mukherjee, Haridas and Uma Mukherjee. 1957. *The Origins of the National Education Movement (1905-1910).* Calcutta: Jadavpur University.

Mukherjee, Tapan. 1998. *Taraknath Das: Life and Letters of a Revolutionary in Exile.* Calcutta: National Council of Education.

Mukherjee, Jadugopal. 1956. *Biplabi Jibaner Smriti.* Calcutta: Indian Associated Publishing Company.

Mukhopadhyay, Bhudev. 1862. *Swapnalabdha Bharater Itihas.* Calcutta: n. p.

Mullen, Bill. 2003. 'Du Bois, Dark Princess, and the Afro-Asian International', *Positions,* 11(1): 217–39.

Münzenberg, Willi. 1931. *Solidarität, zehn Jahre Internationale Arbeiterhilfe, 1921-1931.* Berlin: Neuer Deutscher Verlag.

Muthu, Sankar. 2003. *Enlightenment against Empire.* Princeton: Princeton University Press.

Nagrath, Radhika. 2007. *Swami Vivekananda, the Known Philosopher, the Unknown Poet.* Kolkata: Meteor Books.

Nanda, B. R. 1972. *Socialism in India.* Delhi: Vikas Publishers.

Nandakisandas. 1934. 'Utkal Report for 8 Months Ending 31-3-34', *Harijan,* 19 October, vol. 2, p. 282

Nandy, Ashis. 1987. *Traditions, Tyranny, and Utopias.* Delhi: Oxford University Press.

———. 1988. *The Intimate Enemy.* New Delhi: Oxford University Press.

———. 1995. 'Defiance and Conformity in Science: The World of Jagadish Chandra Bose', in *Alternative Sciences: Creativity and Authenticity in Two Indian Scientists.* Delhi: Oxford University Press, pp. 17–87.

———. 2004. 'The Savage Freud: The First Non-Western Psychoanalyst and the Politics of Secret Selves in Colonial India', in *Bonfire of Creeds,* pp. 339–93.

Narayan, Jayaprakash. 1950. *Selected Writings.* New Delhi: Indian Print.

———. 1956. *Socialism to Sarvodaya.* Madras: Socialist Book Centre.

———. 1971. *Socialist Unity and the Congress Socialist Party.* Bombay.

Nehru, Jawaharlal. 1941 reproduction (1939). 'A.I.C.C. and After' in *The Unity of India: Collected Writings.* London: Drummond. pp. 160–68.

———. 1950. *Selected Writings.* New Delhi: Indian Prints.

———. 1962. *Autobiography, With Musings on Recent Events in India.* Bombay: Allied Publishers.

———. 2003 (originally published in 1936). *Jawaharlal Nehru, an Autobiography.* London: John Lane.

Nettl, J. P. 1966. *Rosa Luxemburg*. Oxford: Oxford University Press.

Niebuhr, Reinhold. 1944. *The Children of Light and the Children of Darkness*. New York: C. Scribner.

North, Robert Carver and Eudin Xenia Joukoff. 1963. *M. N. Roy's Mission to China: The Communist-Kuomintang Split of 1927*. Berkeley: University of California Press.

Northrup, David. 1995. *Indentured Labor in the Age of Imperialism*. Cambridge: Cambridge University Press.

Overstreet, Gene and Marshall Windmiller. 1959. *Communism in India*. Berkeley: University of California Press.

Pachter, Henry Maximilian. 1982. *Weimar Etudes*. New York: Columbia University Press.

Pal, Bipin Chandra. 1958 rpt (1911). *The Soul of India*. Calcutta: Choudhury & Choudhury.

Parmanand, Bhai. 1912. 'Greater India', *Modern Review*, February, 11(2): 152.

Parrinder, Patrick. 1995. *Shadows of the Future: H. G. Wells: Science Fiction and Prophecy*. London: Liverpool University Press.

Petrie, David. 1972 rpt (1927). *Communism in India, 1924–1927*. Calcutta: Editions Indian Publishers.

Plamenatz, John Petrov. 1954. *German Marxism and Russian Communism*. London: Longmans Green.

Polanyi, Karl. 1944. *The Great Transformation*. New York: Rinehart.

Pomian, Kzryztof. 1984. *Ordre du temps*. Paris: Gallimard.

Poster, Mark. 1975. *Existential Marxism in Postwar France: From Sartre to Althusser*. Princeton: Princeton University Press.

Pradhan, Sudhi. 1979. *Marxist Cultural Movements in India: Chronicles and Documents*. Calcutta: Santi Pradhan.

Prashad, Vijay. 2007. *The Darker Nations: A People's History of the Third World*. New York: New Press; Distributed by W. W. Norton.

Puri, Harish. 1983. *Ghadar Movement*. Amritsar: Guru Nanak Dev University.

Qureshi, Naeem. 1999. *Pan-Islam in British Indian Politics*. Leiden: Brill.

Rabinbach, Anson. 1997. *In the Shadow of Catastrophe: German Intellectuals between Apocalypse and Enlightenment, Weimar and Now; 14*. Berkeley: University of California Press.

Rafael, Vincente. 2005. The *Promise of the Foreign: Nationalism and the Technics of Translation in the Spanish Philippines*. Durham: Duke University Press.

Raj, Kapil. 2006. *Relocating Modern Science: Circulation and the Construction of Knowledge in South Asia*. Delhi: Permanent Black.

Ramaswamy, Sumathi. 2002. 'Visualizing India's Geo-body', *Contributions to Indian Sociology*, 36(1–2): 151–89.

Rancière, Jacques. 2004. *Politics of Aesthetics: Distribution of the Sensible*, trans. Gabriel Rockhill. London: Continuum.

Ray, Rajat. 1979. *Urban Roots of Indian Nationalism: Pressure Groups and Conflict of Interests in Calcutta City Politics*. Delhi: Vikas.

Ray, Sibnarayan. 1995 rpt (1984). *M. N. Roy, Philosopher-Revolutionary*. Delhi: Ajanta Publications.

———. 1998–2007. *In Freedom's Quest: A Study of the Life and Works of M. N. Roy*. Calcutta: Minerva.

Ray, Sibnarayan (ed.). 1989. *For a Revolution from Below.* Calcutta: Minerva Associates.

Raychaudhuri, Tapan. 1988. *Europe Reconsidered: Perceptions of the West in Nineteenth-century Bengal.* Delhi: Oxford University Press.

Reznikov, A. B. 1979. *The Comintern and the East: The Struggle for the Leninist Strategy and Tactics in National Liberation Movements.* Moscow: Progress Publishers.

Rostow, W. W. 1953. *The Process of Economic Growth.* Cambridge: Cambridge University Press.

Roy, Dipti Kumar. 1990. *Trade Union Movement in India: Role of M. N. Roy.* Calcutta: Minerva Associates.

Roy, M. N. 1918. *India, Her Past, Present and Future.* Reproduced in Sibnarayan Ray (ed.), Selected Works, vol. 1: p. 64ff.

———. 1922. 'The Political Situation', *Vanguard,* 15 October, vol. 5: p. 2.

———. 1923a. 'Revolution versus Reaction', *Vanguard,* 12 January, vol. 2: p. 4.

———. 1923b. 'Struggle of the German Proletariat', *Vanguard,* 15 July, vol. 2: p. 11.

———. 1923c. 'The Uses of Patriotism', *Vanguard,* 1 June, vol. 2: p. 8.

———. 1924a. 'Appeal to the Nationalists', *Vanguard,* 15 December, vol. 5.

———. 1924b. 'Europe is Not the World', *Inprecor,* 31 December, 4(90): 1045–46.

———. 1924c. 'Mahatma and Bolshevism',*Vanguard,* 15 October, vol. 1, p. 7.

———. 1924d. *Political Letters.* Zurich: Vanguard Bookshop.

———. 1924–25. 'Who will Lead', *Inprecor,* 9(11): 55–65.

———. 1925. 'Foundation of Democracy: The American Experience', *The Masses of India,* September, vol. 1, p. 9.

———. 1927. *The Future of Indian Politics.* London: R. Bishop.

———. 1930. *Revolution und Konterrevolution in China.* Berlin: Soziologische Verlagsanstalt.

———. 1932. 'My Defense'. Reproduced in: Sibnarayan Ray (ed). 1990. *Selected Works of M. N. Roy.* Delhi: Oxford University Press, pp. 573–646.

———. 1938a. *Fascism: Its Philosophy, Professions and Practice.* Calcutta: D. M. Library.

———. 1938b (1936). *On the Congress Constitution.* Calcutta: Independent India.

———. 1938c. *Our Differences.* Calcutta: Saraswaty Library.

———. 1938d. *Our Problems.* Calcutta: Barendra Library.

———. 1939a. 'Fresh Blow to "Forward Bloc"', *Ananda Bazaar Patrika,* March.

———. 1939b. 'Gandhian Policy Must Go', *Hindustan Standard,* 4 June.

———. 1939c. 'Mr. M. N. Roy's Call to Muslim Youths', *Amrita Bazaar Patrika,* 5 April.

———. 1940a. *The Alternative.* Bombay: Independent India.

———. 1940b. *Science and Superstition.* Dehra Dun: Indian Renaissance Association.

———. 1941a. *The Ideal of Indian Womanhood.* Dehra Dun: Indian Renaissance Association.

———. 1941b. 'New Federal Scheme for India', *Independent India,* 9 March.

———. 1941c. 'Our Task', *Independent India,* 24 August.

———. 1942a. *Freedom or Fascism?* Radical Democratic Party: n. p.

———. 1942b. *India and War.* Lucknow: Radical Democratic Party.

———. 1942c. 'International Civil War', in *War and Revolution.* Madras: Radical Democratic Party.

Roy, M. N. 1942d. *Nationalism, Democracy & Freedom*. Bombay: Radical Democratic Party.

——. 1942e. 'The Philosophy of the Twentieth Century', *Scientific Politics*, pp.197–98.

——. 1943a. *The Communist International*. Bombay: Radical Democratic Party.

——. 1943b. *Heresies of the Twentieth Century: Philosophical Essays*. Bombay: Renaissance Publications.

——. 1943c. *Letters from Jail, Fragments of a Prisoner's Diary*. Dehra Dun: Indian Renaissance Association.

——. 1944a. *Poverty or Plenty?* Calcutta: Renaissance Publishers.

——. 1944b. 'War and Revolution', in: B.N. Banerjee et. al. eds, *People's Plan for Economic Development*. Delhi: Indian Federation of Labour.

——. 1945a. 'Constitution of Free India: A Draft', in B. S. Sharma (ed.), *Radical Humanism of M. N. Roy*.

——. 1945b. *Future of Democracy in India*. Delhi: Radical Democratic Party.

——. 1945c. *Jawaharlal Nehru*. Delhi: Radical Democratic Party.

——. 1945d. *My Experiences in China*. Calcutta: Renaissance Publishers.

——. 1946a. *I. N. A. and the August Revolution*. Calcutta: Renaissance Publishers.

——. 1946b. *New Orientation: Lectures Delivered at the Political Study Camp held at Dehra Dun from May 8–18, 1946*. Calcutta: Renaissance Publishers.

——. 1947. *Science and Philosophy*. Calcutta: Renaissance Publishers.

——. 1948a. 'The Message of the Martyr', *Independent India*, 8 February.

——. 1948b. 'Our Future', *Independent India*, 28 November, pp. 572–73.

——. 1949. *The Russian Revolution*. Calcutta: Renaissance Publishers.

——. 1950. *India's Message*. Calcutta: Renaissance Publishers.

——. 1952. 'Nationalism and Freedom', editorial, *Radical Humanist*, 25 May.

——. 1952–55. *Reason, Romanticism and Revolution*. Calcutta: Renaissance Publishers.

——. 1953a. 'The City of the Sleeping Women', *Radical Humanist*, 22 March, vol. 17: p. 138.

——. 1953b. 'In the Land of Liberty', *Radical Humanist*, 15 February, vol. 17: p. 80.

——. 1953c. 'In Power by Proxy', *Radical Humanist*, 19 July, vol.17: p. 343.

——. 1953d. 'In the Land of Revolutions', *Radical Humanist*, 8 March, vol. 17: p. 114.

——. 1953e. 'Stalin's Obituary', *Radical Humanist*, 15, 17 March.

——. 1953f. 'Our Creed', *Radical Humanist*, 1 February.

——. 1955. 'Gandhism, Marxism, Humanism', *Radical Humanist*, 19 June, pp. 294–95.

——. 1957a. *Crime and Karma, Cats and Women*. Calcutta: Renaissance Publishers Private.

——. 1957b. 'Humanism—The Answer to Our Basic Problems', *Radical Humanist*, 7 July, p. 333.

——. 1960. *Politics, Power and Parties*. Calcutta: Renaissance Publishers.

——. 1964. *M. N. Roy's Memoirs*. Bombay: Allied Publishers.

——. 1968. *Men I Met*. Bombay: Lalvani Publishing House.

——. 1970. *From Savagery to Civilisation*. Calcutta: Renaissance.

——. 1971a rpt (1922). *India in Transition*. Bombay: Nachiketa Publications.

——. 1971b. *What Do We Want?* Bombay: Nachiketa Publications.

——. 1973 rpt (1946). *Revolution and Counter-Revolution in China*. Westport: Hyperion Press.

Roy, M. N. 1974 rpt (1939). *Historical Role of Islam: An Essay on Islamic Culture*. Lahore: Sind Sagar Academy.

———. 1981 rpt (1946). *New Humanism: A Manifesto*. Delhi: Ajanta Publications.

———. 1982. *Materialism: An Outline of the History of Scientific Thought*. Delhi: Ajanta Publications.

———. 1987a. Sibnarayan Ray (ed.), *Selected Works of M. N. Roy*. Delhi: Oxford University Press.

———. 1987b rpt (1920). 'Supplementary Theses on the National and Colonial Question',in Sibnarayan Ray (ed.), *Selected Works of M. N. Roy*. Delhi: Oxford University Press.

———. 1989. *Reason, Romanticism and Revolution*. Delhi: Ajanta Publications.

———. 1997. 'Letters to the Congress Socialist Party (1934, 1935, 1936), in Sibnarayan Ray (ed.), *Selected Works of M.N. Roy*. Delhi: Oxford University Press, vol. 4.

———. 2004 rpt (2002). *M. N. Roy: Radical Humanist: Selected Writings*. Innaiah Narisetti (ed.). Amherst: Prometheus Books.

Roy, M. N. and Ellen Gottschalk. 1957. *Fragments of a Prisoner's Diary*. Calcutta: Renaissance Publishers.

Roy, M. N. and Spratt Philip. 1968. *Beyond Communism*. Calcutta: Renaissance Publishers.

Roy, Rammohan. 1906. *The English Works of Raja Rammohun Roy with an English Translation of "Tuhfatul Muwahhiddin"*, (ed. and trans.) Jogendra Chunder Ghose. Allahabad: The Panini Office.

Roy, Sachin. 1957. 'Beyond Communist towards Humanism', *Radical Humanist*, 19 May, p. 251.

———. 1958. 'Existentialist "New Humanism" in France', *Radical Humanist*, 12 May, p. 234.

Roy, Samaren. 1970. *The Restless Brahmin: Early Life of M. N. Roy*. Bombay: Allied Publishers.

———. 1986. *The Twice-born Heretic: M. N. Roy and Comintern*. Calcutta: Firma KLM.

Ruben, Walter. 1959. *Über die Aufklärung in Indien*. Berlin: Akademie Verlag.

Russell, Ralph and Khurshidul Islam. 1968. *Three Mughal Poets; Mir, Sauda, Mir Hasan*. Cambridge: Harvard University Press.

Saich, Tony. 1991. *The Origins of the First United Front in China: The Role of Sneevliet (alias Maring)*. Leiden: New York: E. J. Brill.

Sakai, Naoki. 1997. *Translation and Subjectivity*. Minneapolis: University of Minnesota Press.

Sareen, Tilak Raj. 1979. *Indian Revolutionary Movement Abroad, 1905-1921*. New Delhi: Sterling.

Sarkar, Benoy Kumar. 1912. *The Science of History and the Hope of Mankind*. London: Longmans Green and Co.

———. 1916. *Chinese Religion Through Hindu Eyes: A Study in the Tendencies of Asiatic Mentality*. Shanghai: Commercial Press.

———. 1922. *Futurism of Young Asia*. Berlin: Springer.

———. 1926. *Duniyar Abhaowa*. Calcutta: Raychaudhari.

———. 1927. 'Empire Development and World-Economy: A Study in the New Foundations of National Economy for India', *Journal of the Bengal National Chamber of Commerce*, vol. 2: p. 7.

Sarkar, Benoy Kumar. 1932. *Parajita Jarmani*. Calcutta: Oriental Book Agency.

———. 1937. *Creative India, from Mohenjo Daro to the Age of Ramakrsna-Vivekananda*. Lahore: Motilal Banarsi Dass.

Sarkar, Jadunath. 1912–6. *History of Aurangzib*. Calcutta: Sarkar and Sons.

Sarkar, Jayabrata. 1973. *The Swadeshi Movement in Bengal, 1903–1908*. Delhi: People's Publishing House.

———. 2006. 'Power, Hegemony and Politics: Leadership Struggle in Congress in the 1930s', *Modern Asian Studies*, 40(2): 333–70.

Sarkar, Sumit. 1983. *Modern India, 1885–1947*. Delhi: Macmillan.

Sarkar, Tanika. 1985. 'Communal Riots in Bengal', in Mushirul Hasan (ed.), *Communal and Pan-Islamic Trends in Colonial India*, Delhi: Manohar Publications, pp. 302–19.

Sartori, Andrew. 2008. *Bengal in Global Concept History: Culturalism in the Age of Capital*. Chicago: University of Chicago Press.

Sarvadhikari, Rajkumar. 1882. *The Principles of the Hindu Law of Inheritance*. Calcutta: Thacker Spink.

Sassen, Saskia. 1991. *The Global City: New York, London, Tokyo*. Princeton: Princeton University Press.

Sastri, Sibnath. 1911. *A History of the Brahmo Samaj*. Calcutta: R. Chatterji.

Savarkar, V. D. 1938. Speech at the 19th session of All India Hindu Mahasabha held at Ahmedabad. Lahore: Central Hindu Yuvak Sabha.

Sawer, Marian. 1977. *Marxism and the Question of the Asiatic Mode of Production*. The Hague: Nijhoff.

Scarry, Elaine. 1985. *The Body in Pain: The Making and Unmaking of the World*. New York: Oxford University Press.

Schnapp, Alain and Pierre Vidal-Naquet. 1969. *Journal de la commune étudiante, texts et documents, Novembre 1967-Juin 1968*. Paris: Éditions du Seuil.

Schultz, Bart and Georgios Varouxakis. 2005. *Utilitarianism and Empire*. Lanham: Lexington Books.

Sedition Committee Report. 1973 rpt (1918). London: H.M. Stationery Office.

Sen, Amartya. 2005. *The Argumentative Indian: Writings on Indian History, Culture and Identity*. London: Allen Lane.

Sen, Keshab Chandra. 1954. *Lectures in India*. London: Cassell.

Seth, Sanjay. 1995. *Marxist Theory and Nationalist Politics: The Case of Colonial India*. New Delhi: Sage Publications.

Sharma, B. S. 1965. *The Political Philosophy of M. N. Roy*. Delhi: National Publishing House.

Shils, Edward. 1961. *The Intellectual between Tradition and Modernity: The Indian Situation*. The Hague: Mouton.

Shipman, Charles. 1993. *It Had to be Revolution*. Ithaca: Cornell University Press.

Siegel, James. 1997. *Fetish, Recognition, Revolution*. Princeton: Princeton University Press.

Singh, Bhola. 1985. *The Political Ideas of M. N. Roy and Jayaprakash Narayan: A Comparative Study*. New Delhi: Ashish Publishing House.

Singh, Khushwant and Satindra Singh. 1966. *Ghadar 1915*. Delhi: R. & K. Publishing House.

Singh, Nihal Saint. 1909. 'A message that Japan gave me', *Modern Review*, February 5(2): 154–56.

Sinha, Mrinali. 2008. 'Gender in the Critiques of Colonialism and Nationalism', in Sumit and Tanika Sarkar (eds.), *Women and Social Reform in Modern India*. Bloomington: Indiana University Press, pp. 452–72.

Sitaramayya, Pattabhi. 1946. *The History of the Indian National Congress*. Delhi: Chand Publishers.

Skinner, Quentin. 'Some Problems in the Analysis of Political Thought and Action', *Political Theory*, 2(3): 277–303.

Slezkine, Yuri. 2004. *The Jewish Century*. Princeton: Princeton University Press, pp. 39–40.

Snow, Edgar. 1937. *Red Star Over China*. London: Gollancz.

Sorokin, P. A. 1941. *The Crisis of Our Age: The Social and Cultural Outlook*. New York: Dutton.

Spang, Christian, et al. (eds.). 2006. *Japanese-German Relations*. London: Routledge.

Spratt, Philip. 1948. *India and Constitution Making*. Calcutta: Renaissance Publishers.

———. 1955. *Blowing up India: Reminiscences and Reflections of a Former Comintern Emissary*. Calcutta: Prachi Prakashan.

Stapanian, Juliette. 1986. *Mayakovsky's Cubo-Fascist Vision*. Houston: Rice University Press.

Stein, William Bysshe. 1967. *Two Brahman Sources of Emerson and Thoreau*. Gainesville: Scholar's Facsimiles & Reprints.

Subrahmanyam, Sanjay. 1990. *Improvising Empire: Portuguese Trade and Settlement in the Bay of Bengal, 1500-1700*. Delhi: Oxford University Press.

———. 2005. *Explorations in Connected History: Mughals and Franks*. Delhi: Oxford University Press.

Subramanyan, K. G. 1987. *The Living Tradition: Perspectives on Modern Indian Art*. Calcutta: Seagull Books.

Suleri, Sara. 1989. *Meatless Days*. Chicago: University of Chicago Press.

Suri, Surindar. 1959. *Nazism and Social Change in Germany*. Calcutta: K.L. Mukhopadhyay.

———. 1965. *Der Kommunismus in Südostasien*. Hannover: Nierdersächsischen Landeszentrale für Politische Bildung.

Tagore, Rabindranath. 1917. *Nationalism*. New York: Macmillan.

———. 1936 rpt (1918). *Collected Poems and Plays of Rabindranath Tagore*. New York: Macmillan.

———. 1973. *Rabindra Racanabali*. Calcutta: Prakasa Prabandha.

Tagore, Saranindranath. (Forthcoming). 'Benjamin in Bengal: Cosmopolitanism and Historical Primacy', in Sugata Bose and Kris Manjapra (eds.), *Cosmopolitan Thought Zones of South Asia*.

Tagore, Saumyendranath. 1944. *Historical Development of the Communist Movement in India*. Calcutta: Red Front.

———. 1975. *Against the Stream: An Anthology of Writings of Saumyendranath Tagore*. Edited by Sudarshan Chattopadhyay. Calcutta: Saumyendranath Memorial Committee.

Tenorio-Trillo, Mauricio. 1996. *Mexico at the World's Fairs: Crafting a Modern Nation*. Berkeley: University of California Press.

Terras, Victor. 1983. *Vladimir Mayakovsky*. Boston: Twayne.

Thalheimer, August. 1908. *Beitrag zur Kenntnis der pronominal personalia und possessiva der Sprachen Mikronesien*. Stuttgart: Metzler.

———. 1922. '*Programm der Kommunistischen Partei Deutschlands*', *Internationale Presse Korrespondenz*, vol. 2: p. 194.

———. 1925. 'Über einige Grundbegriffe der physikalischen Theori der Relativität von Geschichtspunkfe des dialektischen Materialismus' in *Unter dem Banner des Marxismus*, vol. 1: pp. 203–338.

———. 1928. *Spinozas Stellung in der Vorgeschichte des dialektischen Materialismus*. Vienna: Verlad für Literatur und Politik.

———. 1932a. *Einheitsfront gegen Faschismus*, Bremen: Arbeiterpolitik.

———. 1932b. *Wie schafft die Arbeiterklasse die Einheitsfront gegen Faschismus?* Berlin: Junius-Verlag.

———. 1936. *Introduction to Dialectical Materialism*, trans. George Simpson and George Weltner. New York: Covici Friede.

———. 1946. *Zurück in die Eierschale des Marxismus?; Zum Existentialismus als bürgerliche Philosophie*. Cuba: n. p.

Thapar, Romila. 2001. *Cultural Pasts: Essays in Early Indian History*. New Delhi: Oxford University Press.

Thomas, Harnisch. 1999. *Chinesische Studenten in Deutschland*. Hamburg: Institut für Asienkunde.

Thomas, Martin. 2008. *Empires of Intelligence: Security Services and Colonial Disorder after 1914*. Berkeley: University of California Press.

Thongchai, Winichakul. 1994. *Siam Mapped: A History of the Geo-body of the Nation*. Honolulu: University of Hawaii Press.

Tillich, Paul. 1926. *Kairos: Ideen zur Geisteslage und Gegenwart*. Darmstadt: Otto Reichl Verlag.

Tinker, Hugh. 1974. *A New System of Slavery: The Export of Indian Labour Overseas*. London: Oxford University Press.

Toews, John Edward. 1980. *Hegelianism: The Path Toward Dialectical Humanism, 1805–1841*. Cambridge: Cambridge University Press.

Torpey, Christopher. 2000. *The Invention of the Passport: Surveillance, Citizenship, and the State*. Cambridge: Cambridge University Press.

Trilling, Lionel. 1951. *The Liberal Imagination*. New York: Viking Press.

Trivedi, Harish. 1993. *Colonial Transactions: English Literature and India*. Calcutta: Papyrus.

Trivedi, Lisa. 2006. 'A National Public in the Colonial World: Swadeshi Goods and the Making of the Indian Nation', in Dane Kennedy and Durba Ghosh (eds.), *Decentering Empire*, (2006). pp. 150–75.

———. 2007. *Clothing Gandhi's Nation*. Bloomington: Indiana University Press.

Tully, James. 1988. *Meaning and Context: Quentin Skinner and his Critics*. Princeton: Princeton University Press.

Turner, Victor and Edith L. B. Turner. 1978. *Image and Pilgrimage in Christian Culture: Anthropological Perspectives*. Oxford: Blackwell.

Usmani, Shaukat. 1977. *Historic Trips of a Revolutionary: Sojourn in the Soviet Union*. Delhi: Sterling Publishers.

Van der Veer, Peter. 1995. *Nation and Migration: The Politics of Space in the South Asian Diaspora*. Philadelphia: University of Pennsylvania Press.

Vivekananda, Swami. 1893. Speech of 1893. *The World's Congress of Religions*. J. W. Hanson (ed.). Vancouver: MacGregor Publishing.

———. 1970. *The Complete Works of Swami Vivekananda*. Calcutta: Advaita Ashrama.

Wardle, Huon. 2000. *An Ethnology of Cosmopolitanism in Kingston, Jamaica*. Lewiston: Edwin Mellen Press.

Washbrook, David. 1990. 'South Asia, the World System and World Capitalism', in S. Bose (ed.), *South Asia and World Capitalism*. Delhi: Oxford University Press, pp. 40ff.

Weber, Hermann. 1963. *Der deutsche Kommunismus*. Cologne: Kiepenheuer & Witsch.

———. 1969. *Die Wandlung des deutschen Kommunismus; die Stalinisierung der KPD in der Weimarer Republik*. Frankfurt am Main: Europäische Verlagsanstalt.

Webner, Pnina. 1999. 'Global Pathways', *Social Anthropology*, 7(1): 17–35.

Weitz, Ulrich. 1991. *Salonkultur und Proletariat*. Stuttgart: Stöffler & Schütz.

Wells, H. G. 1929. *The Outline of History*. Garden City: Doubleday.

Wilder, Gary. 2005. *The French Imperial Nation-State: Negritude & Colonial Humanism between the Two World Wars*. Chicago: University of Chicago Press.

Williams, Raymond. 1996. *Politics of Modernism*. London: Verso.

Williamson, Horace. 1976. *Communism and India*. Calcutta: Editions Indian.

Willis, Kirk. 1988. 'The Introduction and Critical Reception of Hegelian Thought in Britain 1830–1900', *Victorian Studies*, 32(1): 85–111.

Wilson, Patrick. 1955. *A Preliminary Checklist of the Writings of M. N. Roy*. Berkeley: University of Berkeley Press.

Wilson, Woodrow. 1918. *In Our First Year of War*. New York: Harper & Bros.

———. 2005. *Woodrow Wilson: The Essential Political Writings*. Ronald Pestritto (ed.). Lanham: Lexington Books.

Wittfogel, Karl August. 1926. *Das Erwachende China*. Wien: Agis.

———. 1957. *Oriental Despotism*. New Haven: Yale University Press.

Wolfe, Bertram David. 1981. *A Life in Two Centuries*. New York: Stein and Day.

Wolfe, Patrick. 2002. 'Can the Muslim Speak? An Indebted Critique', *History and Theory* 41(3): 367–80.

Wolfe, Patrick. 2006. 'Islam, Europe and Indian Nationalism: Towards a Postcolonial Transnationalism', in A. Curthoys et al. (eds.), *Connected Worlds: History in Transnational Perspective*, pp. 233–58.

Zachariah, Benjamin. 2005. *Developing India*. New Delhi: Oxford University Press.

Zaidi, A. 1985. *Congress Presidential Addresses*. New Delhi: Publication Department of the Indian Institute of Applied Research.

———. 1987. *The Glorious Tradition: Text of the Resolutions Passed by the INC, the AICC and the CWCV (1885–1966)*. Delhi: Indian Institute of Applied Political Research.

Index